conversations with
jack cardiff
art, light and direction in cinema

conversations with
jack cardiff

art, light and direction in cinema

by justin bowyer
foreword by mike figgis

BATSFORD

First Published 2003

© Justin Bowyer 2003

The right of Justin Bowyer to be identified as Author of this work has been asserted by him in accordance with the Copyright, Designs and Patents Act 1988.

Illustrations supplied by Jack Cardiff (unless specified otherwise)

ISBN 07134 8855 7

A CIP catalogue record for this book is available from the British Library.

Printed in Spain by Just Colour Graphic

for the publishers

B T Batsford
The Chrsalis Building
Bramley Road
London W10 6SP
England
www.batsford.com

A member of **Chrysalis** Books plc

Distributed in the United States and Canada by Sterling Publishing Co., 387 Park Avenue South, New York, NY 10016, USA

For Helen and Callum

Contents

Acknowledgements

Primary thanks, of course, to Jack Cardiff for his generosity of time and spirit and his willingness to talk at such length about his life and work. Also thanks to Niki, Jack's wife, for her ceaseless patience and considerable hard work behind the scenes. Special thanks to Mike Figgis for his foreword and to all those who so kindly found time to share their thoughts, reminiscences and tributes: Steven Berkoff, Leslie Caron, Dino De Laurentiis, Freddie Francis, Kevin Macdonald, Phil Meheux, Robert Rehme, Roger Smither, Bill Taylor, John Woodward and Adrian Wootton. Finally, all those who have supported and encouraged the project: Anthony Antoniou, Helen Bowyer, Brett Lake-Benson, Derek Scanlon, Tina Persaud and Nick Walker.

Foreword by Mike Figgis

'Necessity is the mother of invention'

Usually the best ideas in cinema come out of situations where a tricky problem arises and there isn't a piece of equipment around to solve it. Jack Cardiff seems to have spent much of his life and career solving problems. Starting very young and rapidly working his way through the not-so-permeable layers of the film industry, he quickly established a reputation as a cameraman with an incredible eye for light and a very sound understanding of the psychology and frailty of artists. Being an artist himself must have helped somewhat. Being a natural risk taker puts Jack Cardiff into a more rarified category than most of his peers. There is an anecdote in the book in which Mr Cardiff describes the 'men from Technicolour' coming onto his set and handing him a light-meter and telling him to use it, or the camera would be withdrawn from him. I re-read this passage—did this mean that he wasn't using a light-meter prior to this? Apparently so. Respect to Mr Cardiff!

Film-making has always been expensive. It's always someone else's money and therefore there is always a huge pressure to be conventional. To paraphrase Billy Wilder, 'No-one ever went to see a film because it was conventional' (Wilder actually said 'No-one ever went to see a film because it came in on budget'). Without the Jack Cardiffs of this world, we would never have great cinema.

This fascinating book allows Jack Cardiff to talk us through the history of cinema. He talks freely, but never unkindly, about the greatest actors, directors, producers, designers and writers of the last 80 years. There is a refreshing absence of bitterness or rancour about the things that went wrong, the money that vanished or the things that could have been. There is so much to be learned from this great man—the way actors behave (in certain conditions), the way light behaves (in certain conditions), and the way directors behave (in certain conditions)…

Jack Cardiff is a great cinematographer, one of the best. But clearly he is also a great artist and a great film-maker. I'd like to take this opportunity to thank him for all his work; he's certainly been a great inspiration to me. Thank you, Jack.

January 2003

Jack Cardiff: A Tribute by Bill Taylor

I first met Jack when he shot *Ghost Story* for Universal, back in the late 1970s. In those days, a foreign cameraman working in the studios had to have an American 'shadow', and since I was already working on the film as Al Whitlock's cameraman, I was the logical choice. What a dream experience for a young cameraman, to be paid to watch Jack Cardiff work! He was delightful, generous, and happily answered all questions.

I had expected that a man with his background would use many lights in complex set-ups and work at high light levels. Instead, the first shot I saw him light was a good-size real Vermont church interior, with a total of three 9-light PAR fixtures (one through a window) and some tracing paper diffusion. Of course, it looked beautiful, just as if the pale wintry light outside had done it all.

So my first lesson learnt from Cardiff was: you don't necessarily need a lot of lights if you put a few in exactly the right place.

As it turned out, I learned my craft from two great Englishmen who loved painting. Al Whitlock taught me composition and observation through his matte painting, and Cardiff taught me how to light.

Bill Taylor is Director of Photography at Illusion Art and Vice Chairman of the Board of the Visual Effects Society.

Introduction

In a previous life, before film journalism took its full grip on me, I was working as a visiting lecturer in video production on the Mixed Media Arts degree course at the University of Westminster. As the course title suggests, my students were a disparate (and often desperate) group, from a broad spectrum of disciplines and backgrounds and with an even broader appreciation of the film and video arts. One of my students, an outstanding Scottish fine artist with impoverished garret ambitions, finally challenged me to prove that what I was teaching had any relevance to his chosen field. I sent him away with instructions to watch Powell and Pressburger's *The Red Shoes*, undoubtedly Jack Cardiff's most painterly collaboration with the great filmmakers. He returned the following week full of praise and unbridled enthusiasm for filmmaking, and subsequently created some of the best work I ever saw produced on his or any other course at the University. I have no idea what he is doing with his life now, but I sure as hell hope he's making films.

Jack's continued influence on film and filmmakers cannot be underestimated. He has worked with the finest directors and most accomplished actors to create a body of work—approaching 100 features, shorts and documentaries—that is unequalled in its breadth and depth or artistry. Directors as diverse as Alfred Hitchcock, Richard Fleischer, Henry Hathaway, King Vidor, Mike Newell, Laurence Olivier and Michael Winner have called upon his gift as a cinematographer, and actors ranging from Sophia Loren and Maurice Chevalier to Humphrey Bogart and Marilyn Monroe have relied upon his unfailing eye to light them at their very best.

Often overshadowed by his accomplishments as a cinematographer are the films that Jack Cardiff has helmed as director, an eclectic range of titles from mad scientist monster movie *The Mutations* (1973) to psychedelic road-movie *Girl on a Motorcycle* (1968) and the sublime and multi-Oscar nominated adaptation of D H Lawrence's *Sons and Lovers* (1960). This book redresses the balance as Jack talks at length about the trials and tribulations associated with the director's chair.

In a career that has spanned almost 90 years since Jack first stepped in front of the camera as a child star in 1918, there have, inevitably, been projects that have fallen by the wayside: his collaboration with Orson Welles on *Ulysses*, the ill-fated *William Tell* project with Errol Flynn, the discussions with Peter Sellers about casting him in a James Joyce biography, and Jack's long-held ambition to direct a film based on the life of Turner, to name but a few. We can only wonder what these collaborations might have yielded.

Despite the complete mastery of his craft, Jack is the last person to describe himself as in any way technical ('a mathematical dunce … a technical ignoramus'), but as in any industry, the film business has its share of jargon and arcane terminology. For the uninitiated. the specialized terms that have arisen in this book are explained in the Technical Glossary. As for the definition of cinematographer itself, it has been described in literary allusions thus: while it is the job of the director to define the paragraphs, it is the responsibility of the cinematographer to render the sentences.

It is perhaps a flowery definition, yet one Jack wholly supports, but for further clarification his extensive definition of the art and responsibility of the cinematographer can be found at the beginning of Chapter Two. The only film term that Jack quite regularly uses in conversation is the abbreviation 'NG', simply short for No Good and liberally applied to all situations —film related or not.

The 20-plus hours of interviews that have formed the core of this book were conducted over the long summer of 2002, interrupted only by Jack's frequent departures to film festivals, awards ceremonies, speaking engagements and, on one occasion, a brief trip to America to shoot a new film. At the age of 88, Jack managed to cover three continents while we worked together, an impressive feat and a tribute to his continuingly tireless efforts to define (and on occasions redefine) the art of cinematography. This book is not a tribute to Jack—his films perfectly fulfil that function—but a glimpse behind the curtain at the collaborations, personalities, and craftsmanship that have created some of the cinema's most enduring images.

1 Into the Light

- A theatrical family
- An education … of sorts
- The early British studios
- First acting roles: *My Son* and *Billy's Rose*
- Alfred Hitchcock
- Behind the camera on *The American Prisoner* and *Loose Ends*
- Freddie Young
- Sir Alexander Korda
- *Knight Without Armour* and Marlene Dietrich

'With his painterly use of colour and light, Jack Cardiff pushed the boundaries of motion picture photography, creating memorable images that will live forever.'
Phil Meheux BSC—President, The British Society of Cinematographers

'Jack Cardiff's career as a cinematographer and a film director just about encompasses the entire history of British Cinema. His contribution to filmmaking is truly extraordinary, both in photographing masterpieces, like Powell and Pressburger's *The Red Shoes* and John Huston's *The African Queen*, and in directing notable British films such as *Sons and Lovers* and *Girl on a Motorcycle*. Jack has continued to work into the 21st century and remains a massive influence and inspiration for new generations of filmmakers.'
Adrian Wootton—Executive Director, Regus London Film Festival

JB You were born in 1914 into a theatrical, vaudeville world of limelight and greasepaint, which is easy to romanticize, but the reality must have been far tougher.

JC Of course, I didn't know any different or know what reality was *supposed* to be like. I was born into an atmosphere that was wonderful. Later on, I could see that other people didn't have the same experiences, but for the first few years of my life, perhaps until the age of six or seven, I thought it was a perfectly natural existence. Obviously, thinking about it now, it wasn't!

JB The year you were born also saw the outbreak of World War I; your father was never called up to fight?

JC   No, and I'm trying to think why that would have been. In 1914, my father would already have been 30 or 40, so he would have been getting on a bit.

JB   It sounds as though it was a very close and loving family, despite the unusual circumstances.

JC   I was extremely lucky because my parents were so very happy together. You hear so many stories where the father got drunk and beat the wife up, but that didn't happen with me at all. My parents were very much in love with each other and I was in this splendid cocoon of innocence and happiness. Of course, the whole background is exciting to a young kid: the lights, the greasepaint, the fact that it was all make-believe. That was the pure essence of my childhood. Contrast that to someone who's born of a man who goes to London to the office every day and you only see him at weekends or whatever … my surroundings were pure fantasy.

JB   A child's dream, I would think!

JC   Oh yes, it was. Of course, my father was a comedian and as such was wonderful to get on with, and in turn got on with everyone. He was very popular and a hero to me right away. My mother was a doting mother, as all mothers are. She appeared in the shows too; she was always at pains to point out that she had a bit of 'patter' too. Which simply meant she had a line or two in the shows.

You see they weren't repertory entertainment players. My father considered that not to be of his world at all, because that was for the intelligentsia. My father's metier was just happy-go-lucky vaudeville and pantomime. Ah yes! So that was part of my youth too— *Mother Goose* and *Ali Baba and The Forty Thieves*—all kids' stuff, and that fitted into my perfect happy life.

JB   Did you consider the lives of the 'ordinary' children you met as you travelled around to be rather prosaic?

JC   Well, I don't remember thinking that specifically, but let me explain the routine to you, which was disastrous for me from an education point of view: each week we would arrive on the Sunday afternoon in a new town and the next morning my mother would have organized a school place for me. I don't know how it was possible to do it so quickly. as we were only in each town for a week; but she did it. So I would be put into this school or that school for one week and obviously the teachers weren't a bit interested in me at all; what could they do with me? They had no idea if I had any aptitude for education or inclination for any particular subject, and really no time to find out. So I would be given the most basic sets of questions, a modicum of subjects with no depth. I learned practically nothing.

Jack Cardiff's parents, the musical hall 'Pros'.

JB And friends?

JC Well, of course, being the new boy for just one week meant that you weren't really known to anybody, the kids didn't know me and so I had no time to make friends.

But I did have one trick up my sleeve that was very useful: there was some kind of reciprocal arrangement that those who were connected to the show at the theatre could go to the cinema for free, and vice versa. So I could go to any cinema for nothing and I could also take a friend or two. Obviously that would make me an instant hero to the other kids.

JB Most of the constants in your life, in terms of friends, would have been the adults from the theatrical company, then?

JC Of course, the company was only constant for the period of the show, which might last several months on tour and then you would start another show. I suppose, unless it was a tremendous success like *My Fair Lady*[1], it would never be more than a few months. The pantomimes like *Mother Goose* would be automatically engaged on a season of perhaps six weeks, but no more. In other words, you only worked with these people in the company for a few weeks or a few months. So even that wasn't really constant. Sometimes you would meet the same people again later, on different shows.

In my little world, I used to make friends with the chorus girls. I would be in their dressing room and as I was only six or seven they didn't regard me as any threat to their privacy. I used to think nothing of them peeing in the washbasin; it was as if it were the most natural thing in the world!

JB This vaudeville existence of your childhood was very similar to Charlie Chaplin's. Did your father work with him or ever meet him?

JC Yes, he did a bit, though not much[2]. Years later, when I lived in Switzerland for a while, I lived close to Chaplin and we had dinner once or twice. He was a fascinating man, and the first time we met, I mentioned that my father had worked with him, and mentioned the show, and he remembered it. Of course, when my father knew him, Chaplin was unknown and he didn't stay long in England. He went to America very early when films were already being made in Hollywood on a fairly large scale and he walked right into them.

He told me that once, just for fun, he had entered a Charlie Chaplin lookalike competition. He came third!

JB   Did the cinema make an impression on you as a child?

JC   Well, in the very earliest times, when I say 'went to the cinema', one rather imagines going to some grand, purpose-built picture palace, but in those early days it was just a town hall, a silent film and a piano accompaniment. But the time I am talking about, say 1920, there was a little bit more sophistication in the presentation, I would think. I do remember the huge Wurlitzer organs rising up out of the floor. Perhaps they were just coming in at the time.

JB   How did the music hall 'pros', as your parents liked to term themselves, view film work? Did they consider it to be beneath them, somehow frivolous?

JC   No, it was just a different ballgame. When we finished a show, it was called 'resting', which just meant you were out of work. At those timesm, we used to go to digs [lodgings] in London, usually in Kennington. They were pretty awful digs, with bugs on the walls, and I remember my father burning them off with a candle. Generally speaking, we would spend a couple of weeks in London, depending on how long it took to get the next engagement for work. More or less every morning, we would get the bus up West [the West End of London], to where the theatrical agents' offices were, and see what was happening for jobs.

It would sometimes be the case that the agents would say that a show was starting in a month and perhaps rehearsals in two weeks, so there would be gaps, but work was fairly continuous. My parents were very much in demand and my father, who had appeared before King Edward VII, had very good reviews, which kept him in demand as a dancer and later a comedian.

JB   So they just fitted in film work where they could?

JC   The thing was, there was always the odd day here and there to fit in a bit of film work. Again, that was a very happy thing for me, going with them to work as an extra and other odd things. I had the occasional part too.

JB   How did it compare to the theatre?

JC   To me, it was just like the stage, only bigger; you had exterior lots where you had all of the fantastic sets, but they were still just sets, and I was very used to those. I got to see behind the fantasy of moving pictures, cranking the handle on the camera, and the lights and the make-up … Leichner make-up—Leichner number five, I think it was. Because it was monochromatic film, it didn't show up the red colour band very much, so we used to have very dark red-lipped make-up.

Still, there was this thing of not going to the same school for more than a few weeks. There was one time—I know this sounds ridiculous—we were living in Brixton [in south London] and my mother and father put me into a local college where we had to wear a cap, which I thought was fantastic! One of my regrets in life was that I never worked hard at Latin; I'm still working on it, to tell you the truth. So I had my first lessons in Latin at that college. I was probably only there for a total of five weeks and didn't learn too much.

JB   The great painters heavily influenced your later career. When were you first exposed to them?

JC   The thing in my life that has made such a huge shining light, 'shining light' being very much the right phrase, is painting. I remember one thing about all the digs and little apartments all over England, and that is, I don't think I ever saw a single painting in any of them. They were very humble places and they might have had the odd drawing on the wall, but maybe not even that. I had never even a painting at that time. I tried to think the other day what age I would have been when I did, and I think I couldn't have been any older than seven or eight. At this particular school, the teacher said: 'Today, children, we are going to see art.' See art! Well the word itself really meant nothing to me, but we traipsed along to this building—in the north of England somewhere, I forget where—but I remember it being very grey, which made what was about to happen even more of a stark contrast.

We got inside this large room and there were *literally hundreds* of coloured pictures. This was a fantastic and overwhelming surprise and I was instantly fascinated. I don't remember what paintings I saw, and I don't suppose it had all of the wealth of the top painters that say the [Royal] Academy in London had, but I vividly remember being overwhelmed by so much colour.

JB   Did you then decide to take matters into your own hands as far as your artistic education went?

JC   In a way, because after that I had a complete fixation with seeing more: I wanted to *know* so much more. From then on, every time we went to a new town, I would find the galleries, and over the next few years I picked up more understanding and learnt to recognize the great painters. And I have had this great love of painting ever since.

Not long after that, I remember a point when it hit home very forcibly that the thing that motivated the artists, beyond their choice of subject, was this one word: 'light'. I realized that whether it was a long shot of a country field, or just a bowl of fruit, light was the all-important thing. So I began to study this motivation more and more, particularly the way a *good* artist uses the light.

JB Were there any artists specifically that stood out?

JC   I realized that Rembrandt was hugely innovative because most artists had this 'north light' in the studio, but he was never content with using the orthodox 45-degree top light, which made shadows around the eyes and under the nose. He would experiment with really weird lighting. He was very brave.

This fascinated me, but please understand that wanting to learn about light had *absolutely nothing* to do with me wanting to be a cameraman. It was just that I associated it with painting and I was madly in love with painting.

JB Did you complement those visits to the galleries with books? Was this when you started your collection of books on the great artists?

JC   No, not at all. If I had been a bit more intelligent, I would have realized that I could have gone to a library, but I was far too young and probably wouldn't have been allowed to join. Today there are so many books on painters, but at a price. I was completely without money in those days, so even if they had been available to me, I wouldn't have been able to afford them.

It's quite extraordinary when I think about it, that at that time I had no ambition to do camera work or photography; I barely knew about photography. What was so interesting was that the pictures were so much larger than life and so dramatic.

JB Were you yet equating what could be achieved on canvas with what could be done in film?

JC   I don't think so. I wasn't of an age to analyze these things. All that I had an interest in was the wonderful, exciting pictures that were so moving to me.

JB The scale of film production in Hollywood was already vastly outstripping what we had in England at that time. What do you remember of the early studios here?

JC   Well, at St Margaret's Studios,[3] I remember that the general setup was that there was a very pleasant and happy country background. My mother, father and I would catch a train down to St Margaret's and walk up to the studios. It was all countryside and I clearly remember these huge Klieg lamps that were used. When Technicolor[4] started years later, all the experts said that you had to use a lot of light, which was true because you had three films running through the camera at the same time, but the same was true of light in the early days of filmmaking. The film stock was so slow, you needed

A young Jack Cardiff

just as much light. All of the terrific light that the Klieg lights gave off was still a very flat light, though.

JB   And things were predominantly shot outside, even for the interior scenes?

JC   Yes, I remember at Wharton Hall they used to shoot a lot outside. I also remember that the camera had a handle at the back and not at the side, as you might imagine. Very awkward to operate, I would think.

JB   Then you were already starting to take notice of the technical paraphernalia surrounding filmmaking?

JC   Not when I was a child actor, no. I still had no ambition to find out about cameras; I had no interest at all. I was always interested in the fantasy of filmmaking, though.

JB   Your first acting role was in 1918 with *My Son* when you were aged just 4.

JC   I remember that there was a scene on a lawn with Violet Hopson[5], who I remember thinking was a very pretty woman, but I obviously don't remember any details of what I had to do or say.

JB   And by 1922 you were taking the starring role in *Billy's Rose*.

JC   What was sad was that when I was doing *Billy's Rose*, the film was a real sobbing weepy. My sister in the film, Little Nell, is very dangerously ill, and the one thing she would love to have is flowers. So my character goes out looking for some and I see a woman throwing some roses out of her Rolls Royce and I run over to pick them up and get run over.

So I have this scene where I am on a bed dying, and what is truly touching is that my parents had lost a child before I was born. His name was Jack too, Jackie. He was very talented on stage and had great potential, but when they were on tour in Wales he caught some sort of infection and died, a terrible thing. So when I was acting in this film, dying in bed, my father and mother played my father and mother in the scene, and my mother was crying her heart out. They were genuine tears and it was very sad indeed.

JB   Do you remember seeing any of these films you had appeared in? Taking your new friends from school to see them?

JC   No, this was such a long time ago—70, 80 years ago. But I wish sometimes that these films could be rediscovered. Funny things do happen and somebody at the BFI [British Film Institute] was telling me that someone in Brighton had been looking through an old bin and found some film that had been thrown away. So it does happen that things are rediscovered.

JB   You were telling me that you were watching some footage recently and you saw your father.

JC   Yes, that was fascinating. I knew he had done some acting at Elstree Studios[6] and had worked on a film called *The Informer* [Arthur Robison, 1928], which was really the last silent film. I had worked on it as a tea boy and a general gopher. I had a still of my father from that film, but that was all.

There was a possibility that my hands were going to be in the film, because there was a scene at a board meeting and the director wanted my hands right up in the foreground. Well, I went to see the archive footage at the BFI and my hands were on screen for about half a second. Then, just as they were about to shut the film off, I saw a cave on screen and said, 'Hold it just a moment!' And my father enters this cave and does his scene. Having a still picture of a dead relative is normally as good as you get, but here was my father in movement, smiling and laughing and living. A very interesting experience.

JB While you were working on *The Informer*, Hitchcock was shooting *Blackmail* [1929] in the same studios. Did you meet him at this time?

JC   No, not on *Blackmail*, but shortly after that on *The Skin Game* [1931], I think it was called. On that one I was the numbers boy, a pretty lowly role, and obviously I didn't know he was going to become 'The Great Hitchcock'. But what was already very evident was his diabolically cruel sense of humour; he was always playing jokes on people. I was close enough to him on that film to see this sense of humour and he certainly liked to tell funny stories; he was a great raconteur. I remember him making a few sketches on set and now of course, I own a few of those myself.

He did have this extraordinary sense of humour. But then, in the film business there is this thing—I don't know what you might call it apart from a 'film humour'. And it even happens when you are working on pictures with very prestigious people and great big stars. The camera department, for instance, would have an almost secret sense of humour—they could whistle a tune for example, which would *mean* something. It was a laconic, mysterious sense of humour. That sort of thing goes on all the time.

JB Does that come from the fact that despite the preconceptions, there is very little glamour in working on a film and a hell of a lot of hard work?

JC   Yes, that's true. There is a propensity to the ridiculous that you might not get in an office if you were dealing with figures and market prices. On a film set, people are making mistakes and perhaps being conceited and the director may be shouting and putting on a big act—then the sense of the ridiculous comes out. Also, the fact is that in film, ever since I started, you can be lucky and find yourself working on *The Importance of Being Earnest* [Anthony Asquith, 1952] and be on stage every day; or you can find yourself, as I have so many times in my career, in the middle of the Sahara Desert and in terrible trouble. So the humour is a backdrop and maybe an antidote to that tough life.

Most seem to develop this humour in the film business. I know that Dick Fleischer,[7] one of my best friends in the business, has a fantastic sense of humour.

JB Had you left school behind completely by this point?

JC   Not quite yet. What happened was that in 1926, just a few weeks before my twelfth birthday, my family and I moved from our digs in London to live permanently at a film studio, where my father had been offered some kind of job. It was so cheap and we rented a cottage for practically nothing; it was right outside the studio gate. So I was then put into a permanent school. It was called Medburn and was about $2^{1}/_{2}$ miles away. It was very pleasant and I was very happy there and it was around this time that I read

Frank Harris's *My Life and Loves*.[8] He was a very well educated man and even went to Germany so that he could learn German and read Goethe in its original form. So he was a bit of a hero to me. He had a reputation for being a terrible liar. He told Oscar Wilde once that he had been to every stately home in England and Wilde replied, 'Yes, dear Frankie, *once!*'

So he wrote his five-volume memoirs, *My Life and Loves*, and 70 per cent was, I think, outrageous lies about his prowess as a lover. I bought it and something stood out, again rather like the paintings had. I suddenly realized: 'My God! What a world!' I went to Foyles bookstore in London and I bought every book that he mentioned and I read them and each book led me to another—a lot of classical books.

Jack Cardiff as camera operator. Date unknown.

JB   How did you first come across *My Life and Loves*?

JC   I just remember it was so cheap to buy! It was an education in itself.

JB   So you began immersing yourself in books as much as you did paintings?

JC   Yes, but also, at about the same time, I started to buy a magazine called *The Magnet*.[9] The first one came out in 1911, before I was born. It was about a school called Greyfriars and the popular boys in the comic were idolized almost like film stars are today. Wonderful characters, and to me they were very grown up. I became engrossed in these weekly stories and it became like my public-school education and formed my ideas of behaviour and manners—to be honest and to stick to your guns. It probably sounds very naïve today to talk about it, but I learned so much from *The Magnet*.

JB   Going back to *The Informer*, this was the point that you really got your hands on a camera for the first time, isn't it?

JC   Remember that at this time I had no ambition for photography—I didn't carry a No.2 Brownie camera and take snapshots.

But on one occasion, just a few weeks before my 14th birthday, something happened on the camera crew, someone was away or ill or something and they wanted somebody to work at changing the focus on the lens and I was called over. My father was ill by this time, really in bad health, and so I had to work to provide the money. I earned the enormous salary of 15 shillings a week, which even in those days was not very much. So I was called over and the first assistant on the camera said, 'Now look here, sonny, this lens has some figures on it and I've made a few pencil marks on it. During the scene, when I tell you, I want you to rotate the lens from one pencil mark to the next.' So the scene was shot and I twisted the lens around when I was told to and afterwards I said, 'What did I just do?' and he said, 'You followed focus, son!'

JB   So your big break came and you were hardly aware of it happening?

JC   Yes, but although that was my first break, I still wasn't that keen. I never thought, 'Ooh, I must do more of this!' But what *did* happen was that I realized the camera department often seemed to be going abroad on films and I thought it would be marvellous to be paid to travel abroad. What a wonderful idea, I'll join the department!

JB   Did your plan work out?

JC   Of course, not at first because the next job I got was *The American Prisoner* [Thomas

Bentley, 1928] where I had to haul all these camera cases all over Dartmoor, tremendously hard work, and I had to reload film at night when everyone else was having a great time. I was down in the cellars reloading the film—a tough beginning. So it took about a year until I crossed the sea and that was just to the Isle of Wight for a day and a half!

JB **Not quite the romance of travel you had imagined …**

JC   No, but then a dramatic thing happened to change that. My friend Ted Moore,[10] also a camera assistant, called me and woke me up and said, 'Our studios are on fire!' So I put on some clothes over my pyjamas and rushed over and, sure enough, the studio was ablaze.

I remember because I was the smallest person there and the windows were very small, I was the person who got pushed in through the window. I dropped inside and opened the doors and everyone rushed into the hall and we saw everything ablaze with the roof timbers falling down. We thought we would just have time to get the cameras out, figuring they were worth a lot of money. We managed to get something like ten cameras out and the next morning we found that the management weren't very happy at all at our actions because they were heavily insured!

However, one camera, a Debrie,[11] a French camera loaned on approval, had not been insured and was worth a lot of money. So Debrie gave Ted Moore £10 as a reward and offered me a trip for three days to Paris. So I was off! First time abroad!

That seemed to break the curse of not going abroad!

JB **Was the Debrie the camera you were using most of the time at this point?**

JC   Mostly Debries. *The Informer* was silent and the next year I worked for Richard Eichberg[12] on *The Flame of Love* [1930]—what a title! Again that was using a Debrie. On *The Informer* we shot at 16 frames per second, but for sound the speed was 24 frames. At that time, if you switched the camera on and it was running at 24 pictures, it would jam, because it was such a violent action. So it had two switches: the first cranked it, like the first gear of a car, at seven or eight frames, and then you switched the next one to get it to full speed.

One of my jobs on *The Flame of Love* was to switch the camera on and the entire crew was German and I didn't realize that the German word for 'on' is 'auf', which sounds just like 'off'. So every time we were due to start the scene, the cameraman would call 'auf' and I would say: 'Yes, yes, it's *off*.' I got a good whack around the head for that …

in fact, they used to whack my head a lot on that picture. I fell off a scaffold at one point and the director, Richard Eichberg, caught me in his arms and I was very grateful because it was a good eight-foot fall. But then he gave me such a whack for daring to fall off his scaffold. I eventually picked up enough German.

JB What sort of films were you working on now and what was your role on them?

JC *The American Prisoner* was quite straightforward stuff with Carl Brisson[13] and the lovely Madeleine Carroll.[14] I was the numbers boy and again had to carry lots of equipment. We had a lot of location work on that, which was tough. The tripod had a head on it that was solid steel and very heavy. But it was all the cameraman's rites of passage.

Madeleine Carroll was so charming and years later, it must have been 1940-something, I was in Rome with my assistant Christopher Challis.[15] The hotel we were staying in had a huge circular dance floor and Chris turned to me and said: 'I'm going to ask that girl over there to dance—she's very pretty.' He was just getting up and making his move towards her and I said: 'Hang on, better not, that's Madeleine Carroll.' Who knows, she might have agreed, but I doubt it.

JB So you were finally enjoying the glamour of travel to some extent by now?

JC Funnily enough, when we were staying in the same hotel, some time earlier, there was this big crowd outside and they said that Hitler and Mussolini were about to drive past. I had a camera magazine case, quite big, and as I couldn't see properly I stood on the magazine. Along came the car with Hitler and Mussolini, passing no more than 20 feet away. I still have the most vivid impression of seeing the Führer and Mussolini, but just as I was enjoying the moment, I was dragged off by the police, because they thought I was standing on explosives and was attempting an assassination. Eventually they looked in the magazine and just saw film. I could have changed world history there: if only I had …

JB At what point did you meet Freddie Young[16] for the first time?

JC Well, when I went to B&D[17] as an assistant, the chief of the camera department was Freddie. His operator was Francis Carver (son of Lord Carver), the focus puller was John Wilcox, the second assistant was Kenneth Wilcox, the make-up girl there was Sonja Wilcox. Gwen Wilcox was the chief make-up girl and the editor was Derek Wilkinson, who was engaged to either Gwen or Sonja. So they were *literally* one happy family.

But Freddie ran the camera department beautifully: everything was in tremendously good shape, even the stools we had were wonderfully painted. Freddie ran it like clockwork.

JB That practice was quite uncommon for the period?

JC I certainly don't remember any other department at the time that ran with such a high profile. He was called 'chief' and his word was law. I worked on occasions for Freddie when they had more than one camera on something.

Also, and I know this was quite uncommon at the time, the cameraman would shoot a quick couple of feet of a difficult set up and then I would take the magazine off and take it into the darkroom to develop the strip in a thermos flask. I could then dry it quickly and make an enlargement: a photographic print. So within a quarter of an hour I would be bringing them a photograph of the scene. It was a real luxury and very innovative.

Freddie had all this wonderful equipment and Ted Moore, who later won an Oscar for *A Man for all Seasons* (Fred Zinnemann, 1966), was my focus puller. So he was in charge of maintaining the camera, keeping it well oiled and in pristine condition, and on this front he did a wonderful job. But the problem was, the viewfinder was an inverted prism so that you would see things upside down and reversed left to right. When you were trying to pan left to follow an actor it was terribly difficult not to pan right. We worked our arses off getting that right!

JB Was the fact that Freddie Young was turning the camera department into a real art form resented by the directors?

JC The directors at B&D, apart from Korda,[18] were on their own and rather isolated, but they were very well served by people like Freddie.

I was really working on the complete opposite end of the scale, though, because I had been working on 'British quota pictures',[19] which was a really tough schedule and you couldn't make any mistakes as the operator.

JB Was Freddie Young's way of working and his department setup something that greatly influenced you?

JC I think so, yes, although there was this attitude at the time that we, Ted and I, were the Cinderellas, doing all of the rough stuff, with no time for mistakes or retakes. It was quite terrifying, but wonderful training. I became very fast.

JB Alexander Korda was already building his empire at that time …

JC He was a family man again—like Wilcox, who had all his family working in the business—and Korda did too. He had his brother, who was a director, then another brother, Vincent Korda, who was an art director—quite brilliant, and incidentally he used to go to Paris and buy wonderful paintings for Alex, incredible bargains, he even got a Van Gogh at a knocked-down price! Later, when Alex had a sale, they made huge profits. So anyway, there were plenty of other relatives around.

JB   Alexander Korda was a mix of shrewd businessman and great visionary artist. What are your memories of him?

JC   The great thing about Korda was that he managed to get his backers to invest millions although they lost everything. He built a complete empire with the money. He built Denham Studios[20] and a funny story happened: I had finished *Ghost Goes West* [René Clair, 1935] and I took a holiday in France just as the construction of Denham was being finished off. I was under contract there: £15 a week, a lot of money in those days.

So I had just finished working with René Clair[21] and I drove to St-Tropez to his house. He had invited another woman from England, who had just flown in, and I had taken a week or several days to drive there. Well, we had lunch and she said, 'Isn't it awful news about Denham?' I said, 'What?' and she told us that it had burned to the ground. So at the earliest opportunity I went to the nearest village to a phone and called England and found out that a complete stage had been destroyed by fire, but not quite the disaster it could have been.

JB   We really don't have anyone like the Kordas today, do we?

JC Korda was a great entrepreneur. No, today we don't have enough Kordas or Sam Spiegels,[22] we are terribly short of good producers and that is our tragedy.

My son and I were discussing this and one of the problems is that we don't have any proper studios in England any more. In the early days, you worked for a *studio*, but now they are just what are called 'four-wall studios'; it's just an empty space that you hire for three weeks or two months. In the old days, you had the big studios that had a full time, permanent staff, and that included the actors. They would give an actor a script and say, 'There you go, Mr Cooper. You start on Monday.' No argument. It was a job of work for an actor and no matter how big or humble, they had to work for the company.

Now there is no company and the actors today have become so big and so terribly powerful. Now the studios go to the stars and beg them to read the scripts. The star has script approval, director approval, co-star approval and even cameraman approval. It has even happened that actors have demanded the final cut of a film.

JB   Korda wouldn't have had much truck with that!

JC   No, he wouldn't believe the changed position today. I guess he saw the start of it before he died, but still …

JB   You worked with William Cameron Menzies[23] on *Things to Come* [1936]. He was a fearsome talent.

JC   Yes, he was a truly great art director. I was working at Denham with Korda and we also did a little work at Wharton Hall Studios, which were sometimes used as extra studio space.

JB   This was predominantly special effects work?

JC   Yes, I was working with a chap called Ned Mann,[24] who was the head of the special effects department and my job really was still just an operator, but this was highly technical work.

JB   What sort of technical work?

JC   I remember one scene in *The Man Who Could Work Miracles*[25] [Lothar Mendes, 1936] and it was a shot of a shoe that had to get larger and larger in the frame. So we had an expert from London who could carve beautifully and he made this shoe out of plaster or Plasticine or some such, and it was painted. It looked absolutely realistic and we would shoot one or two frames of that—everything was fixed, so you couldn't move anything—then the sculptor would take off a thin layer. We were shooting in reverse, and we would take the next shot, and this went on all through the day and through the night. Two frames, re-carve, two frames. We went on until something like three in the morning before we finished. It was terribly difficult and onerous, but with wonderful results.

When we had to do shots where people had to suddenly appear as if by magic, we would have a big hall and I had a big 10 x 8 camera and when the actor was due to disappear Korda would shout, 'cut!' and I would make a quick sketch on the glass plate on the back of my camera. Then the actor would change costume and I would get him back in the same position according to my drawing. Those films were full of complicated tricks and I wasn't truly happy there. But at least I was working.

JB   And things were about to get even worse …

JC   Well, outside of my area, there must have been at least five other operators working on films, and a man arrived from Hollywood called Hal Rosson,[26] and he started a picture with René Clair and he was a demon who wanted perfection.

He wasn't happy with his first operator and he fired him, then fired his next one too and the one after that. The manager, David Cunningham, called me into his office and told me that I might have to go and operate for him. I told him I didn't want to go because I didn't want to be fired like the rest, and that was inevitable. I begged him and he said that it was up to me, but I might have to go sooner or later. Well, he fired the next operator too, so I was the last one left and *had* to go and work for him.

I was furious that I was going to be fired by this monster, but I went to the set and he was perfunctory with me and rather snappy. I called him 'Hal' instead of 'Mr Rosson', which was risky. And then he tried to show me these handles on the camera for operating it and tried to tell me it was the best way. I said: 'Well, *Hal*, you may think so, but I feel differently and *I'm* the operator.' I was so sure I was going to be fired that I hardly thought it mattered, but after that we got on perfectly well, partly because I tried these handles out and they really were very good. I worked with him over the course of two years following that, but he was a weird character.

JB Do you think directors often project this image purely for effect?

JC There is certainly a lot of it in the film business. John Ford is a case in point and I have heard the most terrible things about him. If an actor told him they didn't like a scene, John would say, 'Don't you?' and simply tear the page out and leave the actor with nothing to do. He was impossible at times.

JB Henry Hathaway was another one.

JC Well, of course, Hathaway, at one time, was Ford's assistant. You could make a film about Hathaway. If anyone had a tough time getting to be a director, it was Henry. He wanted it so badly and he was a prop man to start with—a real labour job. He did become an assistant director and was very tough; in fact, he fired a cameraman for being late. An assistant director firing someone! He was impossible, but very often right.

JB You had a slightly easier time on your next film, *Knight Without Armour* [1937], which was directed by Jacques Feyder.[27] And you met Marlene Dietrich.

JC She took an interest in me in quite a motherly way. I was just out of my teens, I suppose, and she was always very kind to me.

Knight Without Armour was with Harry Strandling[28] on camera. Dietrich was so charming and so was Jacques Feyder, the director. Looking back on it, I was young and pretty naive, but I knew he was a good director. He had made a film called *La Kermesse Héroïque* [1935], a big classical French film. He was a very *French* director; he had a long overcoat that went almost all the way to the floor and it always had a little bottle of Cognac inside, which he would sip at.

I learnt a lot from him, he knew the angle and the composition he wanted. He would cut in close, perhaps across a shoulder or even the top of the head; what I later equated with Degas—a clipping technique. Degas had gotten it from the then-new vogue for stills photography that often cut in. So Feyder had the same idea of getting *into* a scene, something that Hitchcock later used, getting as close as you could because there was no point of getting lots of air around someone.

Harry Strandling was a very fine cameraman. A lot of so-called creative people put on a bit of an act and all that crap, but Harry Strandling was this genial American who really knew how to light quite simplistically.

Jack Cardiff as camera operator on *Knight Without Armour* (1937)

JB   Did Dietrich ever discuss her relationship with Josef von Sternberg[29] with you?

JC   She spoke about him as if he were a god and she always referred to him as '*Mr* von Sternberg'. He really made her what she was. He was a great director and Dietrich obviously thought the world of him.

What was amusing was that Dietrich had worked so much with Josef von Sternberg, who was a great cameraman as well as a director, and she learned everything about lighting from watching him. She was probably one of the first stars to realize what all the great stars in Hollywood now know: that they must be well lit, as their future fortunes can depend on it!

Years later, Faye Dunaway carried a little mirror around with her because she had bags under her eyes and would say, 'Jack, do you think the key light is a bit too high?' And I would deliberately put it too high so that I could bring it down when she asked me to the point that I wanted it in the first place. That way, she was happy.

But Dietrich was the first to learn all of this. She knew that a light at forty-five degrees would make a little shadow under the nose and on her lips and with her physiognomy it looked splendid. So regardless of her being in a cellar or under a waterfall, she would always have that key light.

JB   She had the power to demand that?

JC   Oh yes. And she had a full-length mirror positioned by the side of the camera, which she would adjust her hair and clothes in. Very funny. She would say to Harry sometimes, 'Harry, is that kicker light high enough?' And Harry would always say to me, 'You know, she is always right.' And she was, she really knew her stuff.

Marlene Dietrich takes a bath for *Knight Without Armour* (1937)

2 Painting the World in Colour

'*Western Approaches* represents one of the greatest achievements of Britain's wartime filmmaking. Its compelling story and determinedly documentary approach are immeasurably enhanced by Jack Cardiff's Technicolor camera work, most of it secured in extraordinarily difficult circumstances.'
Roger Smither—Keeper, Film and Video Archive, Imperial War Museum

JB Perhaps this would be a good time to ask you to define the job of a cinematographer.

JC   Well, it's quite a complex situation: the cinematographer is engaged to photograph a film, but he certainly doesn't decide what to shoot; that is decided by the director, who has already worked it out from his script. The cinematographer then works with the director to achieve an atmosphere—poverty or high gloss or whatever. It is up to the cinematographer to use his skills to produce that result. Of course, the closer the cameraman works with the director, the better the results will be.

I forget the name of the film, but there was a director on location who saw clouds scudding across the sky and the light was going in and out with impossible contrast. The cameraman said that he couldn't shoot under those conditions and the director insisted that it was a lovely effect and he wanted the scene shot like that. The cameraman shot the scene as instructed, but he wrote on the numbers board, 'Shot under protest'. It turned out to be a brilliant sequence and the cameraman won an Oscar. So that explains how the situation works; there has to be mutual trust and cooperation.

JB It often sounds more complicated than it should because the terms cameraman, cinematographer, director of photography and lighting

cameraman are all bandied about. In fact, they are virtually interchangeable names for the same thing, right?

JC   Yes, there is really no difference. When I first started out, the cameraman did everything; he did all of the lighting and he operated the camera, there were no pure operators. Then, of course, the lighting became much more complicated and there was no longer time to operate the camera itself.

However, even today, some cameramen like to operate themselves. This I will never understand because you have to do so much when you are lighting and you are thinking about that all of the time; you don't have time to physically prepare and work on the camera. A camera operator pans the camera with great finesse; he is trained to make lovely movements. If I were a cameraman and were operating the camera, I would be concentrating so hard on the movements that I wouldn't be able to notice if someone had missed a light or something. I could never do it.

With a cameraman who is just starting and who perhaps doesn't yet have a big reputation, it is tough if he is asked to make things look lousy and dirty, because in his heart he will want to brighten things up a bit. Once you have a big reputation, it matters less if you make some hideous mistake and don't put a light where it should be. People will still say, 'Brilliant cinematography—how bold!' This happens from time to time.

JB   When did you first become aware of Technicolor?

JC   I had just got home after a hard day's work and my mother said, 'You had a call and you have to go back to the studios.' I was pissed off because of the long drive. She said it had to do with 'Techni-something-or-other'. Of course, Technicolor had never been heard of before, but they wanted to interview all of the camera operators. There were probably half-a-dozen of us working with Korda at the time. I was really angry, but I got in the car and drove back.

When I got there, some of the operators had already been interviewed by representatives from this Technicolor Company and they had been asked the most incredibly difficult questions, about optics and laboratory techniques and terrifying equations. They were literally shaking as they came out.

Well, the same line of questioning happened with me about these theories and equations and I said to them, 'I think I'm wasting your time because I'm a mathematical dunce and no good at these sorts of things.' There was a kind of shocked silence and then one of them asked me how I expected to get on in the film business as a cameraman. I told them I loved paintings and that I studied them and I loved light. One of them asked me which side of the face does Rembrandt light and I said, 'This side, the left, but the other side for etchings.' All bluff, but I talked about Pieter de Hooch and other old painters and in the end they sent me out feeling rather silly. But the next morning, I was told that I had been chosen. Very weird, having admitted that I was a technical ignoramus, but there you are.

JB   Who was on the interview panel?

JC   They were people from the Technicolor Company, not Mr Kalmus who was the big chief, but there was a man called George Kay and one or two others who were the chiefs at Technicolor.

JB   What were Technicolor doing recruiting in Britain?

JC   I never got the full facts, but I think they already had plans for starting Technicolor in England. The idea, officially, was that they wanted to find an operator to make him into a Technicolor cameraman to go to Hollywood. Looking back on it, that didn't make sense: why an English cameraman? Perhaps there was some other reason … I think that in the back of their minds it must have been that they wanted to open a plant in England.

You don't make these decisions in a few weeks, it was a long-term thing, and so they were just getting people ready to step into Technicolor. Shortly after that, they did announce that they were going to open up a plant, a laboratory in England, on the Bath Road. And as I had been chosen, I was the first person to be employed by them.

I was very happy, and left Korda—he didn't seem to mind—and there I was, working full time for Technicolor.

JB   But you still hadn't laid your hands on a Technicolor camera at this point?

JC   No, what happened next was that they came over with the Technicolor camera, which was amazing; just like the Rolls Royce of cameras. So beautifully made and technically brilliant, running three films at once.

I had an assistant called Henty Creer and he was an old Etonian. A marvellous little assistant, very young, but a brilliant assistant. He didn't actually work for Technicolor, but he stayed at Denham Studios and worked on the first films with me.

I mention Henty because he was just like a schoolboy and when the war came he worked on the submarines. He actually worked in baby-subs and saw active service, during which he was killed. Absolutely tragic as he was someone that was really making a name for himself.

JB This all ultimately led to you becoming involved in the first British Technicolor feature film.

JC   Yes, of course, almost immediately they made *Wings of the Morning*[1] [Harold Schuster, 1937]. Thinking about it, they must have been jolly quick building the laboratory and making that first film. I think they acquired me and then started to build everything else, which must have taken at least six months.

So anyway, I found myself on *Wings of the Morning* with Henry Fonda and Annabella[2] and I had Henty as my assistant. And, of course, *Wings of the Morning* was made at the Korda studios.

JB Why was *Wings of the Morning* chosen as the first British Technicolor film?

JC   That's one of the things that I shall never really know because these sorts of decisions are made in hotel suites or in the big offices of Mr Korda. The fact was that it portrayed Ireland and gypsies and the Derby horserace, so it was all very colourful.

JB What are your memories of the young Henry Fonda on *Wings of the Morning*?

Shooting the Derby horserace finale of *Wings of the Morning* (1937)

JC   He was a marvellous man to work with, he had a tremendous sense of humour and played tricks all of the time. He was always clowning and if he wasn't working he would disguise himself: the cameraman would be lighting the set and say, 'put on number nineteen', and the light would come on and start going all over the place and then go out … and you would look up and find Henry Fonda working the light!

One time, he pretended to be a madman and rushed through the set in disguise, screaming his head off, and it spread all though the studios that there was a madman on the loose. He was crazy but a very, very good actor. It was a great film to work on.

JB   Did Korda have a solid business arrangement with Technicolor at this time?

JC   Yes, Technicolor right away established themselves, not as a production company to make films, but as a company that studios could hire. Of course, at first hardly anyone would hire them, because it was a very unknown territory.

JB   What were Technicolor like to work for in those early days?

JC   It became apparent to me quite quickly that Technicolor had very strict rules of conduct and technical abilities. The light had to be exact, because they were running three negatives, each of which had to be perfectly exposed and worked out. You certainly couldn't be too slaphappy. At first, Technicolor brought over their own cameraman, Ray Rennahan,[3] who was a real veteran and obeyed all of the rules. Technicolor wanted light everywhere, because they didn't like shadows as they didn't contain controlled colours, and that might affect their prestige. They wanted *all* of the shadows eliminated.

But Ray lit what I would call very 'high key'. In other words, lots of filler light everywhere so that there were no black shadows; but then he used cross lights to keep a sort of three-dimensional gloss. He did a wonderful job and I learnt an awful lot from him on *Wings of the Morning*.

After that, they did a lot more tests, which I worked on and we did some short things. Of course, I was now an operator dying to be a cameraman! That was my great thing. And there were no English Technicolor cameramen, so I was the closest thing as an operator. Even people like Freddie Young had never photographed anything in colour.

JB   And what kind of technical limitations were you working under with the Technicolor system?

JC   The blimp was just enormous and it was so heavy. We tried to treat it like an ordinary camera, but it was difficult to get lights near, because it was so huge. Also we couldn't reload the camera because it was a very tricky job that took far too long. We used to haul the camera out of the blimp, put it on a tripod, and replace it with a second, preloaded camera, which would save some time. They were very tricky cameras to work with.

JB   **Do you recall any rivalry between those pioneering Technicolor in America and those doing so in England?**

JC   A good question, but as far as I know there was no evidence of any jealousy or rivalry of any kind. God knows what happened. In fact, Technicolor in England had gained a rather enviable reputation, where the Americans thought the colour was so good it must be down to the quality of English water used in the processing. Absolute nonsense, of course!

JB   **This sounds like the beginning of a poor vaudeville joke, but you punched King George VI on the nose, didn't you?**

JC   Before the coronation we had this wonderful opportunity to photograph His Majesty the King, in the gardens at Buckingham Palace. Usually you would just have a cameraman and an assistant, but in this case we had to take everybody from Technicolor. We set up the camera where the King was going to come out and it was so rare to get a picture of the King.

When he eventually arrived, he came out with the Prime Minister, Stanley Baldwin; I took a tape measure and ran across to measure the distance to him for the focus. We were all very nervous and I ran the tape out far too quickly and hit him right in the face—Bang! There was a terrible silence and I eventually muttered, 'Ever so sorry, Your Majesty'. He was very sweet, a terribly nice man, and he said it was quite all right.

JB   **Despite your little faux pas, Technicolor then went on to cover the coronation in some detail.**

JC   I think we had four cameras in the country at that time. For the great coronation procession of the King travelling through London, each camera had its fixed position, because the crowds were so enormous that we couldn't move the cameras from one location to another.

So we had these four cameras stationed at the best places. As one of the cameramen, I was perched on a place opposite the Royal Albert Hall on top of a little lodge, at the entrance to the park [Hyde Park]. Once we got up there, we couldn't move for the crowds, there was no escape. We had to get up there around eight in the morning and there was a rehearsal of all the coaches and the like, including the royal coach. I was pretty high up, so that you couldn't see anyone in the coach, but it was a lovely shot and I was panning right to left as it went by. It was a beautiful day with the sun shining, so just for fun I photographed it. You couldn't see anyone inside, so it could have been the Queen of Persia! Then we had to sit down and wait for the real thing and by the time that came along it was pouring with rain, almost impossible to shoot.

When Technicolor saw all of the work the following morning, they couldn't work out how three cameras had torrential rain and I had wonderful sunshine!

JB   Those technical limitations with Technicolor that we have discussed must have really come to the fore on a day like that.

JC   Yes, because Technicolor, as always in those days, were in terrible trouble without lots of light. George Gunn[4] had advanced the idea of shooting inside Westminster Abbey, where there was almost no light; he thought that by cooking up the developer at the laboratory it would be better than nothing. They shot wide open and prayed and it worked. They shot some pretty good stuff. Very *innovative* stuff.

JB   Another incredibly colourful character entered your life at the same time. Tell me how you first came to meet Count von Keller.

JC   What happened was that one of the heads of Technicolor, who became a great friend of mine, was Kay Harrison; in fact, he was the chairman of Technicolor. Anyway, one day a man came to see him at his office on the Bath Road. This fellow was very tall, 6 foot 5, and he was a German Count, Count von Keller. He was living in America and was very anti-Hitler, although he had been a General or something in the German army. He was a lovely man to work with. He liked people who worked hard and he liked to play hard.

He told Kay Harrison that he had been all over the world with this little 16mm camera, taking odd pictures here and there, and his friends thought they were wonderful and encouraged him to make a proper series of travelogues using Technicolor. So he was visiting Kay to suggest that he could take a cameraman and put him in the dicky-seat[5] of his car with a Technicolor camera on his lap, and they could travel all over the world taking pictures.

JB   An unusual request. What was Kay Harrison's reaction?

JC   Kay explained that it wasn't quite as simple as all that—the camera was very heavy, you required more than just a cameraman with a camera in his lap, and so on. He really explained that it was quite impossible.

JB   And von Keller wasn't prepared to forget the idea when he realized how complicated it would all be?

JC   To do him justice and to his credit, no he wasn't. Count von Keller said, 'Well, OK, I'll organize the thing on a bigger scale'—and he did: they became known as *WorldWindows*.

He had this 16-cylinder Cadillac and off we went; first to Italy. He had engaged two or three directors, one of whom was Hans Neiter. We ended up with a big truck with all the equipment in: camera dollies and all sorts and it was an entirely new approach to the travelogue. We had such wonderful equipment.

JB   But with all this equipment it must have been incredibly gruelling.

JC   One of the problems was that the camera was still so heavy and we had it on a very light head, which made it difficult to pan or tilt. It was just so top heavy.

JB   Can you give me an example of the things that you were filming?

JC   On one of the films in Italy, the challenge was to shoot the interior of St Peter's in Rome, which is the size of a football field; quite enormous. And still there was the problem of the amount of light required. It needed something like 650 foot-candles at f/1.5, so almost impossible because I was given just six little 2k lamps—absolutely absurd. I had no more than 10 foot-candles instead of the 650 I needed.

So I had this idea: at the back of the Technicolor camera, there was a small hole with a handle in it, which you would use to wind the film on when you were loading it. So I figured I could use this, and if I turned it very slowly, I could crank the film through and make an exposure of some kind. So I did this and it took forever, and having shot about 15 feet of film, I stopped and took the belt off of the camera and put it on the other side of the magazine so that I was exposing the same film in reverse. I did that two or three times at least, until each frame would have had about ½-second exposure in total. It was a real gamble, but it was perfect—absolutely marvellous. I suppose I was the first person ever to shoot the interior of St Peter's, certainly in colour.

Jack Cardiff during his travels for World Windows

JB   How long did you have to wait to get it developed to find out if the gamble had paid off?

JC   It took several days to get the stuff off to England and then they reported back that it was OK.

JB   Where else did the *World Windows* take you?

JC   After Italy, Count von Keller told me he had plans to go to Palestine, so off we went. That was unfortunate because that was when the troubles were really just starting and we had a lot of problems there. I was invited to dinner one night and my hosts called me just before I left my hotel to say, 'Please don't come, our daughter has just had her throat cut.' Terrible things were happening.

So Palestine was quite an experience, but we shot several pictures there and then we went out to India and then Egypt and Africa. They really took me all over the world.

JB   You shot a lot around Petra.[6]

JC   That was truly wonderful. A difficult place to get to then, and for the last part of the journey you had to go by horseback. Now I think you can go by plane to the best hotels, but when I went, there were no hotels or shops, just some tents—it was so far off the beaten track. Getting into Petra was amazing, riding through this narrow gorge at least 80 feet high and you could look up and just see this slit of sky above you. On the right-hand side you would occasionally see Roman pipe-work, then suddenly you see this fantastic sight: a building, almost like a church,[7] carved out of the rock all those years ago.

JB   How long did you spend there?

JC   We photographed the whole thing over about three weeks. On one occasion, I had an idea: when you looked around, you didn't always notice at first the steps or buildings carved from the rocks, so I suggested we did a 'double take', where we panned across something and then whipped back to it. That worked very well.

Another building couldn't be seen when you were low down, because of this little mound, but as you went up, it was slowly revealed. We didn't have a crane to lift the camera up with, so I had two tent poles lashed together with ropes, and by pulling the ropes, it raised the camera. A perfect crane shot.

JB   People from the local Bedouin tribes were still living within Petra at that time?

JC   There were no tourists then, so yes. I would hate to go there now. I was on horse-back all the time then, and we used the local Bedouin to help move the camera and things around.

JB   You didn't have the relative luxury of a three-day turn around to see your film at this point?

JC   No, no, a little longer than that! But a fantastic place to work. 'A rose-red city, half as old as time', as the poem has it.[8]

JB   Did you go to Wadi Rum, immortalized by Lawrence in *The Seven Pillars of Wisdom*[9] and later used by David Lean when shooting *Lawrence of Arabia* [1962]?

JC   No, I wish we had. We didn't go there because we had a pretty strict schedule and after Petra we had to head off again. It was a wonderful time to visit and I'm quite sure many of these places are ruined now by tourism.

JB   Was von Keller financing all of this himself?

JC   Yes, but the films were done for United Artists. United Artists released them and they were very popular and hugely successful. We did make some marvellous pictures, particularly in India and Egypt.

JB   What were you shooting in Egypt?

JC   Well, the usual stuff: we had shots of the pyramids and all the usual things and we also went down to Aswan.

JB   You told me that you came close to capturing the pyramid climbing record.

JC   Oh yes! That was actually at a later time in Egypt. While I was waiting around, I used to practise jumping up the pyramids. Each stone is at least four foot high, so you have to do a kind of bounding heave-ho to get up each one. I was told that the world record was nine minutes and I did it in 12, which wasn't bad. If I tried it now, I would take about two days!

JB   When did you last visit Egypt or Jordan?

JC   It was quite some years ago that I was in Egypt last. It was for a film, *Death on the Nile* [John Guillermin, 1978]. We had to climb up the pyramids again for that!

JB How was von Keller getting permission to shoot in all of these places?

JC Don't forget that at the time we were going around with von Keller, it was still the days of Empire. We didn't really have to satisfy the locals in most of these places.

His plea to us as his team was that he wanted us to work very, very hard; often late at night or through the heat of the day—however long it takes. But he told us that when we finished it, he promised we would have a ball: parties and as much fun as we liked. That was a great system. We did work jolly hard and shot some great stuff, and when each film was finished we had wonderful parties with dancing and swimming everyday. It was a wonderful time in my life.

JB The outbreak of World War II obviously ended this chapter in your life.

Jack Cardiff climbs the pyramids for *World Windows*

JC Yes, a very sad thing obviously, and I didn't keep up any correspondence with the Count. He really liked adventure, you know, to head off into the desert. It was certainly more interesting than the usual travelogue because we really got inside our subjects and got to know the people. The films are very difficult to get hold of now; perhaps one or two people have a few copies.

So yes, then came the war. I suppose one might be ashamed, but I'm not ashamed: I had just got married, I had a great career and the idea of going off to war and not coming back really wasn't on.

JB   So what happened to Technicolor and your role with them during the war?

JC   I thought I would be called up at any minute, but it turned out that Technicolor could be of great use in the war effort. The manager of the department was George Gunn and he had an invention where they used a huge dome and they could project the trajectory of bombers as if they were going across the sky so that the young trainee pilots could practise tracking and firing at them. It was a brilliant thing; I believe George Gunn was decorated for that.

So rather than Technicolor being dropped until the war was over, it actually became an important part of the effort. At the time, I was working with Geoff Unsworth,[10] who later became a very big cameraman, and Chris Challis was my assistant. We had a lot of technical work to do. I had to go out and photograph machine-guns being fired at a railway sleeper positioned right next to the camera to make it seem almost as if they were being fired directly into the camera. I was protected as much as possible, but it was truly terrifying. We also had to go on ships and film explosive and shell tests. All sorts.

JB   What were you doing at sea?

JC   The Germans had this bomb that was attracted by noise at sea and if a cargo ship or whatever was going along, the noise of the engine would attract it. The antidote was so simple it was wonderful. There would be a trailing cable behind the ship, maybe a hundred yards long, and at the end of it was something that made a lot of noise and that would attract the bomb instead of the ship. So we had to photograph that working.

JB   These were mostly reconstructions I assume?

JC   Well, we would photograph our own ships, of course, and in this case we also had our own bomb, and that's what we would use. No point in waiting for the Germans to come along!

There were lots of things like that. We also did quite a bit of aerial work. I flew over various parts of England and photographed the ground to see how good the camouflage was. So a very busy time, but I was still yearning to photograph a feature film.

JB   Would you have been freed up to go and do that?

JC   Officially I couldn't work on a commercial film, because I was working for the Government at that time, and if I left to work on a commercial film, I would be liable to be called up. So I stayed, doing things for the war effort.

Sooner or later a film did come up, though, *The Great Mr Handel* [Norman Walker, 1942]. This was with Claude Friese-Greene,[11] whose father had arguably invented the film camera. He was the favoured cameraman of Norman Walker, who wanted him to photograph this, his first venture into colour. But Friese-Greene said he didn't know anything about colour and didn't feel he could do it, so Technicolor suggested me. Captain Walker remembered me because I had been a numbers boy on some of his pictures, including *The Hate Ship* [1929], and he still thought of me in that role. So he was insisting on Friese-Greene. In the end, Friese-Greene suggested that they let me shoot the first couple of weeks while he watched me and then he would take over once he had learnt enough to carry on. So that was my first break and that ended the stalemate.

Around this time. the MOI, Ministry of Information, decided to do their big first feature in colour, *Western Approaches* [1942].

JB *Western Approaches* **was their tribute to the Merchant Navy, which you shot for director Pat Jackson.**[12]

JC Yes, it was. It certainly wasn't easy because we were being bombed most of the time. But the MOI wanted to do it, and although they wanted to use their own cameramen, it was pretty obvious that they couldn't, as they had never worked with colour. I was the only one that could do it. So I came on to this film, which was scheduled to be completed in eight weeks, but ended up taking almost two-and-a-half years to make.

I was the only person for the job. Arguably Friese-Green could have done it, but he was rather large and probably wouldn't have fitted in the lifeboat.

JB Two-and-a-half years working continually on that one project?

JC Yes, the lifeboat sequence alone was six months shooting. We sat in a lifeboat and I was seasick every day—I never did find my sea legs. In the lifeboat, it was very cramped: we had the camera on a platform that slid between grooves up and down, and we could move the platform from side to side, so we could get any position. You couldn't take it apart because the sea was rolling like mad. I tell you, the Irish Sea in the winter is diabolical. Even some of the seamen were sick, but Pat Jackson never was.

It is difficult to be creative when you are sick all the time, but we spent six months in this bloody lifeboat in the Irish Sea.

JB But not just in the Irish Sea …

JC   No, finally we went to America in a convoy of, I think, 110 ships. We went to New York and spent a few days photographing things there. Coming back, we left around 8.30 at night. We had a young Irish boy who used to bring us news and he used to knock on our door and we would let him in, if we weren't unloading film. But on this occasion we were unloading and he was banging on the door. Suddenly we heard an explosion and we quickly put the film into cans and rushed out. The whole sky was red. I saw a ship going down with two full trains on it and six Sherman tanks, all disappearing under the sea. There were people in the sea and bangs all around—it was terrible. We thought we were going to die.

The ship ahead of us had been hit and its steering mechanism was gone, so that it was heading round in a circle straight towards us. Our Captain just managed to steer out of the way. Many lives were lost that night.

JB   Were you trying to film this?

JC   Well, we did a little, but you need so much light for Technicolor and this was at night. Everything was dark except for the red glow in the sky. We did photograph a few bits.

After that, we had help from a couple of ships that came and dropped depth charges, but the noise from those was the most frightening thing of all. It was a terrible noise. We carried on and still had another four nights' sailing to go. We slept in our clothes, of course. We discovered that our cabin was over the storage area for the 12-inch shells, so we weren't very happy about that.

JB   Who were the intended audience for the film? Was it going to be screened in cinemas for the general public?

JC   Yes. It was really a documentary to show how brave the Merchant Navy seamen were. It had reconstructions, and started with a lifeboat with 22 survivors in it, and they were trying to get back to England. There was a scene where an injured seaman thought he saw a periscope and no one believes him. Eventually a ship comes into view and they signal to it in Morse just as a U-Boat surfaces. It was a very dramatic story.

JB   How did you get your hands on a U-Boat to use in the film?

JC   Well, there was one that had been captured and we begged them to let us borrow it. Finally they gave in and said it would be at such and such a position, tomorrow morning at 11 o'clock, and it would surface 100 yards away. All we wanted was a shot of it coming to the surface, so we got ready hours before and got into position. Suddenly it appears, not 100 yards away but less than 12 yards from our ship. It came straight

The cramped conditions filming *Western Approaches* (1942)

up and these are big things—the most terrifying thing I had ever seen. We couldn't possibly shoot it so close and it was a complete disaster. Much later—something like eight months later—the Admiralty gave us permission to try again. So we did finally get our shot.

After we got back from New York, we all went out in a cruiser deliberately looking for trouble! We sailed around the Mediterranean hoping that someone would attack us, which was a mad thing to do.

JB Were professional actors involved in this?

JC No, these were real seamen, not actors. The seamen were supposed to have spent something like 15 days adrift at sea and they had beards of 15 days' growth. Some of them were quite rebellious and thought the whole thing ridiculous, so they would shave off their beards and we would have to use make-up instead. Everything that could go wrong, went wrong.

We shot one scene in broad daylight, and then when we got to shoot the close-ups, it was raining and dark grey. So I had to light using a lot of tricks to match the shots. I made sunshine with one light by taking off the blue filter so that it became very orange and then overexposed the film and told the laboratory to correct the orange back out of it. That matched quite successfully.

JB Was it difficult to persuade Technicolor to fool around with the process like that?

JC Oh yes! To start off, I was the *enfant terrible* of Technicolor, the real bad boy that broke all of their rules, but eventually they came to appreciate what I was trying to do.

JB   Didn't you lose a camera under water at one point?

JC   Ironically that was the one shot that we did at Pinewood Studios.[13] It was supposed to be inside the U-Boat and they had built a set in the big water tank there. It was half-filled with water and I had an idea that we could start above the level of the water to see the Germans thrashing about, and then I put the camera on a geared head that you could crank down below the level of the water. This was from behind glass in a kind of underwater booth inside the tank. It was less than a yard wide and I was the one in it, perhaps with Chris Challis, and the camera was on a uni-pod so that we could wind it down. The trouble was that the booth was buoyant, and no matter how much weight we put in, it we couldn't get it far enough under the water.

Finally there was no more room to move inside the booth because of all these weights, so they decided to put planks across the top of it and get people to stand on them. It took about a dozen people on these planks to keep it down and we shot the scene, marvellous, a great scene. Then the assistant director called 'lunch', and everyone jumped off the planks. Because of the sudden buoyancy, we shot straight up and tipped over. We were working like mad to get the camera out of the water and it took us a good ten minutes to finally rescue it. It was sodden wet and it was put in a bath of oil and whisked off to the labs. Everything was fine and they were able to print the film perfectly.

JB   A modern camera certainly wouldn't survive that!

JC   No, I would guess not.

JB   It might be interesting to see again. When was the last time you saw *Western Approaches*?

JC   The film is still in the archives at the Imperial War Museum in London. I can't think when I would last have seen it. I have probably seen bits of it from time to time. I still see the director, Pat Jackson; we still play billiards together.

3 The Golden Years

- Michael Powell and Emeric Pressburger
- *Caesar and Cleopatra*
- *A Matter of Life and Death:* Battles with Technicolor
- David Niven and Marius Goring
- The bloody bore of editing
- Alfred Junge
- *Black Narcissus*
- Studio Himalayas: Alfred Junge and 'Poppa' Day
- Caravaggio and Vermeer by candlelight
- Academy Award
- *The Red Shoes*
- Learning to love ballet
- Moira Shearer and Léonide Massine
- Oscar snub

'Jack Cardiff deserves to be recognized not just as one of the all time great cinematographers but as a great artist in his own right. His films for Powell and Pressburger possess a startlingly unique visual quality that lives on in my mind above and beyond the story or characters. There is a little bit of magic there.'
Kevin Macdonald—Director and grandson of Emeric Pressburger

JB With your wartime adventures behind you, how did your next big break come about?

JC   Well, the situation was that I was working for Technicolor, but still aching to become a director of photography, a fully-fledged cameraman. And I was doing all I could to achieve this.

I was doing work for the laboratories, doing tests and things, lighting shots and doing my stuff. But there is a big gap, of course, between lighting some tests for exposures, and lighting Ava Gardner and James Mason! But at least I was able to do all of these experiments myself.

I did shoot a commercial. They had a few in those days, but really very few. They liked it very much and it was good for me because I was lighting sets and actors and I had plenty of experience just from having done these bits and pieces.

JB   Who was the commercial made for?

JC   Cadburys, I think. But the important thing was that although there were a few cameramen in the country at that time, even people like Freddie Young, the doyen of all cameramen, hadn't yet shot a colour feature.

JB   Do you remember when you first became aware of the names Michael Powell[1] and Emeric Pressburger?[2]

JC   I can't recall exactly. There were always a number of productions going on at the studios, most in black and white. But in Powell's case I had heard that he was a bit of a bright spark. He could be quite difficult, a bit of a live wire, that sort of thing. But I had never gotten near him, although I may have crept on set one or two times to watch him direct.

JB   But you did get some work on *The Life and Death of Colonel Blimp* [1943]?

JC   Yes, I was set to work second-unit on Michael Powell's *The Life and Death of Colonel Blimp*, with a cameraman who was French, Georges Périnal[3]; he photographed *Sous les Toits de Paris* [René Clair, 1930] and many other very big pictures. He was able to shoot the main feature as he had worked with Mickey [Powell] before, although I don't know why he didn't do again later.

Anyway, I was filling in odd jobs on second unit. When the main unit is flat out doing the important stuff and there is just a small shot left to do—say a close-up of something like an ashtray or a letter heading—the main unit wouldn't be bothered to do it and they would leave it to the second unit, who would have a couple of shots to do every few days. It was pretty miserable work because there was nothing very creative. You might make some shadows on an envelope or whatever.

JB   So it was pretty small stuff, but your work on second unit came to the notice of Michael Powell himself?

JC   There was one set that was quite complicated, and it was very rare to have left this for a second unit to do. I was by myself and it was a wall with animal heads on it—it was supposed to represent the period in Colonel Blimp's life when he went hunting all over the world to forget his lost love.

So that was the shot I was left to do: a wall with all these animal heads on. It was incredibly difficult to do, because it obviously needed several lights, but every time you put a light on it, it made shadows of the animal horns on the wall; three lamps on it made three sets of shadows! I had to light these heads, which were heavy, dark faces and required quite a lot of light. I had to put kicker lights all over the place.

JB   A tricky challenge …

JC   Yes, but it was a fascinating problem to work on. I had more or less got it ready and was thinking that it was pretty good, when I heard a voice behind me saying, 'very interesting'. I look around and there was the great Michael Powell studying the shot very carefully. I remember he had his arms folded with one hand up to his mouth and he turned to me and he said, 'Would you like to photograph my next film?'

Well, that was it! The great break in my career. If I had only known that this was the beginning of such a great, great period, I would have probably fainted.

JB   Did you take Powell's offer seriously?

JC   Oh yes. He wasn't the sort of man to say anything facetiously. So I just said: 'Oh yes, Mr Powell, very much indeed.' He told me we started in three months and he bounded off the stage; he never walked anywhere, he always bounded. I thought it was wonderful news; but then again, between now and three months he might get a top cameraman. I was worried that I would be forgotten.

JB   But you obviously weren't forgotten and he lived up to his word. When did you hear from him next?

JC   A couple of months later, I was on second unit in Egypt for Gabriel Pascal's *Caesar and Cleopatra* [1945], with Vivien Leigh and Claude Rains. Funnily enough, Freddie Young was the second-unit director on that and I was the cameraman, which was very odd because I had been his tea boy many years before and he had always been the big cameraman in my eyes.

JB   Was this more interesting stuff than ashtrays and envelopes?

JC   What it consisted of mainly was lines of soldiers marching over sand dunes, some of them on horseback. It was very funny because we were shooting just outside of Cairo and the extras were all Egyptian locals, who didn't like the costumes and they didn't like having to carry the shields about. So when they used to ride out of shot, they would throw their shields away in the desert. Every day, we had to send out people to try and find them again.

So I was in the middle of all this second-unit work, which I still thought was quite boring stuff. When I got back to my hotel in Cairo one night, I had a cable waiting for me from Mickey saying, 'Where the hell are you? We start in three weeks.'

JB   Michael was a very complicated character. What kind of director was he?

JC   He wasn't the sort of director who would shout. He was crisp and decisive and he always knew what he wanted. He could be rather cruel to people who he thought were stupid; he would really tear them to pieces. If there was someone he didn't like on the set, he would simply say, 'You're not very good are you? Who's your agent?' Crushing!

In Michael's autobiography,[4] he says he was wondering what cameraman to have for his new film and wasn't quite happy about the cameraman he had been working with. He then spoke to Technicolor and asked if they had any suggestions and apparently they told him I was a bright young thing worth considering. Obviously for Michael it wouldn't have been good enough to say, 'OK, let him do the picture', just on their word. It just set a train of reflection off in his mind so that later, when he saw me lighting the wall, something clicked and he decided to give me the chance.

JB   In his autobiography, Michael Powell says: 'I never had the slightest doubt that I was born to be a film director.' Did he carry an arrogance about him?

JC   I don't think so, no. He was very lucky to have formed the association with Pressburger, though, because they were two completely opposite types. Michael was the volatile, very openly enthusiastic one—an extrovert with a great sense of humour who spoke fluent French. He was keen, incisive and just occasionally sarcastic. Pressburger was highly intelligent, but quiet and thoughtful.

When Michael would say, 'We're going to do it like this and come from over here and go upside-down ...', Emeric would just calmly say, 'Well, yes, okay Michael but don't forget that in the next sequence we have to consider this or that'—and he was always right. So it was a wonderful combination of two opposing elements that were also creative and constructive individually.

I asked Michael, quite casually, once, 'Are you making pictures so that the audience can know everything you intend or do you not worry about it?' And he said, 'I don't worry about it. If they can't understand what I'm trying to do, that's their problem.' That was so contrary to someone like Hitchcock, who was always worried that the public wouldn't understand, so he had all these rules and regulations. In his supporting cast, everyone

Jack Cardiff taking lunch with Michael Powell on location for *A Matter of Life and Death* (1946)

had to look completely different so there was never any confusion about who was who. Michael was the complete opposite, you see. He just made pictures the way he wanted to.

JB   Isn't that arrogance? Or was he just crediting the audience with a bit more intelligence than most directors gave them?

JC   I think he was just asserting what he considered to be his rights as a filmmaker and he didn't want to be bogged down with 'will they understand it?'

JB   Did Powell's manner influence your own way of working?

JC   I remember working with them [Powell and Pressburger] and doing some second-unit camera work; it was a difficult shot in London with lots of people and traffic. Very rarely for me, I was really pushing people to hurry up and get on with things and being decisive; really being very tough with my crew. I had the strange feeling that Michael was somehow watching me and listening to what I was doing very carefully and I knew he liked someone who was in a hurry. I was always in a hurry and in many ways that was something of a failing of mine. I would work instinctively and sometimes get it wrong, but that was the kind of cameraman that Michael wanted.

JB   The sheer scale of *A Matter of Life and Death* [1946] must have been daunting. Was there part of you that just wanted to run away?

JC   I didn't want to run away, but I was truly terrified for the first couple of weeks, particularly in the studios because I had never had such a gigantic set to light. I appreciated what [production designer] Alfred Junge[5] was doing with the sets, but I didn't want to get too close to him because he would tell me how to light it and I wanted to be free to do what I could.

JB   *A Matter of Life and Death* **contained both colour and black and white photography. Ironically, you had never worked as a black and white cinematographer before, only in colour, so was it your suggestion to shoot those sections in Technicolor and then print out the colour?**

JC   No, not my suggestion, that idea came from the laboratories. We had to do a transition from colour to black and white. So we shot the pure black and white sequences with a black and white camera and the transition scenes with Technicolor. It was nearly perfect, but not quite. What we called the 'Technicolor black and white' had this sort of strange look about it—not pure black and white, but with rather an iridescent sheen on it like a beetle's wing; just some bits of colour around the edges.

A few years ago when they were making a new print, there was a lot of trouble with it. There was often shrinkage on the negative with old Technicolor film; that was a big problem. There were a lot of problems making new prints from the old negatives because of that.

JB   **Did the idea of having to shoot black and white scare you a little?**

JC   The thing is that light, in itself, is light. It doesn't change from black and white to colour. If you look at a light, the only difference is that in colour a light might be warm or slightly yellow and in black and white it would just be bright. But it's still light in terms of the direction, so lighting a film was exactly the same, regardless. It's simply a question of getting the right balance and it can be very delicate. I just concentrated on getting the right level of lighting and it all worked out okay.

JB   **Did Michael know you hadn't previously shot black and white?**

JC   No, it was never discussed and we never talked about it.

JB   **What was Michael Powell's working method like?**

JC   Michael had this way of working that I don't think I had seen before, or since. On the stage, Michael had this big triangular desk, perhaps six or seven feet long, and he had a secretary, and a lamp and typewriter on the desk. He would agree on a setup for a scene and I would go and start lighting it, and he would go to his desk and start writing letters or whatever. Sometimes I would have to go and ask him a question and he would stop and answer it before going back to his work. In other words, he was divorcing himself from the setup and just getting on with other work until it was done. That was quite a vote of confidence in my work.

JB Is the reason why he largely kept the same crew from film to film to do with that trust and confidence?

JC Yes, I think he liked that feeling very much. He was also very loyal to his friends and he knew who he could trust and who he couldn't.

JB Technicolor must have been quite used to your demands on the technology by this time …

JC Technicolor were still very strict and insisted that you had to measure every light precisely. I didn't do that, I always used to light it and look at it and do it mainly by vision. I realized quite early on that if you kept to the strict letter of their law, you quite often lost the effect you wanted.

There was one shot where there was light coming through a window and I had a big lamp and it looked great. But then one of these Technicolor technicians came up with his light meter and said, 'Jack, that should have been 600 foot-candles and you've used 3000 foot-candles. You have to take it down.' I did, and the whole effect had gone, so I spotted it up until it looked great again.

JB It sounds as if it were a constant battle.

JC I was always fighting that element within Technicolor—the people with the meters. They called me into the office once and told me that my exposures were not level; which was probably true. They had a scale of 20 printing points so that if you were underexposed you might be printing at 3 and if you were overexposed by quite a bit you might be up at 19. That was the whole idea of their scale. It's a bit like when you take your rolls of film to the chemist shop.

So they insisted that unless I used a photometer (light meter) they weren't going to let me play any more. So I said I would and I did. I used it from then on because it is a fact that your physical eyesight can let you down from time to time. One or two cameramen, like Douglas Slocombe[6]—a quite brilliant cameraman—don't have to use a photometer much, as they have trained their eyes to see any change in the level. But I

The enormous Technicolor blimp—*A Matter of Life and Death* (1946)

started using a photometer just to get the key light, so that I could get that right, and then work from there.

These were the sorts of teething problems I had at first with them.

JB **You can almost understand why Technicolor were so touchy. For example, there is scene where time is frozen in the film, and you lit it with an odd, yellow glow.**

JC On that occasion, I said, 'Michael, this whole sequence is unreal and magical and goes beyond any kind of realistic approach. How would it be if the sunlight in this table tennis sequence had a sort of lemon colour?' I used to use a sort of amber filter on the arc lights to make the sun effect quite warm, but I just thought that this touch of lemon would make it more unreal. He agreed and I did it, but I don't think the effect really came over so much.

Looking back on it now, and it is a little late in the day to be thinking about it, but Technicolor used to do the most incredible things. There was a famous and probably apocryphal story that the letterboxes in Ireland are green but Technicolor printed them as red [to match British ones]. That sort of thing did happen. On one picture, I had a shot with a woman near a window; the light coming in was very strong, but with very little light on her face, which was all quite fitting for the tragic tone of the scene. It was a lovely shot, but when I saw the rushes the next day her face was all 'Technicolor bright' and everything else was overexposed to hell.

Later, on *Scott of the Antarctic* [Charles Frend, 1948], I checked a shot [a tent interior] myself by going inside this tent, and because the light inside was coming through green canvas, there was a green light falling inside. So when we did the actual scenes, I used a soft green filter on the faces. The next day, I had a call from Technicolor saying they had a problem and it would be a few days before we got the rushes. After a few days, we got them and the faces had been printed back to normal white faces; that was what they had spent the time on. A typical attitude.

It is possible that they had tried to correct out the lemon light on *A Matter of Life and Death* because it never did stand out quite as I had intended.

JB You have a tremendous admiration for David Niven. How was he to work with on the film?

JC He was terribly good in *A Matter of Life and Death*. He was such a terrific representative of the typical Englishman, wasn't he? He was great fun and had a tremendous sense of humour and was also a great raconteur. He had so many wonderful stories.

He really had an extremely lucky life. To start off with, he wasn't trained as an actor, but somehow he just managed to get there. He told me once that in Hollywood, when he had his first tiny speaking part, it was in a ballroom scene with hundreds of people and he was absolutely terrified. He did the first take and he knew that he was so nervous he could hardly speak, but at the end of it the director called 'cut' and said they were going to do it again. Two or three of the extras came up to him and said 'you were great, absolutely marvellous!', and he said 'Really? Do you think so? Oh!'—and in the next take he was much better. The director had told the extras to praise him to get the performance out of him!

JB You also struck up a long-running friendship with Marius Goring[7] on the shoot.

JC Yes. He was such an intelligent man and we got on straight away. Later, when I directed *Girl on a Motorcycle* [1968], I cast him as the bookshop keeper. He was great fun and there is the famous scene at the beginning of *A Matter of Life and Death* when Marius, as Conductor 71, comes down to earth and walks out among the flowers and says: 'One is starved for Technicolor up there!' I don't know whose idea that line was, probably Michael's, but it always gets a big laugh whenever I see it screened. I have had to sit through it dozens of times at festivals and the like.

JB Do you get bored of watching it?

JC Oh yes! If I have to do a talk, either before or after the film is screened, when I sit down I always get a seat near the exit so that I can duck out during the film.

JB I understand that Marius Goring had tried to persuade Powell to cast him in the David Niven role; did you know about that, and did it cause any friction between him and David?

JC Really? That's news to me. It could be true, because Michael had his favourites like Kathleen Byron, who he used on two or three pictures. He did like to stick to the actors he knew.

JB *A Matter of Life and Death* was intended as a propaganda film[8] in a sense, wasn't it?

JC I had read that Churchill had been horrified at *Colonel Blimp* because it depicted the British army heads as idiots, and he tried to get it banned.[9]

JB So was this film a conscious effort to redress the balance?

JC I really don't know. I think *Blimp* was a very amusing film and a marvellous story and that was all.

JB Michael Powell and Emeric Pressburger were always credited together as 'Powell & Pressburger', as if they didn't have individual identities. Do you think that they ever resented that?

JC I guess that is true, but I think that a lot of the idea behind coupling the names was directed towards getting contract agreements and getting a film off the ground. It was a more formidable thing than just saying, 'I'm Michael Powell' or 'I'm Emeric Pressburger'. It was a team approach and a very wise thing.

I know Mickey didn't resent that joint credit, because as soon as we started shooting a film there was only one man and that was Michael Powell. He was 'The Captain'.

It was sort of a gimmick really, something different. It might have just been an agreement that worked between them. It was a stunning beginning to a film to see that arrow go plonk into the centre of that target.[10]

JB I understand that Michael Powell disliked the editing process but Pressburger enjoyed it.

JC   I wasn't aware of that. But if that's true, then I was a similar character to him with regards to editing. I couldn't bear the waiting about when you are editing; it is such a bloody bore. You go to the cutting room and look at this and that, and you are waiting all the time and sitting in a chair and being bored. It is a slow process with no incisiveness about it.

When I directed *Sons and Lovers* [1960], my plan was to roughly edit the picture as we went along. I had a very good editor and I used to get him on the set and explain the shots to him. Otherwise editors, who are a strange breed, want to contribute creatively, and that can be different from the director's ideas. It happens so many times that a director is busy and the editor is cutting away and when the director finally sees a rough-cut he says: 'No, I didn't want it like that at all.' So I used to get the editor on set as often

On location at Saunton Sands, Devon for *A Matter of Life and Death* (1946). Jack Cardiff, centre, with Michael Powell crouching to the right

as possible so that we could discuss things together and we both knew in which direction we were going.

The other thing with editors is that towards the end of the work, the last two or three weeks, something strange happens and they are a little bit laid back. What has happened is that they are having a conflict of loyalties, because the producer, who often wants to be a director, is asking for something against the director's wishes. It has happened that directors have lost control. Of course, people like David Lean had it in their contract that nobody else could touch a frame of the film, and he always had final cut.

JB   Thinking about it, it would seem ironic if Michael Powell didn't like editing because he eventually married an editor.

JC   Yes, Thelma Schoonmaker,[11] who is considered the best in the world. I think obviously Michael appreciated the usefulness and wisdom of good editing, but he was by nature impatient and he didn't want to spend a long time doing things. It is quite possible that Emeric spent time in the editing.

JB   As you mentioned, the production designer on *A Matter of Life and Death* was the great Alfred Junge. Tell me about him.

JC   When we started to prepare the picture, I immediately became aware of the presence of Alfred Junge, who was a brilliant art director and a terrific authority. He would make the most wonderful sketches, but that skill seems to have faded away now; today art directors don't seem to make too many sketches. But in those days all of the scenes were sketched out in the most wonderful drawings or paintings.

JB   He did have something of a fearsome reputation as an autocrat. How did you handle that?

JC   The one thing that stood out right from the word go, was that he was attempting to dictate to me where the lights should be on his sets. That's okay up to a point, but when it comes to lighting whole sequences, you have to light actors and so on; it's a bit more than just lighting a set.

So we didn't have any antagonism towards each other, but once or twice he would say, 'You must give me light over here!' And I would have to explain why I couldn't, for whatever reason. I managed to get my own way, but it kept me on my toes.

JB   Junge's sets for the film were quite monumental and obviously complex for you to work with.

JC   Really it was quite a frightening experience because his sets for *A Matter of Life and Death* were unique, in a sense. We had the entire stage at Denham, which was huge, with this huge white rock in the middle that needed to be lit. We also had this aurora borealis effect to light behind it. Looking back on it, I think I could have done much better. At the time, Alfred had the idea of these shivers of light. Strangely no one has ever said that they didn't like it, but in my heart I have always felt I could have done something more vibrant.

JB There is also the stunning stairway sequence.[12] In fact, *Stairway to Heaven* became the American title, didn't it?

JC Yes, because the Americans didn't want to have the word 'Death' in the title. Never mind that it also had the word 'Life'!

The stairway wasn't easy to light. It had cost something like £160,000 to build, a huge amount of money. It also had a very small engine in it to power it and it went right to the roof of the stage, which must have been a height of 60 feet or more. It worked beautifully and was incredibly silent. It started beautifully and always stopped in just the right place—quite extraordinary.

There was a vast backing behind it that had to be lit, and these huge statues either side of it that also had to be lit. There were several shots that had to be done later with special effects, long shots mainly. But otherwise it was all done on a real set.

JB It wasn't all studio work, though, was it?

JC No, we started the picture on location in the southwest of England, in [Saunton Sands] Devon. We had to show the scene with David Niven when he believes that he's in heaven. The first thing was a long shot, taken from quite high up, that is supposed to be David seeing this beach and thinking it is heaven. The morning we shot it, Michael came to me and said, 'My God, the script says "Fade in". That's a corny thing. I wish we could do something different.' So I had this sudden idea and told Michael to look through the camera while I went around to the front of the camera. I breathed on the lens, which fogged it completely, and then after 3 seconds it became clear. Michael said, 'I love it! Let's do it!' So right from the beginning, I knew I was able to suggest things.

Almost always he would say, 'Do it! I love it!' That's why I admired him so; he was very brave and incisive and welcomed ideas.

Going right to the other end of the scale, when I worked on *War and Peace* [1956] years later, King Vidor, the director, was an awfully nice man but he would have these conferences every morning before we started shooting that would last an hour or more, to discuss every shot. There was a case when I know Michael would have said, 'Do it! I love it!', but not Vidor. The scene was with Audrey Hepburn in a carriage and she is told that the man she loves is in this column of prisoners that is approaching and she asks to see him. She is sitting in the back of the coach and she leans forward into the light and when she is told that she can't see him she slowly sinks back, crushed. I had a light fixed on the front and suggested to Vidor that she came forward into the light and when she sinks back she goes back into the shadows, so that

if there is a slight tear it will just glisten. Well, Vidor said simply, 'I want to see her face, Jack.'

It was fascinating to work with someone like Michael who was so ready to accept ideas.

JB You've described Michael Powell to me as 'a cameraman's dream'. Is that for the reason you've just outlined?

JC   Well, he was a dream in the sense that he encouraged the kind of brilliant work that a cameraman can be capable of. Most cameramen would welcome the chance to be that creative, but most directors are too cowardly. Some directors today are more like Mickey.

JB Do you think the secret of the success of the Archer's films was that they encouraged creativity from those around them?

JC   Yes, absolutely true. They were a great combination, with Emeric always in the background ready to put in a wise caveat.

JB We've spoken often of Michael Powell, but very little of Emeric Pressburger. Did you simply have less contact with him?

JC   I saw him socially once or twice. He had a wonderful flat in Eaton Square in London. Today you are probably talking about many millions of pounds for a flat in Eaton Square, but during the war when those flats could have been blown to smithereens by the Nazis, you could have bought one for a couple of thousand. Well, his flat was very nice indeed and I used to go and see his family.

He did used to come on the set a couple of times a week, sometimes more often, but he usually just sat in the chair and watched, and then later had a conversation with Michael. Nobody knew what they were about, but maybe Emeric was just reminding Michael what needed to be done.

JB To nicely round off the *Matter of Life and Death* experience, it was chosen for the very first Royal Command Film Performance. That must have been a great honour.

JC   In those days, a cameraman wasn't considered important enough to be presented to the King or Queen. Actors, directors, yes: but not cameramen. I felt I would have liked to be presented, but that's just kid's stuff. Later, David Lean, who had real power—of course, so did Michael Powell, but he didn't realize he could have used it—insisted that

'Ethel', the enormous mechanical stairway built by the London Passenger Transport Board for *A Matter of Life and Death* (1946)

David Niven and Kim
Hunter on location at
Saunton Sands, Devon
for *A Matter of Life
and Death* (1946)

his cameraman, Freddy Young, was presented. So I did feel a little left out. I did go there that night and it was a very impressive evening.

JB As *A Matter of Life and Death* was finishing, was it apparent that you would work with Powell and Pressburger on whatever they planned to produce next?

JC Yes, I think it was. We got on so well, so I don't think there was any doubt. Maybe there was a point on *A Matter of Life and Death* when I thought, 'I wonder if Michael is going to ask me?' But I don't think there was any question really, it was almost automatic.

Towards the end of *A Matter of Life and Death*, the next film was already being vaguely talked about. Perhaps just the idea that it was going to be in India …

JB And that film, of course, was *Black Narcissus* [1947].

JC Yes, but I'm not certain what interval there would have been between *A Matter of Life and Death* and this, because obviously there would have been editing and there must have been some time off. The big thing was when we started preparing the picture: the whole unit, the art director, the camera department, my crew, all assumed we were going to India. I had already been several times, so I wasn't so thrilled at the prospect and didn't particularly want to go.

But then we had this production meeting very early on and Michael told us we were going to make the whole film in the studio! That was a big shock. One immediately started thinking about the story and how it all took place in India, high in the Himalayas. The idea of doing it in the studio sounded awful.

JB   It was presumably for financial reasons?

JC   Yes, but I think Mickey, on the whole, was an extremely lucky person. In some way, things always seemed to work out alright for him. He wasn't a pushover, but I never knew him to be wretched and dejected and down about things; he was always bright and saying, 'Come on, let's do it!'

JB   The physical environment—the mountains and the wilderness and the wind—is very much a character in the film.

JC   Yes, absolutely. The whole story was about the fact that the place was so beautiful and the atmosphere so thick that the nuns failed in their enterprise. That was the whole point of the story. I think that the fact that this beauty was a key actor in the film is what made it such a joy for a cameraman to work on.

JB   Is that why Alfred Junge also jumped at the chance to be involved?

JC   Absolutely. I forget, but obviously there wouldn't have been any sort of objection to the decision. Michael may have already had a talk with Alfred Junge before he and Emeric reached their decision not to film on location. I'm sure he would have done, just to ask him if he thought it were possible to do in the studios. Alfred would have said, 'Yes, I think we can.'

JB   But the decision to film *Black Narcissus* at Pinewood Studios really passed much of the look over to you and the design team. Wasn't that a heavy responsibility?

JC   At first, we were sort of shattered because we thought that out in India we could get so much more. But when you analyzed it, it would have been incredibly expensive to take a whole unit not only to India—which is expensive anyway because of the fares and hotels and everything—but then this was supposed to be high in the Himalayas. God knows what sort of primitive existence we would have had to live there, or where we would stay. So it really was out of the question that we could possibly do it *in situ*.

JB   You know that when Bernardo Bertolucci[13] was shooting *Little Buddha* [1993] in the Himalayas, he said that the real thing didn't quite measure up to the image you had created …

JC Really? Did he say that? That's interesting.

JB So how did you go about recreating the Himalayas in a studio?

JC The first thing I thought of was backings: we would have to have those, and that was the one thing that worried me very much. At first, Junge and I were worried about paint-ed backings; they can be brilliantly done, by very good artists, but they never look real. They are alright out of focus in the background for one or two shots, but not through the whole picture. It would have been phoney as hell.

It was most probably my idea that we have photographic backgrounds, but then again this was a Technicolor picture and the point was that coloured photographic backings were going to cost more than the whole of the rest of the picture. In those days, it was a tremendous expense to have a colour enlargement of that size, they went back for something like 100 feet. So we decided to make black and white backings and colour them.

JB Colour the backings by hand?

JC Yes. We hadn't started the picture at this point and we were just doing tests. I think we had just one part of the set built, where you could look through a window at the back-ings. Junge started to paint the black and white backings and it was awful, absolutely awful! He didn't paint it himself, you understand, he had it done by someone.

So I made the suggestion that it might be better to just use a little light chalk. Pastel chalk. Which Junge agreed to. I thought that if it were done with a certain amount of delicacy, it would work. And it did. We put a lot of blue in the sky, obviously, and a lit-tle blue and ochre in the mountains and it all worked beautifully.

So that was our first big problem over.

JB How did you then light these?

JC Well, in most cases just with a very flat light, because the actual modelling was in the picture itself. But sometimes I would emphasize something like a snow-capped mountain with just a little extra light on it or something like that. Not a great deal of work.

The other problem was that we had this gentle breeze blowing throughout the picture, so we had the agony of choosing a wind machine—and they were very primitive in those days. We had these sort of electric propellers, which made one hell of a row and meant that you couldn't use any sound. Finally we used a sort of long sleevelike tube that ran straight out of the studio's air control vents. That was silent.

JB But you did have some locations. Just not quite as exotic as the Himalayas …

JC   On the road to Brighton, roughly 25 or 30 miles outside of the town, some chap in Victorian times had bought a lot of land; a huge estate. This man was a bit of a nutter because he had brought back hundreds of thousands of foreign trees and plants and things, which he replanted on this estate. So it was just a huge estate full of the most exotic looking plants.[14]

I don't know how we found out about it, but the estate was there and we used the location for one or two days. One scene was the nuns' departure at the end, filmed at the lake, and another was to show the young prince trotting along on his horse. So those were the only things we did outside.

JB Everything else was inside?

JC   In a way, but the actual palace was built outside in the grounds of the studios, outside the stage on the lot. So right there, near the door of the studios, was built this palace and, of course, if you looked in most directions all you would see behind it was chimneys or whatever from other stages. So what we did then was use the incredible skills of 'Poppa' Day.[15]

'Poppa' Day [Walter Percy Day] had been a painter, but he was now quite passé because he painted very realistically; beautiful stuff. He was almost a Victorian-era painter. But somehow he got started making paintings for glass shots, and they were exquisite. So we could shoot this palace on the lot and he would mask out the chimneys or whatever with his paintings.

JB So the glass was simply placed between the camera and the set?

JC   No, that's a different system. What we did was we would matte out the 'NG' parts of the frame with black card very exactly and then rephotograph the painted glass with mountains and clouds as a second exposure of the film. It worked wonderfully.

It was a great bit of luck having him. It's a very romantic story that a man like him, who was virtually finished in his profession as a painter, suddenly finds himself in a whole new profession where he can become very successful.

It was a combination of elements and people that made it all look so good.

JB Was Alfred Junge still being as irascible as ever?

JC I forget who employed him, but the guy in charge of costumes was Hein Heckroth,[16] who on the next picture [*The Red Shoes*] became art director, and not Junge. He too was a German and the two of them seemed to work together as a good team. I remember distinctly that Junge had these huge rooms for his art department and he used to lord it up and down them. I remember from a distance hearing him have a huge row with Hein Heckroth and they were shouting at each other. I heard Junge simply saying, 'Hein! Remember you are a German!' and Hein just said, 'Ja, ja.'—and that was the end of the argument. I have no idea what it was all about: perhaps simply that Junge meant 'we don't argue like this in front of others because we are German *together*'!

JB To me, *Black Narcissus* is the film that most obviously demonstrates your love of painters, particularly Vermeer.

JC Yes, many people say that, and it's partly true, I suppose. There are two artists I think of: one is Vermeer and the other is Caravaggio. They both lit with very simple light. Many painters did, but with Vermeer and Caravaggio you were very conscious of it; they really used the shadows. Caravaggio would just have one sweeping light over everything so that you were aware of the single light. A lot of other painters cheat like mad and have faces clear when they should be in shadow. In other words, they paint them up.

In Rembrandt's case, he got into a lot of trouble because when he painted his very famous large painting, *The Night Watch*, he was at his most creative. These people had paid a lot of money to be painted in the picture and some of them found that they were out of focus in the back or in deep shadow. They were furious because they would have liked every face perfectly sharp and visible and lit.

JB   Did you discuss the idea with Michael Powell or Alfred Junge?

JC   No, funnily enough. One would have thought one would have done that, but no. Really and truly, I didn't have a great creative friendship with Junge. We were friends socially and we lived almost opposite each other in Kensington and I would go and call for him in the morning sometimes and have a coffee at the breakfast table. He really ruled the house and his poor wife used to have to get up and get breakfast for him and the family. He was very dictatorial.

I had more going creatively with Heckroth, so that really worked out well later on *The Red Shoes* [1948], when he took over. But I think that Junge was apt to be dictatorial and would try and make me do this and that; he wouldn't take ideas too easily.

JB   You employed a lot of candle effects on *Black Narcissus*. Tell me about those.

JC   Trying to perfect the candle effect was like a hobby for me. I did get some marvellous results.

I always loved candlelight effects because they were such a challenge. If you have a candle burning in the middle of a room and that is the only light, you have to exaggerate it. Today you could almost just use a real candle for the light, but with early Technicolor you couldn't dream of doing it, because you needed a hundred times that light. So I would have a 2k lamp up above the candle, hanging down out of shot and it would have a snoot on it, which makes a very small soft light that would just hit the top of the candle. That way, it lights the top of the candle and makes the shadow of the candle on the table. I would get one of the electricians up on the spot rail above to stand with a long piece of wood and nudge the rope so that it would move a bit and you would get the flickering movement of shadows. I also had orange filters on the light and it was on a dimmer so that I could take the brightness up and down.

If you have a shot with just two people, say just you and me, for example, then it's a piece of cake, because if we shoot one way, the light is obviously one way from the candle, so you just use one lamp onto you and it looks like the candle is lighting you. Just one light, that is all.

JB   But that was never the case on *Black Narcissus,* and there was also a lot of movement.

JC   Yes, and when you've got actors walking about, then you really have to work it out carefully. It is possible with incandescent lights that you could fade things in and out on dimmers so, as you walked about, one light would fade down and another fade up. I loved doing that work. But the problem on *Black Narcissus* was that we only had arc lights then, and you can't fade those up and down, except by putting dimmer shutters on the front—which we didn't have. The nature of an arc light is very hard and nothing like candle light, so I had to put all sorts of diffusion on them to bring it down. I got away with it, just! But I knew I could have done much better.

With a candle, the flame lights the top part of the candle itself, going down through the wax an inch or so, making it translucent. So the top would have this sort of ochre glow. What I would do is spray ochre paint on the candle, so even when you didn't have a light on it, it would look like the candle was alight. It was quite uncanny. All these things combined to make marvellous candle effects.

JB   You also diffuse the Technicolor to such an extent in *Black Narcissus* it is rendered almost monochrome. How did Technicolor react to that?

JC   I was, as I said before, rather the bad boy of Technicolor. At one stage, I'm sure they hated my guts, because I was always doing something with the light that they didn't think was normal. But I had gone through all that and I think they had come around to appreciating my work a bit when we started *A Matter of Life and Death*. By the time we started *Black Narcissus,* they were far more on my side.

JB   Did shooting in a studio throw up other problems beyond sets and lighting?

JC   The only thing that was terrible, when I come to think of it, was the all-but-last scene in the picture. It was outside at the palace, which was so huge that often we could work without shooting off the edges of the set.

We had to shoot the scene where Deborah Kerr comes out at dawn, something like 6 in the morning, to ring the bell. So it was to be outside and Michael Powell said that he would really like to shoot it at dawn to get the right light and atmosphere and everything. Now at that time there was a works committee at Pinewood with a big, bolshy, socialist attitude. They insisted that we would have to finish at 5.20 pm on the dot, and if we were in the middle of a scene, the assistant director might call up to the electricians on the spot rail and some of them would be terribly bolshy if it were getting towards the end of the official working day.

Left: Scene from the *Black Narcissus* (The Kobal Collection/ The Archers)

JB   Was that situation peculiar to Pinewood?

JC   No. One time at Denham, I was moving a lamp around to test things out and I was called up to the top office to see the head of the union and he said, 'Jack Cardiff, you don't touch lights, that's an electrician's job! You tell them where you want it and they'll move it.' That's how bolshy they were.

JB   So the scene with Deborah Kerr …

JC   It was virtually the last sequence and Michael wanted to shoot it at dawn and the works committee said that we couldn't do that because the weather in England is so unpredictable and if it rains we would have wasted a whole day at our expense. Michael told them that he was usually very lucky with weather and that he really wanted to do it outside at dawn. They said, 'Right, Mr Powell, but don't forget that we told you, we warned you!' A terrible situation.

As it happened, we all got to the set for 4 or 5 am and the weather was perfect. We got the shots we needed in the dawn light. I suppose I was a bit slaphappy with ideas and I said to Michael, 'I thought as it was dawn I could use a slight fog filter on the camera.' He agreed, but in those days Technicolor, although they didn't forbid it, hated any kind of diffusion on the camera, because the light was all supposed to be as sharp as anything. But I used a number two fog filter, which today a lot of cameramen use all through a picture; it's very soft and just takes the edge off hard light.

The next day we had a note from Technicolor saying that everything we had shot that day was 'NG', it was all out of focus and had to be retaken. I could just imagine the works committee saying, 'We told you so.' I really felt sick, realizing that this was Deborah Kerr's last day and if we had to re-shoot, she was in for an enormous amount of overtime. So this was disastrous.

Technicolor brought the print over to the studios to show us that it was unusable and Michael and I sat in the screening room. As it came on the screen, I could see it was fine and Michael said, 'That's great, just what I wanted, Jack.' He turned to the Technicolor people and he said, 'Why the fuck don't you guys learn something about art?' He gave them such a bollocking. They argued and said that in the drive-ins in America it would look out of focus and he just said that he didn't give a shit about that and this was what he wanted.

JB   *Black Narcissus* had an amazing cast. For a start, Jean Simmons, who was very young at the time, around 17 or 18 years old?

JC   Yes, I had some slight misgivings because I was never happy with putting dark make-up on, but it seemed to work with her—just! She was very beautiful and had a real quality about her.

JB   **Sabu[17] was considered by many to be simply 'exotic', but I think Michael Powell really saw something more in him than that.**

JC   He had just the right voice somehow. I was just the cameraman, of course, so not really present at the big meetings, but I think Michael and Emeric would have talked a great deal about the cast.

He He thought that David Farrar was perfectly cast because he had that combination of cynicism and masculinity and a certain way of looking at Deborah Kerr. He was awfully good. He did several pictures afterwards, but he didn't really become a very big success.

JB   **And Deborah Kerr herself?**

JC   She had a lovely voice and carried herself with a lovely dignity. She was simply wonderful to work with.

JB   **I have read that Emeric Pressburger wasn't keen on Kathleen Byron for the role of Sister Ruth. Do you know anything about that?**

JC   I didn't know that, but the facts are that Michael had her on *A Matter of Life and Death* and I think they were obviously good friends. It might have been that the difference of opinion came because Michael was being loyal to her rather than casting her for being a great actress. Perhaps that was behind it. Nothing came out on set and it would definitely have been behind closed doors if it happened.

JB   **In Pressburger's defence, it has also been said that she had difficulty in accepting that her character was supposed to go insane. Do you remember any problems over that?**

JC   She had to be like that [insane]—it was central—but I don't know. When she went to see David Farrar's character, Dean, and he tells her to get lost and shouts at her, Michael had the idea of using a quick flash of red screen. I thought at the time it worked very well and showed a terrific intensity and a great flash of drama.

JB   **It fits with the colour of the lipstick …**

JC   A lot of people have talked about the fact that when she puts her lipstick on, it is very dramatic. I had had enough experience with Technicolor by then to know that some things were always exaggerated. I warned Mickey that the tests that we shot made it look like they already had lipstick on, because Technicolor exaggerated their naturally red lips. Also because they had the white robes and pale faces, the lips really showed up. Michael agreed at once that we should use a little bit of flesh-coloured lipstick just to take it back down.

JB   **I believe the composer, Brian Easdale,[18] wrote a section of continuous score leading up to Sister Ruth's death, and the sequences were then filmed to the music. Is that right?**

JC   I don't think we ever had playback on the set. That end sequence was bitty to shoot, not like the sequence in *The Red Shoes* where you had a flow. This was a lot of little shots, so I find it hard to believe that we did it like that. It wasn't the kind of thing that would have had a guide track.

JB   **You were telling me that you had some problems grading the film.**

JC   Technicolor usually looked after the print and grade, but on this occasion when we finished the film and it was cut, it was agreed that we should grade the print reel-by-reel by running it in a real theatre, the Odeon Leicester Square—which we could only do when the regular day's programme was finished. So about six of us, the Technicolor people and Michael and myself, would gather at around midnight and we would run these reels and we would make notes: 'That should be warmer and that's too cold and that should be more red.' It took about a week or ten days and was very tiring and we got to the last reel and knew we were all agreed. But as we were getting up to go, I noticed that there were workmen putting up ladders against the screen and I was told that they were about to clean and repaint the screen because it was too dirty. So all the work we had done was rubbish because it would have made it all two or three points lighter! It was a complete negation of everything we had done.

We did a lot of adjustments and it finally turned out to be a very good print of the film.

JB   **Do you remember when you first heard about your Academy Award nomination [for Best Cinematography: Colour]?**

JC   It would be in my diary, but I can't really remember it all. *A Matter of Life and Death* had the Best Picture Oscar, which was wonderful because it was my first picture. I should have been overjoyed at my nomination for *Black Narcissus* and I might have just thought, 'Isn't that fun!' But I didn't really feel like I might win it.

JB And, possibly a redundant question, but how did it feel to win?

JC I didn't go out to the ceremony, of course. I had no thought of going because, for one thing, I was already working on *The Red Shoes* by that point, and for another thing I couldn't possibly afford to go. You have to pay for the whole thing yourself, the flights and the hotels, everything … even in those days it would have cost a pretty penny, and I was living quite austerely. I think my salary was something like £40 per week, which was not much.

JB The Oscar didn't just turn up in the post one day, though, did it?

JC It was sent to Mr Rank, and they had a ceremony somewhere in town. Of course, Junge had one too for the art direction.

I had my first taste around that time of critics, as I was very enthusiastic about going to see the press shows. They would start at 10.30 in the morning and there would be very few people there and I would notice that some of them would wander in about a quarter of an hour or half an hour after the film had started. They would just drift in. Some of them would be coughing and look like they had had a night out and got pissed, and they would make a few notes and leave! I thought, 'My God! This is the press?' How could they possibly judge a film like that? It probably still goes on.

JB And so directly to your third consecutive film with Powell and Pressburger—*The Red Shoes*.

JC Michael asked me on the set of *Black Narcissus* what did I think of ballet, and I said 'Not much'. I thought it was a lot of sissies prancing about. So he asked me if I had ever seen a ballet, and I said 'No'. Touché! He told me that the next film would be all about ballet and that I had better get acquainted with it. He organized for me to have a seat at the ballet several times a week, almost every night in fact. I thought, 'Oh God! No!' But I went and I fell in love with it.

It was magical because Covent Garden was a new world to me and it was such a beautiful theatre. It had such an atmosphere and as the curtain went up, you could smell the greasepaint and the other smells of theatre. The audience was always so enthusiastic there and there was spontaneous applause. I saw [Margot] Fonteyn dance and Moira Shearer. It was a completely new world.

I also had to go to classes and watch them practising.

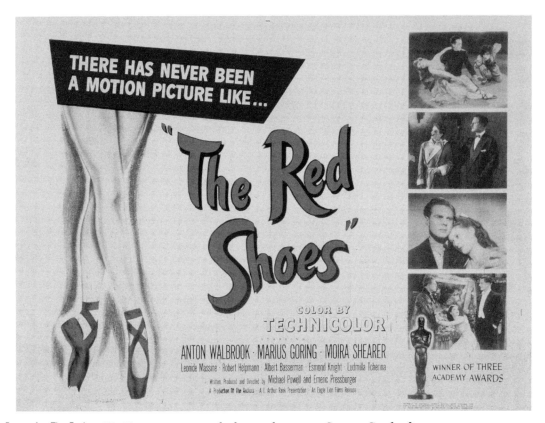

Poster for *The Red Shoes* (1948). *(The Kobal Collection)*

JB You went to watch them rehearse at Covent Garden?

JC No, at a place called Madame Volkova's. She was a strange woman, but she knew all the top people. I remember one day someone came in late, halfway through the class—it was Fonteyn, and instead of going to the front, as was her right as this great ballerina, she just went to the back to the barre with girls that were quite unknown. That was wonderful, there was no 'side' to her at all. But there was a complete spirit of sharing among them all—a wonderful spirit.

It was like religion to these girls. At that time, they only got a couple of quid a week, and most of that went on shoes; I didn't realize that at first until I got into it. They used to wear out so many pairs of shoes a week, which had to be repaired. In other words, they worked for practically nothing.

JB Do you think that part of the reason you fell in love with ballet was because it was reminiscent of your childhood?

JC   Well, very slightly, yes. This was a much bigger theatre than I had ever known, of course, but there was this indefinable smell that was a mixture of size used in the paintings and those things. It was wonderful.

I do remember watching films of the great ballerina Anna Pavlova as a kid.

JB   But now you had to completely immerse yourself in the ballet world?

JC   Yes, but the great thing was that I remember watching a ballet called *Symphonic Variations* and Moira Shearer would dance in that. There were three or four people in it[19] and Moira was just perfect. She was absolutely perfect and looked so beautiful, but when you saw Fonteyn on the same stage, you could see that she had something that Moira didn't have. She had this extraordinary personality that radiated from her and it went far beyond technical ability.

I met her a number of times. Once, when I was in Japan, she was performing and I went backstage and said hello. She was perfectly charming. She truly had a greatness about her.

JB   I believe that a ballet project had been around for a number of years in various people's hands. Do you know why the Archers chose to make it when they did?

JC   What happened was that Pressburger had a contract with Korda to work for him as a writer and Korda had this thing going with Merle Oberon[20] and he wanted to put her in a big picture. Pressburger had been working on a script about ballet and Korda asked him to make it a part for Merle. So he worked on it for Merle!

JB   But Merle Oberon wasn't a dancer, was she?

JC   She had never danced in her life! And it was the most ridiculous thing. She couldn't possibly dance in it.

JB   Had Korda assumed that she could just be replaced in long shot with a real ballerina?

JC   Yes, just use a double and do close-ups of Merle. Ridiculous! So Pressburger had this script and later, when he left Korda, he took it with him. Mickey and Emeric would have been discussing what properties they owned and up came the idea again of *The Red Shoes*. That was the beginning of it.

JB   **Given that Pressburger was Hungarian and was trained in Germany, it was amazing that he managed to write such quintessentially English pictures.**

JC   Yes. Mind you, although they officially shared their credits, everyone knew that Emeric did the basic writing. I think that Michael Powell's influence was probably the 'English influence' and he could simply put the English twist into the dialogue or whatever. Emeric was a good writer, and there is something magical about a good writer. It isn't so much what the dialogue says, but there is something else that they put in that is pure magic. It can be a single phrase that makes a film.

JB   **Michael Powell entered this film without Alfred Junge. What happened?**

JC   Alfred was his usual overbearing self in how he visualized the pictorial side of ballet and Michael didn't want that, so I think they fell apart there. But Hein, who had worked on *Black Narcissus*, had a lot of experience of ballet in Germany, working on several theatrical productions in art direction. He was very well up on ballet, so it was the most natural thing in the world that he should do *The Red Shoes*.

JB   **Did Alfred Junge take that as a terrible slight?**

JC   Absolutely, but something went wrong and they parted company. Michael told me that at one stage Alfred was going to have a new contract and he wanted the right in his contract to instruct the cameraman exactly how to light his sets. Michael made a joke of it, but that was it. Such a shame because he was such a great art director, but he was so sure he was entitled to dominate everything.

Oddly enough, as I mentioned, Junge lived almost opposite me in Palace Gardens Terrace in Kensington and I saw quite a lot of him; but Hein also lived reasonably near and we were great friends. He took an interest in me and my painting, and he told me all about the hazards of being a painter and what to look for. He befriended me in that way.

Hein was the opposite of Junge; he was easy to get on with and ready to help and didn't have any particular 'side' to him.

JB   **Was this house you were living in the one that you had an entire studio come and decorate?**

JC   Yes, I had rented this house in Palace Gardens Terrace just after the war and the whole street was virtually empty, because it had been knocked about a bit by the Germans with firebombs. My then wife [Julie] and I had been living in Slough—a terrible place—

and she had always wanted to live in London. So she looked for somewhere and found number 14, which had hardly been touched by the fires. Also, the rent was only £7 a week for this vast house that had about 20 rooms.

We had a lot of ideas about getting it into shape. Hein used to come around and advise me on how to do things, and he did some paintings for me.

The funny thing was that this was just after the war and it was austerity time and there was a limit of £10 that you could spend on refurbishing. No more. But I knew so many people at the studios and I asked them to come and help me decorate. A whole team of painters came along and painted the whole house beautifully. I wanted a Robert Adam ceiling and the plaster department came out from the studio and made the most elaborate ceiling for me.

JB   And you were never caught for overspending?

JC   Someone from the council did come round and almost fainted when he saw it. He asked me where I got everything from and I told him I was in the film business and had it done for almost nothing. He laughed and said that he used to be in the film business too, so he would let it go. I got away with murder, really.

I had my Oscar celebration in that house with something like 70 or 80 people, and police outside controlling the cars. A fantastic evening.

JB   Back to *The Red Shoes* …

JC   Yes, so on *The Red Shoes* we were all full of enthusiasm and going to ballet every night and we were all full of ideas. But then Michael said: 'Look, we have gone into this and we have decided that the public aren't ready for so much ballet in a film. So we are restricting the ballet sequence to 18 minutes.'

By that time, I had made a lot of interesting camera tests: slow motion; fast motion; stop motion for the paper dance sequence. Michael loved them, but it had been decided to produce the music first and then work to the music. He thought if we didn't do that, we would go crazy and get lost with what we were doing. So some of the test shots might have been done to three bars of music, and in the end we only had one bar to do that shot in. It was quite sad in a way that the length of the sequence restricted all of those things that we wanted to do. But it was still a really fascinating film to work on.

JB   Again, there was some brave casting. How did you find Moira Shearer to work with?

JC   She was the opposite to a film-struck person. She didn't really think a great deal of films. Ballet was her heaven and she wasn't at all star-struck or even thought it was that wonderful to be offered the principal part in the film. She just thought it might be interesting. While others might have given their soul to be the lead in a film, she wasn't that crazy.

I took her to see Russell Flint[21], the painter, who was a friend of mine and who lived quite close by. Well, it was two Scots together, and she would tell him, 'I don't think you've got the leg quite right,' or this or that—very critical. A tough one.

JB   Was she tough to work with on set?

JC   She wasn't difficult to work with. She was no idiot and knew what could be done and how she could contribute to the film.

Even though she was the principal star, after a few days everyone liked her and she was friendly with everybody. She even came up to the camera department and asked if she could get anyone a cup of tea!—first time that had ever happened with the star of a picture. She was like that. Typical of the ballet world, where everyone pitched in.

JB   Were the dancers reluctant about what you might do with the camera? That you might somehow dilute their performance?

JC   That didn't really arise and the only time it might have was when [Léonide] Massine[22] did his big leap on to stage. By that time, I had swatted up and I knew that there had been this colossal jump onto stage in *Spectre de la Rose* [a ballet choreographed by Michel Fokine for the Ballet Russe in 1911]. I thought the only way to get the shot, as Massine was already 50 by then—very fit, but probably not able to make quite such a jump— was that I could get the camera speed altered, just for a second, when he springs onto stage, so that it would increase the time. So as he jumped, I got the camera up to 48 frames and straight back again. It worked beautifully. The ballet purists might have said that was cheating, but we were making a film, not a ballet.

JB   Massine had worked with many of your great artistic heroes such as Matisse, Dali, and Picasso. Did he ever discuss that with you?

JC   That was what awed me. I was amazed to think that this little man, who was very quiet but had a tremendous presence on screen that would always steal the shot somehow, worked with all these people. We had lots of talks and he was an extremely nice man. He had worked with the greatest in the world. During the picture, I was talking to

Massine about one of my favourite ballets, *La Boutique Fantasque*, because I wanted to make a film of it.

At Pinewood, they had previously had a problem where the normal workers, the electricians and carpenters, could never book their holidays because they never knew when they were going to break on a picture. So they tried out this idea where the whole studio would shut down in August for two weeks. They did it that year [1947], but never again, because although it worked out for the workers, the stars and their agents hated it. So we had these two weeks off and I suggested to Massine that I could photograph the ballet on stage during this break; just shoot it straight as a ballet and preserve it for posterity with the great Massine.

He was enthusiastic and very happy to do it, so he and I organized the rights to the music and Moira was enthusiastic to get involved. So then I needed a *corps de ballet*. I went to see Ninette de Valois (founder of the Royal Ballet) and she said, 'No way!' She hated films and thought they were a terrible idea … and that was that! We never made it.

JB   It must have been quite the most dynamic and vibrant set to be working on with such a fusion of creative talents. Did it ever threaten to fall apart under the strain of opposing personalities?

JC   Well, there was what I would call good-natured tension. Massine, at 50, was the hardest-working man on the film. He would always be there early practising at the barre. We had a barre made on set for all the dancers.

What was tough was that the ballet dancers were used to dancing on a stage that was wood and had a certain amount of give and spring in it, but here at Pinewood they had to dance on concrete floors. They were very good about it. But it was so much harder than the stage.

JB   Do you think there was something political about the lack of Oscar for *The Red Shoes*?

JC   That was sad. I had a big friend in Hollywood called Lee Garmes,[23] who had won an Oscar for *Shanghai Express* [1932]. A very fine cameraman and we were big friends from the time I spent out there. When *The Red Shoes* came out the critics liked it very much and when it came to Oscar time several of them said that they knew that my photography would win the Oscar. So I thought I was in with a chance because everyone was telling me I would win.

Then I got a phone call from Lee Garmes, who said, 'Jack, I don't know how to tell you this but we had a meeting with the ASC [American Society of Cinematographers] last night and it was generally felt that you would definitely win and that would put the American cameramen in a bad light.' So the only way to stop me winning was not to nominate me. You can't get the award if you're not nominated!

Most of the people that voted on that are probably under the ground now …

4 Fire and Ice

- *Scott of the Antarctic* and John Mills
- *Under Capricorn*—one-shot wonders
- Method in Hitchcock's madness
- Ingrid Bergman and Joseph Cotton
- Henry Hathaway
- *The Black Rose* and Tyrone Power
- Orson Welles
- Directing Montmartre
- *Pandora and the Flying Dutchman*
- Ava Gardner
- *The Magic Box*

> 'Jack Cardiff is one of the giants of world cinema. The images he creates are beautiful, but they are never empty—they always serve the story being told with both elegance and great power.'
> *John Woodward—Chief Executive Officer, The Film Council*

JB After *The Red Shoes* in 1948, you parted company with Powell and Pressburger. Was there anything behind that?

JC Well, no … the thing was that Michael Powell was getting ready for his next film, and I was rather in demand and already working on another film by the time he was ready to go. That was a shame.

JB After three consecutive films with Powell and Pressburger, did it feel as if some of your safety net had been taken away on *Scott of the Antarctic*?

JC Yes, I suppose I must have noticed the difference. The director, Charles Frend[1], was extremely nice to work with, but I did miss Michael because he was so inspiring and really made you creative.

JB How did you come to work with Charles Frend on *Scott*?

JC They had already shot some footage because they knew from the beginning that they would need some wonderful landscapes with ice, so they hired a cameraman called

Borradaile[2], who they sent out to the Antarctic. Technicolor wouldn't allow their camera to go out there, so he shot it with a system called Monopack, which was terrible film. Everything came back bright blue.

Then they got some more of the script written and realized they needed some more shots, but not quite so far away. So they sent Geoff Unsworth—this was still before I had come onto the picture—to Norway in the winter. Of course, in Norway, in the winter, the sun never rises more than about 10 per cent and gives very orange light—so a complete reverse to the blue film they already had!

Finally they decided that they needed some footage with sledges, so they sent Geoff off to Switzerland to photograph that. This time it was late spring, so the mountains were covered in brilliant white snow. He had to shut the lens down, which made the sky almost black. So they had three different qualities of film by this stage.

JB Didn't that colour disparity concern you? It's not the best way for you to start a film.

JC Oh yes! I was in a terrible state, because today you could fix so many things with effects, but then I could only rely on Technicolor to adjust things in the printing. But there was a limit to what they could do.

I had a little editing machine on set so that I could see where I had to match the long shots in the studio, which was tiny[3]. I used a lot of coloured filters to try and match the footage we already had: blue, orange, and pure black and white.

JB What did you do about snow on the set?

JC We had lots of artificial snow and there was one machine for close-ups that made real snow. It was a huge thing. It put snow on the actors and it used to melt almost at once because of the lights. It was so cold at times, because we had this terrific propeller on stage that must have been 10 feet high and made a great draught. One day I fell ill and was sent home with pneumonia. I had lots of injections and came back very groggy.

JB How did recreating the Antarctic for *Scott of the Antarctic* compare to the creation of the Himalayas for *Black Narcissus*?

JC It was a different character completely. At least in *Black Narcissus* the sets were real and you could light those, no problem—what you saw through the windows was supposed to be the beautiful Himalayas. In the case of *Scott of the Antarctic*, all you had was white floor and a white backing and a wind-machine and artificial snow. It was a real headache.

JB It is a tremendous *Boys Own* story—was Scott a hero of yours?

On set at Ealing
Studios for *Scott of the
Antarctic* (1948)

JC   Yes, he was a great hero of mine.

JB And how did John Mills do filling those famous snowshoes?

JC   It was a wonderful performance, but they were all good on that film. It was so very
moving. He was fine to work with, but there was another actor in it called Harold
Warrender, who played his scenes with Mills all the way through [Warrender played
Edward Wilson]. The problem was that Johnny was very small, shorter than I was and
Warrender was 6 foot 1. So we built a kind of ramp for the two-shots and John would
walk slowly up this ramp so that by the time he reached his two-shot with Warrender
he would only be a tiny bit shorter.

JB Oddly the film didn't do that well commercially.

JC   It had a Royal Command Performance but wasn't a huge commercial success, perhaps
because of the old theory that the story of a failure doesn't make good box office. A
funny thing, that.

JB At this point, Hitchcock re-entered your life with *Under Capricorn* [1949].

JC   Yes, he did. Well, once you get a few good pictures behind you, the offers start coming
and perhaps my agent put my name forward. I can only say modestly that I did have a

More snow is delivered to the set on *Scott of the Antarctic* (1948)

good reputation. Hitchcock wouldn't have remembered me from when I was a kid.

JB You don't think he remembered you from *The Skin Game*?

JC I wouldn't have thought so for a moment. But he was very friendly and still a great character. It's funny thinking that here is the man who is the master of the macabre. Terrible things: juicy murders and horror, horror, horror! But also very funny. Isn't that odd?

JB But often his humour was equally macabre, wasn't it?

JC Yes. He had several kinds of humour. It could be very cruel, I suppose. In America, his assistant director was getting married and wanted to go down to Mexico for his honeymoon and he told Hitch about this and asked him, as he had several cars, if he could borrow one to go on holiday. Hitch agreed and the assistant director sets off on honeymoon; the moment he is gone, Hitch phones the police and tells them his car has been stolen! So when this man gets to the border crossing, he is arrested and spends his first married night in jail. That's a diabolical thing to do! Quite disgusting!

He was always doing things like that. That's something quite psychologically weird, isn't it?

JB Did his famed pre-production stifle the creativity for you?

JC   Yes, that was the great difference. He was the most meticulous person in preparing a picture and everything in the script had to be absolutely perfect. For instance, a script page would have to be, say, two minutes to the second long, and he would try out the dialogue and if he found that it was over, he would adjust the script so each page was the same.

He had a tremendous amount of creative ideas, though. But, really the opposite to Mickey [Powell]. Once that script was finished, he would never touch it and never change it on the set. He would stick to it completely.

JB   **It must be tough to work like that, no?**

JC   It was, because I didn't even know what he had in mind in his script. But he made sketches for me that he would show us. It was all down to a fine art, and very precise.

JB   **Hitchcock famously referred to actors as 'cattle'. Did this dismissive attitude extend to his crew?**

JC   No, no. I think he had a certain attitude to actors, where he thought that the worship of actors was over the top and exaggerated; which was as true then as it is today. I spent a long weekend with him and his wife in San Francisco and I had a lot of long talks with him. He really just had so many good ideas about things to try out in films. I have heard and read things since, about certain fetishisms that he had, and I don't believe many of them—they are just being sensationalist. He was still the most extraordinary man.

Alfred Hitchcock
directs the action for
Under Capricorn (1949)

JB   Do you think some of it was an act?

JC   On the contrary, he never put on an act on the set. He was a very quiet man, not like John Ford or Henry Hathaway and people like that, who scream and fire people and whatever. Hathaway was looking for trouble all the time.

          If people were late on set, Hitchcock wouldn't say a word, but at the end of the day, he would go to the production office and see the production manager and make his statement for the day about how everyone had been, or who had been late. So he would get the front office to do the dirty work rather than create a scene on set.

JB   Maybe it was more a media thing that presented him like that then. He did become almost a parody of himself?

JC   Oh yes, I know what you mean. He was everywhere, in magazines, short stories. That was all part of either his or his agent's policy to become a worldwide figure. The sales point of his films weren't the big stars; it was Hitchcock himself.

JB   Hitchcock's idea for *Under Capricorn* was really an extension of his experimentation on *Rope*[4] [1948]. Tell me about that.

JC   That was amusing in a way. *Rope* was a setup that would save an enormous amount of money on the picture, because you could make a whole first-class film in two weeks— which is preposterous when you think about it. Just by shooting reel-by-reel did mean a lot of rehearsing, but rehearsing is cheap.

          It was perfect for *Rope* because it all took place in one room and the analogy is there from the beginning, because, as most people know, a television play, in most cases, is shot in one night and they have lots of lights and they light every position. Well, that works fine and it worked for *Rope*, because all they had to do was track and pan all around the room, and the characters were trapped in a cage. An ordinary film goes outside with cars and fires and buildings, and you could obviously never do that in one reel.

JB   And so the idea for *Under Capricorn* was to repeat this single-reel, ten-minute take process?

JC   With *Under Capricorn*, it wasn't quite that bad, but it was still largely one-reel takes. It wasn't that every single shot was ten minutes, but every few shots were ten minutes or eight minutes long.

          I remember one shot in this big mansion, which was built on a stage. They had taken from the Warner Brothers cinema circuit a whole year's supply of cinemas' carpets, and covered the whole stage with it, and then they built the set on top of the carpet.

JB   And it was then all shot using a crane of some sort to move the camera around the sets?

JC   Yes, we had an electric crane, which could travel in any direction on this carpet without having to lay tracks.

Joe Cotten[5] told me one time that he was terrified of this bloody great electric crane, because it was quite quiet on these big tyres as it snaked around. He could just hear it at his back getting closer and closer and he was terrified he was going to be run over.

It did come to rest on Hitchcock's foot once. I watched him and he was in agony, but he didn't say anything until the shot was over.

JB   Back to the shot in the mansion …

JC   OK, we went through the front door, turned right and went down a little passage to a kitchen, where there was dialogue. Then we came back again to a circular hallway with a stairway. We went through the hallway and turned left down another passage into a big drawing room. There we would shoot something like six or seven minutes of dialogue. Shooting this way and that way and back again. Then in the hallway again and up the circular stairs and to another passage. Through that passage to the bed where Ingrid Bergman was laying and, so that we wouldn't have to go high up and look down on a close-up of her face, the whole bed was designed to tilt towards us as we tracked

The huge crane at rest.
Under Capricorn (1949)

straight in. That was probably about ten minutes. So I had about ten sets to light at once and that was terrifying, absolutely terrifying.

JB And the sets were built specifically to accommodate this technique?

JC Yes, but it was full of compromises because we could only push things so far. The art director would make some of the walls so that they could slide open. We quickly gave up the idea of any natural sound because the noise of the tracking and the sliding doors and sets and people running with lamps and hiding out of shot under tables was pure bedlam.

Usually we would rehearse for a day on a big scene and the next morning we would shoot it, sometimes two or three takes of it. And when we had the take of it we would print, and the unit would leave the studio apart from the sound department and the actors and Hitch. I think I used to stay behind sometimes, and the actors would do the whole thing again, except this time there would be no crane, no camera and no noise. They would just speak their lines. They would walk about the same positions for their timings and somehow it all worked.

JB The film is set in Australia, but it wasn't shot there, was it?

JC No, it was supposed to be a small town in Australia but it so happened that Warner Brothers, who were making the picture, had on their lot what one might almost call a large village set of buildings from that date. They were in perfect condition so we went out to Hollywood and shot those sequences there.

JB How did Ingrid Bergman cope with such an unorthodox filmmaking technique?

JC Well, our Technicolor blimp was a monster and she had what she considered a very important scene. It was only about four or five minutes, but she said to Hitch that she would really like that done in the old-fashioned way, without the full four or five minute take. Also, she wanted it done without arc lights because I was having to use a lot of those and they also made a hell of a noise. She asked me to light it with incandescent lights so that she could have a quiet scene, and as it happened I could—just—by filtering the light. So it was perfectly quiet and she was so happy and we shot the scene, but it was 'NG' because, for the first time in history, we heard the Technicolor blimp! That's the way it goes.

JB Bergman projected a very icy screen persona. Was she generally tough to work with?

JC   Not so much with the crew. She was wrapped up, as most people like that are, in the story and her performance and so on. She would be very pleasant on the set and I got on well with her, but I don't think she was terribly happy about using this terrible technique. It's not the sort of thing that induces good acting, is it?

JB   **How did the other actors feel about it?**

JC   There were so many positions for the actors during these ten-minute shots. Joe Cotten had a very subtle sense of humour. For example: if you have two characters face to face talking in front of the camera, which is called a two-shot, and one of them starts to go back up the stage, the one in the foreground has to turn to talk to them and the camera will be on the back of the head: hence the phrase 'up staging'. I'm sure Bergman didn't intend to do it, but she kept going back up the stage; Joe Cotten would laconically call that 'a Swedish 50:50'.

JB   **Why do you think *Under Capricorn* is such a little-known film? It is really considered one of Hitchcock's very few failures.**

JC   It wasn't a huge success and I can tell you one reason why, as I have thought about this a lot: the essence of filmmaking from the director's point of view is in the rhythm of the shots and the editing. If you have two people talking, then depending on the nature of that scene, you might talk fast or slow or whatever, but it is always under control. To simplify, this is what you might shoot: the two of us over here talking; then a shot over my shoulder onto you; then the reverse—over your shoulder onto me; then two separate close-ups of you and me. With that combination, you have everything covered, you can take away my dialogue or vice versa. That is the essence of getting rhythm in a scene. If you are doing it the ten-minute take way, then there is just one camera tracking in and out and around, and this slows everything down and you lose any rhythm that would usually exist. It removes the possibility of fixing anything in the edit. You are stuck with it.

Quite often, I know that scenes like that have lines of unnecessary dialogue which slow things down, or just don't work, and they have them taken out. It's an obvious thing and I'm amazed that Hitch didn't see it.

JB   **I would also have thought that the studio financing it might have noticed the inherent problems.**

JC   Ah! Well, you see that's an interesting thing. When *Rope* was made, they must have thought: 'Boy, we're on to a bonanza here! We can make a film in two weeks—imagine the money we are going to save!' Even in those days it cost a fortune to make a film and always took a minimum of six or eight weeks, maybe 15 or 20 weeks. If you could do a film in two or three weeks, all that cost is just wiped away, so the producers were all for it, regardless of what technical problems we might face.

JB   So although you never worked with him again, you would consider the collaboration with Hitchcock a fruitful one?

JC   Oh yes, I enjoyed it very much, because he was a fascinating person to talk to. When I went to stay with him in San Francisco, we used to talk about all sorts of things and he would tell me his ideas for things he wanted to try out in his films. Just little ideas. All these ideas in his mind.

JB   Is that where his films came from, from these odds and ends of ideas?

JC   Not just that. He read a lot of books. In his house he had the whole collection of the Everyman Library[6]—something around 600 in the collection, and he had every single one, just to have around as a reference. He also had arrangements with publishers where he was automatically sent the best new books and stories.

I think it had happened to Hitch that people had stolen ideas and things from him and claimed them as their own. He had a rule that he would never open any correspondence addressed personally to him in case it was a script or an idea, just in case he later did something similar and was accused of stealing the idea or story. It is so easy to sue.

JB   After Hitchcock, you worked with the equally fascinating Henry Hathaway. Did he talk to you about his long career?

JC   Well, yes, he told me the story of how it all came about. He yearned to be a director and he talked to friends and even management and asked them what he should do. One of the management said, 'Hathaway, you're not an educated man, so you'll never be a director.' So Hathaway talked to his friends and asked how he could become educated and they told him he had to read a lot. So out he went and bought the Readers' Digest! So that didn't work and his friends suggested he try travel to expand the mind. So he took his savings and came from America to Europe and made a quick trip around, but still with no luck.

He decided to try and see Thalberg[7], who was the boss. He goes to his secretary and she says, 'You must be joking, Mr Thalberg is absolutely booked, he doesn't have a second for anybody.' But then she relented and told him that if he turned up every morning at 8.20 and waited, eventually he might get a minute or two. So that's what Henry did every morning until one day he was granted exactly one minute. He runs in and explains his ambition and Thalberg says, 'Take this script, and maybe we will do it.' He has this date set to go back and tell Thalberg that he loves the script, but on the day, when Henry was on his way over, he stopped at a diner for breakfast and was told that Thalberg had died in the night!

JB   But that obviously didn't stop a man like Hathaway.

JC   No, finally the studio gave him another chance and another script and they say to him, 'Can you make this script for $200,000?' and Henry says, 'Yes, sir.' And they say, 'Can you do it in eight weeks?' And he says, 'Yes, sir.' So he gets the job and starts work. Well, the film took a year to make and cost something like $2 million—but it was *The Lives of a Bengal Lancer*[8] [1935]. Not a bad start. A pity he didn't write a book about it, really.

JB   He had a terrifying reputation for being a complete tyrant. Were you intimidated by him when it came to working on *The Black Rose* [1950]?

JC   He was formidable, but he had had a strange life, really a life of adversity. He had worked with some of the toughest directors in the film business, including John Ford.

He was a prop man and I think that the treatment that he endured made him a very tough character in turn. It really trained him to be a tough guy. As a prop man, he had been very, very good. One of his first jobs was to work for Cecil B DeMille[9]. DeMille used to walk about the set and if he wanted to sit down, he would just sit down right where he was, because he knew there would be a guy following behind him with a chair ready to plant under him the moment he showed signs of sitting. This was one of Hathaway's jobs—can you imagine that?

JB   But your working relationship was a good one?

JC   I got on all right with him because I didn't kowtow to him and I was honest and I said what I thought. I never tried to make excuses.

There was one incident on *The Black Rose*, that first film with him, where we were supposed to be at an abandoned French Foreign Legion camp—just the remains of mud huts. Hathaway hated the British in general because he thought they were always taking tea breaks. 'Goddamn British and their tea!' he would always be growling. He used to make me laugh. We were just settling into the set, this camp, and we were unpacking and there was a tea break in one of the mud huts. Hathaway saw this and glared and grabbed a piece of paper and stuck it up on the notice board and wrote on it, 'In future, the British will have their tea standing up!'

Henry Hathaway with
cigar, shooting *The
Black Rose* (1950)

He told me to come with him and look at the next locations and I said to him, 'Henry, you have just made an enormous mistake.' 'What the hell you talkin' about?' he demanded. So I explained to him that the British crew had a certain amount of respect for him—they didn't like him—but they had a respect, and this business with the tea was so ridiculous that they would lose that respect. I told him he had had it with the crew. He drove off, growling, 'You're full of shit!' After about 10 seconds, he turned the car right around, drove back, marched into the hut and tore down the notice.

That was the relationship that I had with him: we were always very frank with each other.

JB So he at least appreciated your way of working?

JC I think there are many different types of cameraman. I think in a way I had a strong sympathy with directors and I understood their problems. You do get cameramen who say, 'I can't do this because it's not good for me. The light is not right.' Or whatever. They don't seem to realize what the director is going through and quite what his responsibilities are. Just being on set each day is costing them thousands—millions, sometimes.

So I used to shoot in any kind of light and I think that's why Hathaway had a good regard for me. There was a sequence, if you can imagine, which was set in a courtyard with the sun going overhead throughout the day from east to west. In theory, the sequence is only supposed to be two or three minutes and the sun should be in the same spot throughout. But that didn't bother Hathaway, so I had to try and balance it with certain tricks so that no one could tell where the sun was supposed to be in any one shot. I think Hathaway liked that and he was appreciative.

JB   Was Hathaway better with his actors than with his crew?

JC   His way of working was pretty good on the whole. His whole thing was to please the actors. He might be hell to work with for the technicians or whoever, because if they were noisy or something he would just fire them, but when it came to the actors it was a different story.

He hated it if the assistant director said something like 'we only have just enough footage for one take and then we will have to reload'—because now the actor thinks the film is going to run out in the middle of their scene. Or they overhear a focus puller talking to the director and know they are going to be out of focus in a shot. It was all these psychological things. He dealt with actors very well.

For instance, he didn't like marking the positions of the actors' feet[10] because he thought they would become more concerned about hitting their mark than their performance, or remembering their lines.

JB   This must have been a marked difference from working with Hitchcock, who reportedly didn't like actors at all.

JC   Oh yes! Hitchcock naturally chose very good actors anyway, and he did admire good acting. They do say that he called all actors 'cattle', but a lot of Hitch was just publicity. He got where he was because he was a great director, but also because he is this figure, this big man.

JB   Tyrone Power[11] was the star of *The Black Rose*. How did he relate to Henry Hathaway?

JC   Tyrone was not really a dedicated kind of actor, but he was extraordinarily good looking and had a terrific star following and the young people really adored him. He was a passable actor and he was very easy-going. He would come on set and make himself up, not that he bothered too much. Instead of bothering about his dialogue and performance and being nervy, like most actors, he would just stroll on to the set and say 'hello everyone'—just chatting away and not bothering about the scene at all. Hathaway didn't like that one bit.

JB Orson Welles also had a smallish role in the film. How was he to work with?

JC He was playing in it, but it was only a small part and I suppose he was only out with us for two or three weeks before he went off the picture. I thought he was a great character and I liked him very much.

JB How did Welles react to Hathaway's directorial style? As a director himself was he difficult to direct?

JC No, not at all. Only there was one scene in a tent that was quite terrifying. We were shooting in a tent in Morocco and it was very hot. Orson had a long scene to do and he had told Hathaway that he couldn't remember all of it at once and that he would have to break it up. Hathaway explained that he couldn't, or wouldn't, and so the duel commenced. Orson would go so far and then try and fluff his lines. Hathaway guessed that Orson was just trying to make his point about remembering it all the way through, so he would just say 'One more … One more …' We did maybe 30 or 35 takes in this hot tent and Orson was sweating in his very heavy costume.

Eventually I think Orson realized that the director always has the last word because Henry would have let that go on for days if he had to.

JB A lesser director would have given in to Welles. Do you think he respected Hathaway more after that?

JC Well, no, I'm not sure about that. Orson was so mad and you could see that his eyes were so deadly. When the make-up man went up to him between takes to pad the sweat out, he retreated very quickly because Orson just gave him this deadly look. Looking back, it was a very dramatic couple of hours, let me tell you. But Henry got his scene.

JB Orson Welles had already had a tough time in Hollywood, partly with _Citizen Kane_[12] [1941], but more specifically with _The Magnificent Ambersons_[13] [1942].

JC So many dirty tricks were played. He wanted me to photograph _Ulysses_[14]—not the James Joyce _Ulysses_ but the classical one. Of course I said I would love to, but it was a case of waiting for him to accumulate the money to start.

We had a couple of evenings when we went out for dinner together. He just mentioned it once, just as a passing comment almost, that he should really be on a picture right until the end, to supervise the editing. It was a reference to *Magnificent Ambersons*, because the studios took him off the picture in the end and I think another director may even have re-shot a couple of bits. Certainly the editors changed the ending around. Diabolical. He was such a brilliant man.

JB   Was Welles embittered by his experiences?

JC   I don't think so, no. He had tremendous balance and had a great philosophical view. He was such a genius, in fact, and he wasn't going to be overridden by these factors against him. The tragedy was that the people around him didn't realize what wonderful things he was capable of.

Gradually he was kept at bay, and in the end it was so pathetic to see him working on television commercials for lager or whatever.

JB   Almost like Hitchcock, Welles became something of a parody of his own persona towards the end, didn't he?

JC   Yes, he did, although he did make one last wonderful film, *F for Fake*[15] [1973]. I thought that was a brilliant picture, because he was such a showman and a bit of a conjuror, and a certain cynicism was in that picture; you got to see his real character in a way.

JB   What happened to the *Ulysses* project?

JC   It died. He had probably around half-a-dozen films that he had either started or prepared that he had to leave off because he didn't have enough money. Of course, the big one was *Don Quixote*[16]; that was a tragedy because it would have been a wonderful film.

JB   Probably a redundant question, but would you have liked to photograph for Welles?

JC   Oh yes, very much. He had Gregg Toland[17] photographing *Citizen Kane* and he had a very deep regard for his work because he was a wonderful cameraman. I think that he had great respect for what a cameraman could do. He encouraged experimentation and if his cinematographer suggested that they had a character in very deep shadow, Orson would be like Michael Powell and always say, 'Let's do it!' Nothing frightened him, nothing. What Orson also had was a very deep psychological understanding of things.

When I saw *The Magnificent Ambersons,* I remember a scene where he broke all the rules, as he often did. He had these characters all leaving a house after a party all saying 'thank you very much' and things like that, and he had them all overlapping with each other—all speaking at the same time. I was very impressed with that, and later, when I shot one of my first pictures, I had a lousy script and I had a scene that I thought was very flat, so I thought I'd try out this idea from Orson. The sound man told me it couldn't possibly work, but I did it anyway and it worked very well. If it was good enough for Orson Welles …

JB *Kane* **had been very innovative with its cinematography, pushing the limits of light and shadow and depth of field.**

JC Absolutely; it was marvellous.

JB **Going back to Hathaway, what did you learn from him as a director? Did you later use any of these 'tough love' techniques when you were directing?**

JC Going forward a number of years to when I was directing Michael Redgrave on *Young Cassidy* [1964], he came to me just before the last big scene of the picture, which is where he had a big power speech to make, outside this theatre. He came to me in my caravan and said to me, 'Jack, I'll never get through all of this.' Exactly the same as Orson Welles, and obviously he too asked me to break it up.

But I played it a different way: I said, 'Michael, of course, we'll break it up for you, don't worry. But I have to do a rehearsal to check on the rain and the lights and everything else, so do your best and just go through it and we can time it.' So he was happy and he went right through the scene from beginning to end—perfect, and a marvellous bit of acting. He came over and said, 'Oh Jack, if only we had been shooting that!', and I said, 'We were.'

JB **Was he mad with you for that?**

JC   No, he roared with laughter at it. But that's the thing: you have to treat actors very carefully because they can be so pent-up. For example, Henry Hathaway wouldn't have anyone behind the camera watching.

JB **You mean actors?**

JC   Anybody! He would say, 'Jack, please don't loiter behind the camera. I know you have to watch, but please just hide behind something.'

After a while, he told me why he did that. He told me he had a system where he would tell if an actor was a 'one-take actor', which was rare, or a 'take-three man', where he knew instinctively that he would be no good on the first two, but would get it on the third. He knew when he was going to get a performance. Anyway, one time he was working away with an actor and he had gotten to take four, and Hathaway knew that take five was going to be the one. On that take, though, the actor went to pieces and Hathaway couldn't understand it—he was absolutely bewildered. Then he looked behind him and saw one of the actor's friends, who had strolled on to watch. So from then on, he would have no compunction in clearing the whole set, because what was most important was to get a good scene with good acting.

Hathaway would always get on the set before anyone else. He used to take me in his car every morning to Pinewood studios. If the call was for 8.30 am, he would get there at 8 am and start yelling, 'Goddam it! Where is everybody?' I would say, 'Henry, the call was for 8.30.' But his argument was that if they really liked their work, they should be there for 8 am to be ready for 8.30!

Hathaway was prepared to die for his pictures, that's why he was perhaps not liked, but certainly respected. He was quite a character.

JB   You next went to Paris to direct your own documentary. How did the chance to do that come about?

JC   I had worked for a producer called Jean Bernard. He was a funny little man who, when he was young, had worked in London as a garage attendant. He spoke French-Cockney, which was highly entertaining; he was a nice man, though.

I had photographed a short in Paris about the Seine, a ten-minute short rather like a [James] Fitzpatrick film[18]. And Bernard had talked about doing a film on Montmartre, which interested me very much. So I worked with him on a script and I wrote most of it.

JB   Were you taking a break from the 'day job'?

JC   I could do things like that between film productions because you always have a month or two off between pictures and in that time it was fun to work on something that you really enjoyed doing. So I worked on this. I had several ideas and in the end I wrote the script, I directed it and I photographed it.

I probably made half-a-dozen visits with the Technicolor camera and my crew to Paris to make the film. We worked like hell, but it was great fun. We would organize it in such a way that we could even go on stage with the girls performing the can-can. We shot almost like a newsreel crew and had to work very fast. It wasn't like a regular feature film.

JB What kind of things were you shooting for it?

JC   For example: I shot a scene in the Place du Tertre where I wanted to do a transformation from the winter to the summer. In the winter, I put the camera with a wide-angle lens on the balcony of a house that overlooked Place du Tertre. Everything was very black and grey and rainy and the trees were completely bare. I photographed about 100 feet of the empty square (well, it was almost empty: right in the middle of the scene a dog came right up and peed in the middle of the picture!) I went back the next summer and put the camera in the same position and created something like a 50-foot dissolve from the winter to the summer, so that gradually you saw come on the trees and these street artists arriving to sell their paintings. It really was a wonderful shot and I had a lot of fun.

JB What about the finance?

JC   Well, it wasn't an expensive picture, but it was in Technicolor and I had worked on it for some time. I did some of it, then went and worked back on a 'regular' film, and then came back to this.

JB You did have money troubles at one point, didn't you?

JC   Yes, I had shot a lot of stuff and put it all together and it really was shaping up into a marvellous film. I think it was intended to be a two-reel finished film, something like that. Just before we were finished shooting the whole thing, Bernard told me he didn't have quite enough money to finish the last bit.

So he went back over to England and took some of the stuff with him and when he came back he said that he had been given a further £2,000, which was enough to finish it off. But he didn't tell me that there were any conditions with that money. So I finished it and made my cut and then I found out that the conditions were that they wanted a four-reeler. What he had done was re-cut it using all of the 'NG' shots and all of the padding stuff that I had shot. I was furious, but as it happened it ran for five months in London and was very popular.

JB You shot two documentaries, *Montmartre* and *Montmartre Nocturne*, and there is also a short called simply *Paris* [all 1950], which Jean Bernard is credited as directing …

JC   No, that's the confusion. One is my version and the other is the trumped-up version that Bernard had released. It was successful, but I hated it because it wasn't what I had intended it to be. Bernard later broke the film up into two or three pictures and also released them that way! They were all the same film.

JB   Your love affair with Paris has lasted all your life, hasn't it?

JC   Oh yes, I was there just a few weeks ago. It is full of wonderful characters and the more you go back, the more fantastic *everything* is. When I was first there, it was the golden age of cafés and was wonderful. In the days of the Impressionists, they were theorizing about everything and they would have their meetings at the big cafés; they would meet almost every night and have these often very violent discussions about art and what they should and shouldn't do. I was fascinated by all of that side of Paris.

JB   So you were always drawn to *Paris* as the spiritual home of the artists you admired?

JC   Yes. Oh yes. And certain things haven't changed. When I was making *Montmartre*, I went to the places where the Impressionists had been. The Bateau-Lavoir was an incredible great place that had no running water or heat, but Picasso lived there for a time. These were very dramatic scenes that you could still visit.

JB   Had the move from cinematographer to director always seemed like a logical progression for you?

JC   The thing is that you have to remember that I was born and brought up on the stage; I was used to actors and sets and lighting and things. I was brought up with it all and understood it. It was my background. So it seemed perfectly natural to me.

I remember a difficult scene on *Black Narcissus* with Deborah Kerr. She had done this scene so well and when Michael Powell called cut, he turned to me and said, 'Oh God. I suppose you want to do that one again? Did you see that light go out?' I told him not to worry about it, it was a great performance, absolutely perfect, and I knew we wouldn't get another. So perhaps I was already thinking more like a director.

JB   Your next job was again as a cinematographer and the film was *Pandora and the Flying Dutchman* [1951].

JC   Al Lewin[19] was the director and he had been one of the big shots at MGM and had also produced a number of very big films, so he was a very important man. He was only about 4 feet 2 inches in height, something like that. A truly tiny man, but charming, and he had plenty of money.

He had a wonderful apartment on Fifth Avenue in New York, which was quite something. After the picture, I went several times to see him there. He was very fond of very modern art and he had the most wonderful pictures. Anyway he was the most intelligent man and a great director.

Pandora was also the first time I met Ava Gardner. She was great fun to work with and very beautiful. It was also the first time I had worked with James Mason, and he was a delight to talk to, a very intelligent man and a wonderful voice.

JB   Al Lewin seemed to have had quite a thing for Ava Gardner.

JC   He thought Ava was the most beautiful person ever, and he used to just gaze at her and he would shoot so many close-ups and then say 'do it again!' Always doing extra close-ups. Quite mad.

JB   And this was shot on location in Spain. Was that another country you knew well?

JC   Not very well. I had worked there before and I knew it a little. We worked at a place called Tossa de Mar [northeast of Barcelona] and that has really changed now and is full of tourists, but in those days it was perfectly delightful. We shot all of the beach scenes there.

The art director was John Bryan[20] and so we had some wonderful sets, so with Al Lewin directing and a very good cast it was a great picture to be on.

JB   You fell in love with ballet while working on *The Red Shoes* and on *Pandora* you fell in love with bullfighting.

JC   It is, of course, fascinating, but nine out of ten people today would question how you could possibly like it. The way the bull is sometimes killed is of questionable taste.

I thought that the great thing was that it is a tremendous display of courage with a man facing this beast that is so tremendously strong and powerful. These bulls can toss a horse in the air, they are so strong. A bullfighter has to literally and completely understand the bulls; it's not just a question of moving away from them.

Miguel Dominguín was the big bullfighter then and later he and Ava had this big affair.

Dominguín invited my wife and I to go and spend a couple of weeks on his farm with Ava and they rowed all the time. Fighting and making up all the time.

JB You sound like you really enjoyed the experience of working on this.

JC It was a very pleasant film to work on because it is what I would call an 'artistic film'. Everyone concerned was very artistic.

Al Lewin was very grateful to everyone at the end of the picture. He wanted to buy me a present and he told me to go to the camera shop and buy the best 16mm camera I could find. I told him he might not realize quite how expensive that might be, but he said he didn't care. So I went and I bought the cheapest that they had, which I regretted later.

I still have the camera and I photographed a lot of things in *The African Queen* [1951] with it.

JB Naturally the press had a field day with the film's star, Ava Gardner, and her penchant for bullfighters.

JC Oh yes. But there was nothing in it at the time. She was the sort of person that was the product of Hollywood in a way. She could never have a quiet evening at home or just go to a nice play; it always had to be something more. At that time, she was passionately in love with Frank Sinatra and they were phoning each other every day.

When we got back to England after that picture, Frank came over to London and he and Ava and I went out for two or three evenings, which was more than I could take because it

Jack Cardiff and James Mason on location, *Pandora and the Flying Dutchman* (1951)

wasn't just a nice dinner and then home, it was on to a nightclub and then another nightclub and another and we would end up at six in the morning in the dawn light. I was exhausted.

But Ava lived on a kind of tension, which drove her.

JB   When you have spoken about Ava before, you have always sounded very protective of her. Was she someone who needed protection?

JC   Yes, in the sense that she was really quite an ordinary girl who came from somewhere in the Midwest,[21] and if there hadn't been a film industry, she would have worked in Woolworths and just turned a few heads. But the film industry made her a goddess and in some way that made her quite neurotic, I think. She was then never content with simple things.

JB   After *Pandora*, you worked on *The Magic Box* [1951] for the incredible John Boulting.[22]

JC   He was a funny character. He had had a very good education, and not that he was snobbish, but he had a slightly supercilious manner. He knew what he wanted and he would get it.

Again John Bryan was the art director on that, and on one occasion he had made quite a small, simple set because it was only needed for one scene and we were on quite a low budget. But Boulting was furious and gave him a terrible dressing down in front of me and one or two others. I thought that was a bit mean because John had only done that to satisfy the budget.

JB   Did he treat you in a similar manner?

JC   No, he was always quite pleasant to me and we were quite friendly together. Of course, by the time I directed *Girl on a Motorcycle*, he was in control at Shepperton Studios and he came on as an overall producer.

Unfortunately I wasn't that familiar with the true facts of the story of *The Magic Box* and the life of William Friese-Greene. There were still many uncertainties about a lot of his life, although I do believe he was one of the inventors of the film camera. Friese-Greene had also worked on several things appertaining to the development of the film camera, like emulsion film. He had a shop opposite the Ritz Hotel in Piccadilly, where he had a room in the cellar for performing these experiments, and apparently there was always a terrible chemical smell coming from it. It's a shame that he has never really received that much recognition for the work that he did.

JB It must have been interesting to work on the film because you knew and had worked with William Friese-Greene's son, Claude.

Ava Gardner and Jack Cardiff, *Pandora and the Flying Dutchman* (1951)

JC Yes, I had worked with him several times. He never really talked about that, though; he would only have remembered him as a father, I think.

JB A young Richard Attenborough was in the cast too. I say young—he had already been making films for a decade by this point.

JC Well, he was younger than he is now! He is very venerable now with his white hair and beard. It was a nice little film and he was great in it.

5 Legends

- Hell in the jungle: *The African Queen*
- Huston, Bogart, Hepburn and Bacall
- *The Master of Ballantrae*
- In with Flynn—*Crossed Swords*
- Gina Lollobrigida
- Almost a director—*William Tell*
- Joseph Mankiewicz and *The Barefoot Contessa*
- Ava Gardner
- *War and Peace*—King Vidor
- Dino De Laurentiis
- Lighting the duel
- Audrey Hepburn
- *Legend of the Lost*: Sophia Loren and John Wayne
- Olivier and Monroe

'Not only is Jack one of the greatest cinematographers of all time (as further demonstrated by his well-deserved Honorary Academy Award), but he is also a man who always got the job done, never wasting time and always bringing fresh ideas and incredible imagination to any picture. During the filming of an exterior duel scene between Henry Fonda and Helmut Dantine in *War and Peace*, for example, we were discussing with King Vidor how best to shoot it when Jack surprised us all by suggesting we film it indoors by building the set on stage. The result was a truly wonderful scene with snow softly falling on the actors that, thanks to Jack's extraordinary lighting, nobody could tell had been filmed on stage. Jack Cardiff is a true master filmmaker.'
Dino De Laurentiis—Producer, War and Peace

'I wish I could be the way you have created me. You are the best in the world. I love you.'
Marilyn Monroe—Actress, The Prince and the Showgirl

JB Had anything you had done previously prepared you for the arduous location work on *African Queen* [1951]?

JC Oh yes, because don't forget I had worked on the *World Windows* travelogues. We shot in the desert, carrying equipment, and made five little films in India. This wasn't cosy studio conditions, so I was fairly used to it. Of course, *African Queen* had a lot of production money; not a lavish budget, but we were well looked after.

I liked John Huston very much because he was so laid back. Having worked with people like Hathaway, who was the very opposite, I noticed that nothing seemed to bother Huston. He did have this iron control and would never be talked out of anything that he had set his mind on—but he would always get his own way in the nicest possible manner.

JB   Was he aware of the travelogues you had shot? Was that part of the reason he chose you to work on the film?

JC   I really think I just had a certain reputation by this point and was sort of on top of the tree, so when they were casting a picture, there were certain people they would look for, rather like picking a football team.

JB   So it was off on location again. Where were you shooting?

JC   We were supposed to make the film on British territory, in Uganda; that was part of the deal. Huston went out on a recce while I was still on *The Magic Box* and he sent a message back to the English producer, John Woolf[1], saying that he didn't like the Ugandan locations. And then he just disappeared for something like two weeks. Maybe he had been eaten by a crocodile—we just didn't know.

But then we got this cable saying that he had found a wonderful place in the Belgian Congo. The place was two days outside of Stanleyville [now Kisangani], right in the wilds of the Congo. This really affected the production, but it was what John wanted.

JB   So you knew you were in for a tough one?

JC   When we arrived, we couldn't believe it. They had already prepared a number of little huts, which were made of dried leaves. It was a pretty ghastly location and a terrible jeep drive from Stanleyville. So yes, right from the beginning it was very tough going.

JB   This was an intelligent and experienced crew and studio. Did anyone have the slightest concern about dragging major stars off into the 'heart of darkness'?

JC   Well, they might have had, but that's the film business for you. It so happens that if there had been any real trepidation about the danger, John Huston would still have got his way. It wasn't unusual then to go to wild and tough locations. The philosophy was you got the rough with the smooth; sometimes you had a very nice location or were in the studios and other times you had to go out into the wilds.

JB   You had already recreated the Himalayas and the Antarctic in the studios. Was there no question of shooting this on a set too?

JC   That is something that Huston would never have agreed to. He had a very quiet way of getting what he wanted. For example, what he insisted on, in his very quiet way, was that the engine noise from the boat, the *African Queen*, was to be left running so that the actor had to speak above it. He was quite right because it made it far more realistic. So we shot almost all of the film with that terrible engine noise going.

So he was a fine director.

JB   Did Humphrey Bogart's tough-guy screen persona translate to his real-life character?

JC   Yes, in a way, but the funny thing was that he was an extremely nice guy and he wasn't really tough, but he put on the tough. You would say, 'Good morning, Bogey.' And he would always reply, 'What's good about it?' It was part of his manner, and the films he made created that part of him, I suppose.

Bogart could be a little argumentative when he had had something to drink, and on *The Treasure of the Sierra Madre* [1948], which Huston also made with him, they had a big argument and Bogey started swinging at John. John was very tall and had a tremendous reach so he just reached out and grasped Bogey's nose and left him there thrashing about until he had cooled off.

JB   Katharine Hepburn proved herself to be pretty tough on the film.

JC   We all had this terrible sickness and Kate was as sick as the rest of us. Of course, Bogey and Huston were never ill and the joke is, it was because they only ever drank whisky and never touched the water. The rest of the unit were very ill and so was Kate, but she was very brave to go in front of the cameras and act like that, because her face was often white or sickly green. She sometimes had a bucket just out of camera range, which she would throw up into between takes.

Of course, at the time, we didn't know it was the water making us sick, but the irony was that it was known that Kate was using bottled Evian water to wash her hair, which was considered very wasteful. If only she had drunk it instead of washing in it, she would have been fine.

The flotilla of boats used for filming *The African Queen* (1951)

JB **And Bogart's wife, Lauren Bacall, was along for the ride on the shoot too.**

JC Oh yes. They had this amazing dialogue between them and whatever they talked about together, it was slightly challenging. It was very much like a parody of the films they had made together, particularly *To Have and Have Not*[2] [1945]. They really were like that.

They weren't argumentative and she took it all very calmly, but Bogey would grumble sometimes, mainly because he had a yacht of his own back in California and he thought the whole flotilla thing was crazy, and would try to take over as if he was the admiral.

JB **What do you mean by 'flotilla'?**

JC We had this meeting to discuss how we were going to make the film and Huston said he wanted to put the boat, *African Queen*, on a raft and go down the river on that, so that we could be on the raft but outside the boat filming. It was funny really, because that made it like a stage and we had gone to such lengths to go out into the wilds. Perhaps 80 per cent of the film took place on this little boat.

The raft was towed, which was a wonderful idea, but also I had two lamps. It's amazing, but I made most of *African Queen* with two lamps. John Woolf had said, 'My dear Jack, you don't need lamps, you'll be in Africa where all the sun is!' But I did need lamps to light out the shadows. In fact, for the first week or two, it rained a lot and we were able to keep shooting with these lamps. So they paid for themselves. But the lamps needed a generator and that meant another raft, and then the sound department had another boat, and then a boat for Kate Hepburn's dressing room, and another for props. So we had a whole flotilla going along the river like a string of sausages. It was fine going straight, but when we went around bends, things often just crashed into the bank.

JB   But Bacall was happy to come along and put up with this hellish location misery?

JC   Yes, she was, and I'll never know why she did such a crazy thing, but she came out and I don't really remember her being sick; perhaps she drank whisky too, I really don't know. But the fact was, she would bring us our food when we took a break for lunch. We had these weird sort of lunch boxes that probably came from Stanleyville or some-where, and she used to bring them out on the set. I told her she was the most expen-sive waitress in the world. She was very nice.

JB   You have taken many beautiful photographic portraits of stars over the years; didn't you take any of Bacall?

JC   No, I didn't. Of course, it would have been impossible on location apart from horrible snapshots and when we got back, it just didn't work out. She was very beautiful, though.

JB   Huston, I understand, was just as interested in shooting animals as film. Is that part of the reason why he insisted on real locations?

JC   Oh definitely, I think that might have coloured his choice of location to a certain extent. Although I don't think he realized there wasn't much where we were, apart from croc-odiles, and there's not much sense in shooting a crocodile because we had hundreds in the river. It would have been like shooting at fish.

We got quite used to them and they never attacked us, although we wouldn't swim in the water, of course. The water was jet black and the crocodiles were on the bank and then would just slither down into the water. They never bothered us.

JB   Did Huston get to hunt any big game while he was there?

JC   No! Kate had a certain masculinity and she used to go walking in the jungle sometimes with John, who would have a rifle. But we never heard it go off. Kate was a strange per-son, she was all woman, but she hated to be considered a frail female. If you offered her your hand as she was getting off the boat, she would slap it away, because she wanted to just jump off like the men did.

You couldn't legally shoot animals anyway because there was a law in the Congo that you needed special permission to hunt. So it was a disaster for John from that point of view.

JB   Have you seen *White Hunter, Black Heart*[3] [1990], Clint Eastwood's dramatization of the filming of *The African Queen?*

JC   I saw some of it, but to tell you the truth I didn't have the heart to really watch it. I think it is a very loose adaptation.

JB   Do you still consider that the toughest shoot of your career?

JC   I think so, yes, because it was so painful working like that. We had temperatures of 104 or 105 degrees. The sound man got malaria.

JB   How long were you out in the Belgian Congo?

JC   There were two main locations: one was Beyondo, which was in the Congo, and that, I suppose, was about eight weeks, perhaps a little more. Then we had this very long journey by train from Stanleyville. I clearly remember the *African Queen* being loaded onto a train. And we went from Stanleyville across to Uganda.

We thought we were over the hard times and that Uganda was going to be a holiday. We were going to be on this great big liner, that we would work on and sleep on. But the moment we got there, we felt even sicker. It finally turned out that we were drinking water that wasn't being filtered so we were really drinking hippo droppings.

JB   What were you doing about communicating with London when you were out there? And how about the rushes from Technicolor?

JC   Sam Spiegel, who always wore beautiful white shorts and a white hat, would make the trip every few days to Stanleyville and then from there he would phone England. There we would have an editor, who had to be completely trusted, and he would see the rushes himself and report back. The director never really has the chance to see the rushes for himself on such a location.

Huston, like Hitchcock, was no fool and really knew what he was going to get just from looking through the camera. That's why I can't stand to see modern directors who just watch on a video monitor, because they just can't see the nuances on an actor's face— they are missing the human factor, like a glint in the eye.

JB Sadly that's perhaps because today many directors know that their films will predominantly be seen on the small screen.

JC Yes, indeed, I know what you mean. In that case, they should be perfectly happy with what they see on their little televisions, but in my day it was all for cinema, of course.

Later, when I worked on *The Far Pavilions*[4] [1984] in India, they used to send out tapes of the rushes for me and I could run them in my bedroom each evening. That worked quite well.

There used to be times, when working on location, when a whole lot of rushes, which we hadn't seen for some time, would arrive all at once and we would set up a projector, like a hastily organized Christmas show, and project on the wall of the hotel. It's certainly never easy to watch rushes on location.

JB With the cameras being so heavily blimped was there less chance of getting hairs in the gate and that kind of thing?

JC No, that was a big problem for years. Most of these little hairs in the gate are tiny fibres, often from the black paper that the film comes wrapped in. They can be a pain in the arse. You do a wonderful scene and then the camera assistant tells you that there is a slight hair in the gate and the big question is: is it going to be noticeable on the film? In most cases you have to do it again, for safety.

JB There was some respite at the end of *The African Queen* with a little studio work.

JC Yes, because there are scenes where Hepburn and Bogey have to get out and pull the boat and we couldn't do that in Africa because there is a terrible disease called bilharzia that comes from being in the water. So we had to do that in the studio.

We had a very good set with all these reeds and things. It was quite easy to do and a good match.

JB You had been offered, and turned down, the chance to be paid for *The African Queen* by taking a percentage of the box office. Is that right?

JC With *The African Queen*, a funny thing happened. On the previous picture, *The Magic Box*, which was a prestigious film selected for the Festival of Britain, the producers offered us half salary with the other half coming from the box-office takings. Well, it was a very nice film, but not a big financial success and didn't make a lot of money at the box office. So we never really got the other half of our money. So when the contracts for *The African Queen* were being drawn up, Sam Spiegel, the producer, offered me a profit cut and I said, 'No way!' and turned it down. That's got to be the silliest thing I ever did—it made so much money that I would have been a millionaire.

JB   You worked next with Errol Flynn on William Keighley's[5] *The Master of Ballantrae* [1953].

JC   Yes, we started the film at Elstree Studios and then had some location work in Cornwall. I only saw the finished thing once, at Errol's. He was a terrific swordsman and really made it thrilling to see. He was like a ballet dancer and had a quite brilliant manner.

JB   Your old friend, Roger Livesey[6] from *A Matter of Life and Death*, was on the picture too.

JC   Yes, it was good to catch up with him. He was a fine actor, and strangely enough, years earlier—I must have been about 11—I had worked with his father on a stage play, *The Octoroon*[7].

That was one of the few times I appeared on the London stage and I was thrilled about it. I had to open the show and I had black greasepaint on (I was supposed to be a little coloured child). It was at the Little Theatre near Wardour Street and I remember my parents couldn't go on the first night because they were rehearsing another show, but I finished the show and took the make-up off my face and rushed to get a tram. I saw people staring at me with incredulity and disgust, and I realized I had forgotten to take the jet black greasepaint off my legs.

JB   You formed a very close friendship with Errol Flynn. Did that strike you as unlikely given that you were such different people?

JC   Absolutely. To start with, I didn't really drink; I liked wine, though. I think Errol just seemed to have a regard for my capabilities and we talked about a lot of things. He trusted me, which is the important thing.

JB   His reputation has taken something of a battering since his death, but he was simply viewed as something of a rogue at the time, wasn't he?

JC   He had this attitude that any girl was a piece of cake and he could go to bed with them, no problem. He was married, of course, at the time. Later, when *William Tell* [1953] was

finishing and I was about to start on *The Barefoot Contessa* [1954], I went to several get-togethers that Errol had. He had just made friends with the ex-king of Egypt, Farouk. Now Farouk was like Flynn, but perhaps far worse; he was girl-crazy. I saw him follow one girl out as she went to the loo and he came back with a big red slap mark on his face. He and Flynn were a great couple and had all the fun in the world together.

JB Your next film, *Crossed Swords*[8] [1953] was also with Flynn. Was that pure happenstance, or had he requested you?

JC I think again it was just that I had a certain reputation. Flynn was the boss and as we had just worked together, he knew I was all right.

The film was an interesting story about this ageing Don Juan character, which was Errol, who teaches young chaps how to escape from irate husbands. I know Errol was very happy about the story.

JB Was his drinking even heavier by this time?

JC He was really on the booze at this time, and halfway through the picture Flynn collapsed. He was taken to the hospital in, I think, Naples, and kept there. Barry Mahon[9] phoned the hospital and asked when Mr Flynn would be available to return to work. The hospital said that really he had no liver left, that the booze had taken

Jack Cardiff presents
Gina Lollobrigida with
a gift. *Crossed Swords*
(1953)

his liver, and that perhaps his relatives should be contacted. They thought he was going to die at any moment.

The doctor, when pushed, said that he thought it would be at least nine months to a year before he could come back to work, if he ever could. So ever optimistic, what we did was use this very good stand-in, an Englishman that looked ever so much like him. We used him in all the long shots, and for the closer shots on Gina [Lollobrigida], we would have him with his back to the camera. We did a lot of work like that and got through quite a bit.

But after just a few weeks, Flynn rolled up on set. The doctor had said it was a miracle, but he must never touch a drop of drink again—ever! Flynn came on set looking terrible and in his hand he had a glass of neat vodka.

Well, he finished the picture and still went on for another few years. He must have had a gut like no one else.

JB **What did his co-star on *Crossed Swords*, Gina Lollobrigida, make of his antics?**

JC   There was never anything between them. She was married to a guy who was very nice and very good looking, and they were very happy together[10]. I think Gina was not a sophisticated woman, in the sense that she was just a very ordinary, uncomplicated Italian woman—not dumb, but just simple and honest. I think that she would have been horrified at the idea of leaving her husband or having an affair with Errol Flynn. She was too pedestrian; she was just decent and honest. Of course, it is quite possible that Errol tried it on!

JB   He was clearly already drinking himself to death at this stage, was he still doing his own stunts?

JC   Yes and no. He did the duelling and that's what impressed me, he was so good. We had an Italian who choreographed all of the duelling scenes and he was quite brilliant. He might have made it quite easy for Errol, because he had this stock kind of movement with his quizzical expression and one eyebrow raised.

JB   Do you think he was being deliberately self-destructive with his drinking?

JC   I think basically he must have been. But he was a tough character.

JB   Tell me about the *William Tell* project that you and Flynn developed together.

JC   Well, my chance to direct came in a strange way. After I had worked on those films with Flynn he went off and I began working on something else. Then I had a phone call from him, from Rome. He said, 'Jack, come on over to Rome, it's great fun. Come and do a picture.' He wanted to make a film of the William Tell legend and he wanted me to direct it.

I worked on the script with John Dighton[11], who was ever so good.

JB   As a first-time director, did Flynn's drinking reputation concern you?

JC   People said to me before we started the picture, 'Jack, you're mad having your first film with Errol. He'll get drunk all the time and won't show up on set.' So I brought my own caravan from England and I had it all cleared out and fitted up as a bar for Errol. In this caravan, there was every kind of drink that he could want and it was right on the set. He was delighted and he was never drunk on the picture because he had it there if he wanted it, and there was never any question of sliding off somewhere. This worked psychologically very well.

JB   How was it to be financed?

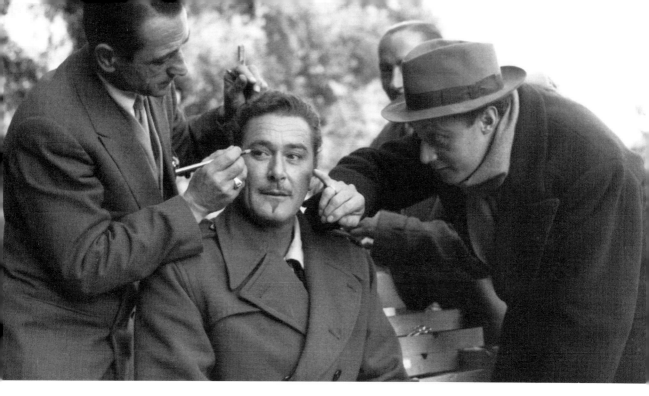

Touching up Errol
Flynn's makeup on
location for *Crossed
Swords* (1953).

JC Well, Errol and his associate, Barry Mahon, who was an American ex-pilot, had a system: so many people, particularly in places like Rome, were trying to get Errol Flynn
in their picture that they would ask him and then go to the banks and say, 'Look, we
need money for our film, but we have Errol Flynn in it.' And the banks would give
them the money. So Flynn's system was that he would tell anyone who had a proposi-
tion for a film for him to be in, that he would only consider it if they could put $60,000
in cash on the table while they discussed it. That kept the phoneys away and made Errol
some money.

There was a chap called Count Fossataro, who said he could finance *William Tell* and
organize everything. He must have talked Errol out of the $60,000 thing because the
bank told him and Barry that Fossataro was wealthy and owned a lot of property in
Naples. They said his account was in good standing, but later we found out that the joke
was that in Rome, if you had $10 in the bank you were considered to be in good stand-
ing! So it all added up at the time to seeming like Count Fossataro was the right man.

We were to shoot in Eastman Color and in CinemaScope. It would have been only the
second CinemaScope film ever made. So we were in good shape and Fossataro was to
pay for the Italian crew and the locations and the hotel—those sorts of things.

I started work on it and this was the big break of my life.

JB Where was it going to be shot?

JC We had this wonderful location in Courmayeur[12], which is very near Mont Blanc. You could pan around in a complete circle in the Alps, and wherever we looked, there were these amazing snowy views. It was the perfect location.

Location scouting for *William Tell* (1953)

We had a wonderful art director and he built this wonderful village made from real stone; it was fantastic.

JB And so you were all set to go.

JC Yes, I had a good cast and started off with fine enthusiasm, but after a while it became apparent that no money was arriving to pay the crew. Well, this was quite usual for the Italians, it does happen.

Barry went to Rome and got in touch with Fossataro, who gave him a cheque, but when he went to cash it, it bounced. Then the truth came out that Fossataro didn't have a lot of property in Naples; it was all in his wife's name. He had nothing, and very little money; so that was the beginning of the tragedy.

JB How long did you manage to keep on going?

JC We carried on shooting and the Italian crew were wonderful; they were used to not being paid on many films. But eventually the electrical crew, who had a strong union, sent an order to confiscate the lamps. So the lamps were taken away and we used

Cast and crew of
William Tell (1953)

reflectors for a few days and then the reflector people took the reflectors away! So we made our own reflectors from the silver paper in cigarette packets. At last, the hotel people commandeered the two CinemaScope cameras and locked them up, and that was that!

We went back to Rome, hoping we could sort it out, but no one would take the finance over because at that time, you see, Errol's reputation was on the way out. No one would dare to take over.

JB **David Niven said of him, 'You can count on Errol Flynn. He always lets you down.' Yet you pursued your feature début with him!**

JC Yes! That's a lovely saying, isn't it? But I found him very genuine and he tried so hard. He and Bruce Cabot, his co-star, had been buddies for years and had fooled around with women together in Hollywood, but in the end it got nasty, and Bruce sued Errol and confiscated his cars, I think. The whole thing just dissolved.

But I still have the telegrams from Errol when he had gone to Rome to try and get more finance and they say, 'Don't worry. Stay with it, pal!'

JB **How much had you shot?**

JC I guess there is no known record, but I think I shot about half an hour's screen time in about six weeks.

Now there is a company in Hollywood who want to make the film and have asked me to come in on it in an advisory capacity. I certainly wouldn't want to direct a film any more at my age. But I think things are going ahead, although you can never tell in this business. The original script is quite good.

The New York laboratories sent our original rushes over, but somewhere along the way the soundtracks went missing, so it was all silent.

JB Did you ever work with Flynn again?

JC No, but I saw him occasionally in Rome. I was in terrible financial trouble because I hadn't been paid anything. But then Joe Mankiewicz[13] came up to me in a restaurant and asked me to come and photograph his picture, which was *The Barefoot Contessa*.

JB Mankiewicz had been a writer before turning to directing. Did that encourage you to direct?

JC He knew that I had the tragedy of *William Tell* behind me and he told me I should stick with it.

JB He had an amazing career behind him as a screenwriter.

Jack Cardiff takes up arms on the set of *William Tell* (1953)

JC   Oh yes, he was a brilliant writer, one of Hollywood's best. But for a long time he didn't realize it and people were taking advantage and friends would ask him to do them a favour by reading scripts that had been sent to them. They wanted Joe to tell them if it was any good. All of a sudden one day he thought, 'What the hell am I doing this for? I'm an expert and I'm giving free advice.' So that's when he started to say, yes he would read it but that it would cost $10,000. That soon put a stop to that.

What really made him, furious, though was that a writer completes a script, gets his money, and says goodbye to it. He may have been well paid for it, but once he has done it and it's gone, it is a fact that many producers, directors, and even actors want to change the script.

So Mankiewicz used to get hopping mad about this, because he liked his work. So he then organized things so that he would direct as well as write—that way he had much more control. If he was directing, his script wouldn't be changed.

JB   And this was the case with *The Barefoot Contessa*?

JC   Yes, when he was making *The Barefoot Contessa*, he had written it, was directing it and he was the producer. So no one could touch his script: not even a question mark or a full stop.

The only problem there was that he did write beautiful stuff with wonderful dialogue, but on a page of script, instead of having an inch or two of dialogue, he would have half a page in one go. Humphrey Bogart used to complain that he couldn't remember it all, and I think that was fair enough. Mankiewicz was a very clever director, though, and fairly bold.

JB   So you think that he had started directing purely to protect his written word?

JC   Yes, although he liked directing anyway, he liked the drama of it. A good writer is sensitive to good drama, and as a director, he then knew how to direct a scene. He knew how to do it and he would bloody well do it that way!

JB   In addition to working with Mankiewicz, did the thought of being reunited with Ava Gardner attract you to the film?

JC   I guess so, because she was so nice to work with and pretty easy-going.

JB   How did she get on with her co-star, Humphrey Bogart?

Above left: Directing Errol Flynn on *WIlliam Tell* (1953)

Below left: Jack Cardiff takes the director's chair on *William Tell* (1953)

JC   I wish I could remember, but I just recall that she was loyal to the picture and she did her job well. I don't think Bogey was really a troublemaker; he was what I would call a 'surface man'. He would say funny things, but he would never really complain much, so it was fine.

JB   Dino De Laurentiis[14] contacted you at this point to ask you get involved with *War and Peace* [1956]. Did his reputation precede him?

JC   I never thought about it before, but he did come from very lowly origins—he was a taxi driver in Naples, so they say. He was far more astute than, say, Sam Goldwyn[15], although Sam Goldwyn did have a genius about him.

Dino made a big impression on people with his grand gestures and his, 'I make you a great-a big-a star!' and 'we make-a the greatest film-a!' To his credit, he certainly got *War and Peace* together! I forget who financed it, but it had a huge cast.

JB   It was a massive undertaking all round, just tackling Tolstoy for a start.[16]

JC   Yes, indeed. Of course, by the time I came onto it, they had already gone through the agonies of the script, although it was still formidable.

JB   Was King Vidor[17] already attached to direct?

JC   Oh yes, I think so.

JB   What was Vidor like to work for?

JC   King Vidor was very earnest and really laboured with his direction. He would call a meeting every morning on the set to go over everything and we wasted so much time doing that. But that was the way it worked.

JB   And De Laurentiis had the whole thing set to shoot in his native Italy by this time?

JC   I know that Dino must have suffered because he wanted the best of everything for the film and that included the biggest stages. But the Americans, bless their hearts, in the same way that they have taken over all the cinemas in Europe, had already hired all of the biggest and best stages at Cinecittà.[18] So it was impossible to get the stages he wanted. In his own country! Here were these bloody Americans and they weren't even using them, they had just hired them.

JB **What was De Laurentiis's solution?**

JC   Well, right opposite Cinecittà in Rome, right on the other side of the street, is another little studio called Sperimentali. The actual stage size was nowhere near as large as the one not being used at Cinecittà, so can you imagine how Dino was feeling?

We had to build this huge interior set of a palace hall. Against all of the fire rules, Dino ordered it built to within about a foot of the studio walls—usually you had to have at least 5 or 6 feet so that you could run in the case of fire. Someone probably paid a few bob to get away with it.

What was unbearable about it was that the stage was incredibly stuffy and we started shooting there in the middle of summer. The cast, who were supposed to be freezing in Russia, were all wearing big fur coats and capes. They were absolutely collapsing with the heat.

Jack Cardiff and director King Vidor discuss a scene on *War and Peace* (1956)

Later on, some weeks after we started, the stages at Cinecittà became free. We were nine months shooting the film.

JB   All studio interiors?

JC   No, of course, we did the battle of Borodino[19] on location!

There were also exteriors in the snow with lines and lines of soldiers and that was a terrible difficulty for me to match with the studio stuff. The big stage at Cinecittà was covered in snow and I had so many arc lamps, probably two hundred, around the stage with architects' tracing paper across each one to diffuse the light. It gave a blank softness like a day without sun. It matched very well in the end.

JB   You were reunited with Henry Fonda on this. Was he still playing his old tricks?

JC   No, and I don't think he was terribly happy with King Vidor, he hated all of these long discussions. I don't think Henry remembered me from *Wings of the Morning*, though.

In one scene, Fonda was supposed to walk for miles through the snow and Johnny Mills had left him in the previous scene, I think he had been shot. Well, Johnny's character had given Henry his dog and he then had to carry this dog on this long walk through the snow.

Fonda just kept saying, 'I don't want that bloody dog!', but he had to carry it. We would be on a dolly following, and when we got to the end and Vidor called 'Cut!', Fonda would just open his arms and drop the poor dog straight down in the snow. Every take. Poor bloody dog! How it survived I'll never know.

JB   Can we talk about the amazing duel scene that you shot?

JC   Yes, there was this famous duel scene, of course. The amazing thing about Cinecittà was that although it had a huge stage the spot rails were quite low, perhaps only 25 feet from the ground. We did the duel scene with a wide-angle lens for a long shot at dawn, and of course, with a wide-angle you got all of the spot rail in the picture too.

So what I did was put the camera on a six-foot rostrum and I put a big piece of glass, about six foo by four, six feet in front of the camera. I got the same paint that they had used for the backing and I spray painted it onto the top of the glass so that it masked the spot rail. The first time I tried it, not being a professional spray painter, it all ran down the glass just as Dino De Laurentiis came on to the stage. He demanded to know what

was going on and wanted to know why I was taking so much time. I assured him it would be okay, and I had another go and this time it blended perfectly. I lit it very carefully and it was a wonderful effect.

I shot the long shot of the duel with a slight fog filter on to take off any hard edges, and when Dino saw it in the rushes, he went mad with joy and would show it to all the visitors to the set. From that moment on I didn't have any problems with Dino.

JB *War and Peace* **was the first time you met Audrey Hepburn, wasn't it?**

JC   Yes, she was lovely and, of course, very beautiful. The only thing was, we had a ballroom sequence on another colossal stage at Cinecittà, and she was in it wearing a very low-cut dress. Now she really had no breasts, she was a model and very thin, a typical model. I suggested that she wear a necklace or something with this low-cut dress and she said, 'Jack, I'm just me. I am what I am and I haven't done too badly like this.' But you could really see her ribs.

We shot the scene and when Dino saw it, he went mad. She was very silly because there was no need to accentuate her ribs.

JB **One of your most beautiful photographic portraits is of Audrey Hepburn. Was it at this time that you photographed her?**

Jack Cardiff with Audrey Hepburn and Henry Fonda, *War and Peace* (1956)

JC   Yes. I just told her one day that I would like to take some pictures in the lunch hour and would she mind? It was a very daring thing to do in the sense that you can't really achieve much in a twenty-minute lunch break. I used two lights and set them the best I could with some filters. I had to work like mad to get those pictures, and when you see them, I don't think it's obvious that they were done in a terrific hurry. She liked them and it all worked out okay.

JB   **Are they the portraits you are most proud of?**

JC   I think so, yes. She had such a lovely face and the portraits have that light, dark, light, dark combination that worked very well.

      Someone had told her that her eyebrows were too thick, but that was part of her. She was a sensation in England and girls, as they still do, copied the stars. They copied her eyebrows, and thick eyebrows became the vogue.

JB   **What was the public reaction to *War and Peace*?**

JC   I remember going to the opening in London and Audrey was there with Mel [Ferrer], her husband. It went down extremely well. Today we have instant notoriety or instant fame and it is all overstatement, but that didn't happen then with *War and Peace*. The press were very good and they thought it was well made. Of course, Dino made a lot of money from it.

JB   **Have you ever seen any of the later versions?**

JC   I have seen pieces. I saw the big Russian production.[20] Of course, they had the advantage over Hollywood and Dino, in the sense that they could take years to make it in the real Russian locations. They did wonderful work on it.

JB   **On *Legend of the Lost* [1957], you worked again with Henry Hathaway. So your previous encounter with him hadn't put you off?**

JC   No, we were quite chummy. His wife was called Skipper and she was a remarkable person, because to spend a large part of your life with Hathaway must have been a terrible strain! He was always looking to have a row with someone, always looking for trouble.

      He had an unerring instinct about people who had something to hide, and when he was on set and someone had come in a little bit late, he would always discover it and make their life hell.

JB   At what point did you get involved with the film?

JC   I was involved from quite an early stage, which was a privileged position to be in. Most cameramen wouldn't have been involved so early with the script discussions and the like.

There's the scriptwriter, Ben Hecht,[21] was a very famous Hollywood scriptwriter, and Henry and I went to see him. He had a large room and all the way around it on desks and tables were dozens of pencils in pots: literally hundreds of pencils. And they were all sharpened; he had an electrical sharpener for them.

He would say, 'Well, how about this?' And he would grab a pencil and a piece of paper and he would write a scene in half a minute. Hathaway would read it and say he didn't like it and Hecht, would screw it up, throw it away and write another one. That was how the whole script was written, which is so Hollywood. Always keep your pencils sharp!

JB   An unusual approach to constructing a story!

JC   Yes, but we thought we were on to something good, although the story was rather preposterous when you came down to it. John Wayne played a drunk in the French Foreign Legion and Rossano Brazzi[22] played a character who was an explorer and was looking for his long-lost father. Brazzi wanted to go to Timbuktu to look for him, and he uses John Wayne as a guide. Then Sophia Loren comes along and joins them, and she is sup-

Audrey Hepburn, Mel Ferrer and Jack Cardiff examine test shots for *War and Peace* (1956)

posed to be a sort of tart. It was all so preposterous and really just a case of them think-ing that they had to have a woman in it. It didn't add up. She looked gorgeous and wore this very sensible dark green dress that went down almost to her ankles, but it was very un-sexy. She didn't look a bit like an Arab tart.

JB   This was another gruelling location shoot—the desert this time.

JC   Yes, the Sahara. The places where we slept were just a few dusty old buildings and it was so hot. In the morning it would start off very cold and by 11 am it would be unbearably hot. The Technicolor blimp still weighed a tonne and we would have to carry it about.

We also used a place in Tripoli that had a lot of old ruins but looked nothing like Timbuktu. Absolutely ridiculous!

Hathaway used to go mad if anyone wandered about, because they would make imprints in the sand and spoil the shots. He used to really scream. It was a real nightmare.

JB   I don't think the press were too kind to the film, were they?

JC   I went to one of the trade screenings. The press can be lethal and I could tell from the beginning that they thought John Wayne was crazy in the role and Loren was much too beautiful for her part. It was the most embarrassing time of my life, because it really wasn't my responsibility and Hathaway wasn't there. They tore it to pieces.

In one scene, Wayne and Loren follow this sound of sobbing and they find Brazzi on his knees in front of three skeletons and he sobs, 'I knew my father was dead, but to see him like this!' I went to a trade show with the press, and when that line came up, they all fell about laughing. To make it worse, John Wayne then says, 'Which one is your father?' Well, that got another big laugh.

JB   Wayne wasn't the world's greatest actor, and when he was playing anything but his cowboy persona, he often looked terribly lost. He even played Genghis Khan[23] once, didn't he?

JC   That's right. Of course, Ford had wanted to mould him into a great big star, and he did. Later I think Ford wanted to do the same thing with Rod Taylor.

Jack Cardiff and Sophia Loren on location with *Legend of the Lost* (1957)

The funniest thing was, that despite the fact that John was supposed to be a French Foreign Legionnaire, he was always dressed as a cowboy with his Stetson and guns and holsters. He had to wear the cowboy outfit in every film.

JB When it came to *The Prince and the Showgirl* [1957], I understand that Marilyn Monroe insisted on you photographing the film for her.

JC I don't know about insisted, but she had mentioned me to Larry [Laurence Olivier]. You get a certain reputation, I suppose. I had never met her at that time so maybe she had seen something that I had done or she knew of my reputation.

JB   And Olivier wanted you too?

JC I had an uneasy feeling that Larry might have had his own cameraman in mind and it might have been that he wanted Marilyn and Marilyn wanted me. So I said to him, 'Is that all right with you? Do you want me to do it?' Well, he assured me he did and that settled that.

Laurence Olivier had an office in London's Piccadilly, close to the house where the Queen had lived as a young girl. One day when we were working there, Larry said, 'Hang on a minute, I want to go outside because the queen is coming by.' So we all traipsed outside and this was so casual and could only happen in England, because there was no fanfare and no crowds. Along came an open carriage with Queen Elizabeth in, and by she went.

JB How did Olivier know she was about to go past?

JC That's a good question and I have wondered that myself. I suppose someone must have told him—he knew a *lot* of people.

But anyway, he had very prestigious offices and I used to go in almost every morning. The very first time I went in was when Larry told me that Marilyn had put in the request for me to photograph the picture.

JB   Had you worked with him before?

JC   Yes, going back some time, I had. When I was an operator at Elstree, I worked on a film of *As You Like It* [Paul Czinner, 1936], which he was in. It didn't make us buddies and I don't suppose he would even have remembered me from back then.

Funnily enough, on *As You Like It* Olivier was the first film actor I had ever lit in a close-up. The cameraman was ill one day and I got to do the shot. Larry had a quite knobbly face at that time and he hadn't quite matured—he wasn't very pretty. I had lit him in a particular way and Lee Garmes, the great cameraman, said 'Let me give you a tip.' And he showed me an easy kind of lighting to do on it: we had lights called 'cans', which had one big, soft bulb—and we put one on one side of his face with a silk on as the key light, and we put a second sidelight about 18 inches away on the other side of the face with about six silks on it. I had never seen that before, and it made him look marvellous. So my first lighting lesson for faces was with Larry.

JB   When did you first meet Monroe?

JC   I went to see her at the house they had rented for her and her new husband.

JB   Arthur Miller? [24]

JC   Yes, Arthur Miller. He opened the door and told me that Marilyn was still asleep. After we had a coffee, Marilyn came downstairs—and I had looked forward to meeting her as she was without doubt the biggest sex symbol in Hollywood—but I was staggered because she had just woken up and her hair was all tussled and she looked like she was about 14 years of age. She had no make-up on and she looked like an adorable little child. I really thought, 'This can't be Marilyn Monroe!'

JB   You clearly fell under her spell! Do you think her naivety was a tool she used or was it genuine?

JC   I think it was 99 per cent genuine. The fascinating thing about her was that I saw a lot of her, I used to go into her dressing room and talk to her and we became very good friends, and not once did I hear her swear. She had this kind of wondering look about her that was incredible, and there was never anything smutty about her and nothing cynical.

JB   How well did she and Olivier get along?

JC   From the first, it was evident that she was going to be a problem for Larry on the film. Most actors will come on the set and chat, but she would never come on the set. I felt quite sorry for Larry trying to act in and direct this film. She went through so many agonized times with Larry because he was, to her, a pain in the arse. She never forgave him for saying to her once, 'Try and be sexy.'

Marilyn had this ghastly obsession with method acting and was always searching for some inner meaning with everything, but Larry would only explain the simple facts of the scene. I think she resented him; she used to call him 'Mr Sir', because he had been knighted.

I saw Larry years later on *The Last Days of Pompeii*[25] [1984], which was made for TV. We talked a lot on set and I asked him one day what he had thought about Marilyn and he just said, 'She was a bitch!'

JB   The film was adapted from Terence Rattigan's play, *The Sleeping Prince*. Was Marilyn familiar with the work?

JC   Well, it's a good point to mention the play, because in the first week or two of the picture Vivien Leigh would come on the set, and she had played Marilyn's part in the stage play.

Vivien was a superb actress, very sophisticated and well educated with a lovely accent, and she would come on and she would terrify Marilyn with this authority that she had about her. I think perhaps Larry should have kept her away. I don't think that Vivien ever stayed to watch any of the acting because that really would have been in very poor taste.

JB   Did you see Marilyn socially?

JC   Larry had this play, *A View From the Bridge*, coming up and I was invited to go with Marilyn and Arthur to the opening. We got mobbed when we got to the theatre; the crowd was just surging in, looking at Marilyn.

When we got inside, we were sitting in the stalls about ten rows back and everyone sitting in front was just turned around looking at Marilyn. It was explained to us that during the interval, to stop her being mobbed, they had fixed up a little room for us. Somehow we all squeezed in.

The first bell to signal the end of the interval went, and we got ready to go, but Marilyn asked for another drink. Then the second bell went and she still wouldn't go. I looked at her and she was obviously terrified about going back and being stared at. That's when I realized that one of her big problems was people staring at her. It doesn't sound much, but if everyone is staring at you wherever you go, it can be a tremendous problem.

Probably that was the reason that she didn't come out on set. She never got to know the unit like most actors would. I'm sure she thought if she came out on set everyone would stare at her. She was in a nervous state.

JB Tell me about the photographic portraits that you took of Monroe.

JC Well, I had said to her that I would love to do some portraits of her because I thought she looked like a Renoir girl. That amused her, so she asked me to come over to the house one Sunday morning, at 9.30 am.

I went along with my camera and when I got there Arthur said that she was still asleep, so we had some breakfast. She was still asleep, so we played some tennis. Still asleep, so we had lunch. Finally she came down at 6.30 in the evening, looking gor-

Left to right: Jerry Wald, Marilyn Monroe, Jack Cardiff and Paula Strasberg.

geous, and I had to work very fast to take the pictures. I probably did them all in less than an hour.

She said to me one time, 'Jack, come and look, I have the most wonderful disguise.' And I went to her dressing room to see it and she took out the most fantastic bright orange wig you have ever seen! So there was really this side of her that was very naive and childish.

JB   You saw Marilyn just a little before her death …

JC   That was after she had done *The Misfits*[26] [John Huston, 1961]. I was staying at a hotel in Hollywood and I found out that she was staying there too in one of their bungalows. I phoned her up and she told me to come on over.

I went over and it was a big room with just one dim light on and yet she was wearing dark glasses; she couldn't have been able to see much. We sat together on the settee and had a drink and she told me what a terrible time she had been having. She told me that she went to what she thought was a health farm and it turned out to be a loony bin. She noticed that the door handles were missing on the inside and she couldn't get out. She also realized there was a peephole and they were watching her through it.

She had been told that she could only leave if a relative came and took her; but she had no relatives by this time. She was also now separated from Arthur Miller and in the end Joe DiMaggio,[27] who was a wonderful guy and who had *always* stood by her, came and got her out. She was so upset about the whole thing and had had a terrible time.

JB   Of course, the tragedy of her life and her early death are, in part, the very things that have made her an icon.

JC   Yes, she was such a tragic person. I have read the book *The Assassination of Marilyn Monroe* [by Donald H Wolfe], which states that Monroe was definitely murdered. The reason I believe this is that it describes in great detail how she came to be murdered and how some people had seen Robert Kennedy there that night.

Of course, Marilyn, who was always very silly, had kept a diary while she was with Jack Kennedy, before Bobby got involved, and in the diary Jack had told her a lot of stories about the Bay of Pigs episode, which was hot stuff. But she put it in her diary, and at a certain point Jack had wanted that back. I feel it makes sense to me, because she had this diary. She was just such a tragic figure.

Jack Cardiff stands in
for Olivier with Monroe on
*The Prince and the
Showgirl* (1957)

6 Fighting Vikings and Directing Features

- *The Diary of Anne Frank*
- Richard Fleischer
- *The Vikings*
- Kirk Douglas, Tony Curtis, Ernest Borgnine and Janet Leigh
- Directing at last: *Intent to Kill*
- A second feature: *Beyond This Place*
- *Fanny* and the Oscar nomination
- *Scent Of Mystery*: The first 'Smelly'
- Peter Lorre

> 'Jack Cardiff lit an actress with the caressing strokes of a Renoir—or rather, I should say a Degas, whom he copied at the Louvre while we were doing the interiors of *Fanny* at Boulogne Billancourt, in Paris. Yes, Cardiff was a painter concerned with delicate contrasts, contours and depth and also the balance of colours. He used light for drama and for romance. He worked with almost feminine minutiae, little touches of light here, little touches of light there, I felt part of a beautiful canvas.'
>
> *Leslie Caron—Actress,* Fanny

JB **You worked next on *The Diary of Anne Frank* [1958], but you were only responsible for the location work. Is that right?**

JC Yes, I worked just on the locations in Holland. The director was George Stevens,[1] but I was working with George Stevens Jr, who was his son and one of the film's producers. He wasn't just a kid though; he was a very mature, well-educated and interesting man—a very nice man to work with. So for the location shooting there was just him and me and one or two others, and we had no specific actors because they had finished all of the main shooting. This was just pure location work, which included the house of Anne Frank and one or two scenes of people going through the streets and other external shots.

They had hired an actual truck from World War II. It was a restored van of the sort used for taking away the prisoners of war or rounding up those that were to be sent to the concentration camps; the sort of thing that these poor people would have seen on their streets all the time. We got a number of extras who were chosen because they were particularly thin, and then they were given these dreadful clothes that they had to wear—sort of like prison pyjamas.

JB   Had you read the book[2] prior to starting work on the film?

JC   Oh, yes.

JB   Specifically for the film?

JC   No, no, before that. Although I did read it again when I was asked to go out there and work on the film. It was quite an incredible tale. I was very deeply involved in the story and felt such a deep sympathy for the girl.

JB   This was less than fifteen years after the actual events of World War II. So you were resurrecting some fairly recent memories …

JC   That's right, yes. And, in fact, a really weird thing happened to us. This woman, who lived in a house in the centre of the town, had just gotten ready to do her shopping. She got her bag and left the house. She came down the steps to the street and right in front of her was our van with about fourteen 'prisoners of war' with their heads all shaved and looking very thin and dirty. Now this poor woman had been in that position herself. She had had her camp number burned on her arm and had been a long time recovering from the experience, and she thought that she had gone mad. Well, she screamed and screamed and screamed. They ran up to her and in the end managed to make it clear to her that it was a film being made, but what a nightmare for her. Can you imagine what that must be like to really think that you had gone mad? It brought back everything so vividly because it all looked so real.

JB   Were you able to shoot in the actual Frank family house?

JC   Yes, we did some night shooting at the real house. In fact, we shot all night once, as we had a lot of odd shots to do that tied in with what had been shot for the film so far on the Hollywood sets. They didn't have anything like the actual house to use in America, so we were doing all of that work. Anne Frank was, as you will know, hidden in a secret room at the very top of the family house, although actually it was several rooms together, almost like a tiny apartment, but very cleverly hidden.

Those were the rooms that I walked about in at night. We weren't shooting in those rooms because they had already shot those interior scenes on the sets in Hollywood, but during the various breaks that we had, I wandered about the house. I remember seeing

the wall where she had puts marks during those two years to show how she was grow-ing. Just pencil marks, but they were still there.

Also there was the tiny window that she had to look through—all she could see outside was a large tree, and that same tree is still there, of course. It was very strange and one had a feeling of being there with her. It was so vivid. It was completely silent, as all the tourists had left for the night.

JB   In some ways, it is a story of hope, yet the audience know the outcome. Does that change the way a director has to approach making a film like *The Diary of Anne Frank*?

JC   Well, obviously the audience knows there is no way out. The director can't keep Anne alive, unless you create a structure where the film ends before her capture and murder. But then the audience still know that she is going to be killed, so there is not much you can gain from trying something like that. *The Diary of Anne Frank* is so amazing in itself— it is so pathetic and horrible—that it stands up in its own right.

JB   You later met Anne's father, Otto Frank.

JC   No, not later, it was at that same time [as the film] that I met him; we had lunch togeth-er. It was during this lunch that he told me that he knew the name of the person who

The location shoot in Amsterdam for *The Diary of Anne Frank* (1958)

had been responsible for giving the family away. Now that shook me! I didn't ask him who it was, partly because the name wouldn't have meant anything to me anyway, but also I felt it was in slightly bad taste to ask.

A few weeks ago in the newspaper, I read that Otto Frank had been implicated in the betrayal himself. That is hard to believe. Really hard to believe.

JB   The film was shot in CinemaScope. Wasn't there a danger of losing the sense of claustrophobia with such a large-format film?

JC   Well, I never liked CinemaScope because when I used it myself as a director I always found that you couldn't get the intimacy that you might want. *The Diary of Anne Frank* would have been much better in 185^3, where you can go closer, much closer.

During the first couple of years after CinemaScope started, they said that you couldn't go closer than 5 feet 6 inches from the camera, which is a long way away. When I used it on my films, I had a system going where I got hold of some cheap little lens adaptor from someone in the camera department and that allowed me to go a little bit closer. I tried doing some inserts where I was only about 2 feet away and I found that if I used a lot of light—really fierce light—and I stopped down on the diaphragm [lens aperture], it just held the focus. I tried it on one of the actresses, but she obviously didn't like being burned up by a lamp; it got so hot.

I must say I was relieved when I got away from using CinemaScope. The system didn't last long.

JB   There are also framing issues with very wide-screen formats.

JC   That's the big problem. If you had a close up with, say, just the top of the shoulders at the bottom of the frame, then the rest of the screen would have these huge blank spaces at either side. It was very good for group scenes; you could really go to town with those and have a whole group of people, which was wonderful.

JB   Do you think it was purely a gimmick?

JC   Oh no. I think they really thought it had something going for it. There was an element of a gimmick perhaps, but it was genuine enough and many people really liked it. It was also at this time that they introduced sound which went around the whole cinema, and that was great too. It all gave a super-realistic effect. Panavision now is the accepted format, which gives 2.35:1. And, of course, now with digital it is quite different again. I don't know how it is all going to end up.

Mike Todd[4] was involved in many of these sorts of innovations. It was so tragic when he was killed in that flying accident. I had spoken to him just before he died and he had asked if I was interested in shooting one of his pictures. I had only just rekindled my ambition as a director, so I turned him down, and I was sorry I did that, but I was just so keen to direct my first picture.

JB   Your long-standing friendship with director Richard Fleischer began with *The Vikings* **[1958].**

JC   I forget how we first met, but he had the most wonderful sense of humour. He was laconic and quiet and he would just say things that made you giggle. I took a liking to him at once. He is a very sincere person. He had been to one of the very good universities in America and had also studied to be a director at university in California. He had a good mind and was very un-American in many ways.

JB   But it wasn't exactly a film without its problems, was it?

JC   The biggest problem he had on *The Vikings* was that the actor, Kirk Douglas, was also the producer. At least he was one of the producers; basically he was the man that owned the picture.

JB   Actor-producer can be a lethal combination …

JC   Yes, it can.

JB   You shot on location in Norway, which must have had its own set of difficulties too.

JC   We had a lot of adventures on the fiords where we made *The Vikings*. We had a houseboat, rather like on *The African Queen*, but not quite so disastrous. The cabins were all together and Kirk had the cabin next to me. I could hear him sometimes at night when I was trying to get to sleep, arguing with Dick about the next day's scenes. Kirk always wanted to do it a certain way and Dick was always fighting him.

JB   When Kirk Douglas wasn't fighting Dick Fleischer, did he fight his co-star Tony Curtis? How did they get along?

JC   Okay, but what happened was that Kirk owned the story and had a script written, which was very good and he went around trying to get it off the ground. The usual problems happened and it wasn't easy, but eventually someone agreed to put up the money, but insisted that Kirk as the star wasn't enough, and it needed two stars to

make it box office. So poor old Kirk took that on the chin and looked around for another person.

He approached Tony Curtis and he agreed, but he didn't like his part and really wanted the part that was intended for Kirk. So again Kirk agreed, and they signed the contract, but before they started making the film, Kirk did a bit of rewriting and carefully adjusted the script so that he again had more than Curtis.

JB   Didn't Curtis notice?

JC   Tony didn't realize until halfway through the picture, and then he did a sort of slow-burn take on it.

JB   His then wife, Janet Leigh,[5] also starred in the film. Was that another condition of Curtis taking the role?

JC   I don't know, but she was very good in it. I had a young son, Peter, and when he was on location she used to look after him. She was a very nice person.

JB   Another long-standing friendship was born on the film: Ernest Borgnine.[6]

JC   Yes, he was a great guy. I saw him last year when he came over to England.

There was one scene where Ernest was supposed to be thrown to the dogs in a pit, and these were savage-looking dogs—quite terrifying. But the keeper couldn't make them growl or bark; they were just sleepy. They tried flicking stones at them, but they were just bored, almost yawning and going to sleep. It was a terrible problem.

But then Tony came on the set to watch and he was wearing a funny hat that he had just picked up. When the dogs saw him, they went mad! We quickly started the scene and it was wonderful. What had happened was that the hat had belonged to one of the dogs' other keepers, whom the dogs hated—so when they saw that hat, they went mad! Method acting for dogs.

JB   Did Richard Fleischer encourage you in your directing ambitions?

JC   Dick knew I wanted to direct and he was one of my best friends in the film business. In fact, he asked me to direct a scene one day, just to see how I would handle it. He was convinced that I could direct, and he knew the 20th Century Fox people and suggested that they give me a break. He never admitted afterwards that that's what happened, but I believe it's a true story.

Tony Curtis and Jack Cardiff, with Jack's son, Peter, on location with *The Vikings* (1958)

JB And so, five years after the failure of the *William Tell* project, you did final-ly get another chance to direct. The film was *Intent to Kill* [1958].

JC Funnily enough, I found a press cutting just this morning for *Intent to Kill*. It said, 'This is different; I like it!' It did have some good reviews. It didn't become a smash hit, but it was interesting.

JB You shot it in black and white.

JC That's right. I think we were using Mitchell cameras. I had a lot of ideas scenically for *Intent to Kill*, but I didn't bother myself too much with lighting. I hadn't worked with Desmond Dickinson[7] before, but he was quite good. Looking back on it, it's quite pos-sible that most of that crew was hired because they were quite cheap. I didn't realize that at the time—I was just happy to go on the floor and direct the film. The unit was extremely good.

JB Didn't it seem strange to be shooting in black and white after so long working in Technicolor?

JC Not really, no. As a director I was more concerned with the script and the actors and whatever. It was not an easy subject and we had to go to Canada on location. It was an interesting picture with Richard Todd[8] and Betsy Drake.[9] I enjoyed it.

JB How did your next film as a director, *Beyond This Place* [1959], come about?

JC Well, once you have done one, it is always easier to get another. I must have had an agent at the time and he probably got it for me.

It was not a big picture and it was done, I think, by quite a small company. It was an interesting story and very low budget. It was definitely in the category of a minor film. It was based on the Oscar Slater[10] murder story.

JB Were you finding directing tougher than you had thought you would?

JC It wasn't difficult to make, just a straightforward low-budget picture and it certainly didn't hit the headlines.

I do remember that Van Johnson[11] played the lead, and he was a very strange man. Very nice to work with and quite charming, but for some reason he would love to sleep. He had a dressing room and he seemed to sleep all the time. He was extremely young and

Directing an unconscious Herbert Lom—*Intent to Kill* (1958)

More snow on *Intent to Kill* (1958)

fresh and he was never late, he wasn't the type to be up all night at parties; he led a very sedentary life. But nevertheless he used to sleep all the time.

JB   What films were inspiring your work at this time?

JC   I went to see lots of films. Orson Welles in the marvellous *Citizen Kane*; Spencer Tracy was another favourite of mine; and Charles Laughton too. They had a certain idiosyncratic manner that stamped their personality on the screen. It was always a lesson to see films because you learnt what worked and what didn't. One of the things that always offended me was overacting. The essence of a good actor is that he *underacts* for the camera. It is so important.

JB Are you always watching films for their technique? Can you watch a film just for entertainment?

JC Oh yes, definitely just for entertainment. I live near a good cinema now, and also we sometimes tape things that I think I should see. I have become a bit lazy because the whole thing of going out to the cinema is less attractive as the years go on.

JB You're not a purist about watching films on the big screen, then?

JC No, but I quite agree that at the cinema, when you see a film on a big screen, with the space around you, you really feel the audience reactions. So I would always much rather do that.

JB Did you have problems with overacting on *Beyond This Place*?

JC A little. I remember one time Van Johnson was doing a scene: he was supposed to have come from America to find out what has happened to his father, because he has disappeared. Someone tells him that his father is in jail for murder. So now we cut to Van Johnson's face; Van wasn't a great actor and he made this huge 'Ahhhhh!' face. I said to him, 'Please don't do that. Don't show any emotion at all.' A sharp camera cut to his face would convey the shock and it didn't require overacting.

JB After directing *Beyond This Place*, you returned to cinematography, working with Maurice Chevalier[12] and Leslie Caron[13] on *Fanny* [1960]. Were you still hedging your bets?

JC Well, just a few weeks after I had finished *Sons and Lovers*, when I had been working on the editing, I had this call from Josh Logan,[14] saying, 'Jack, you must come over and work with me on *Fanny*.' I explained that I was a director now, but he was a great wily showman in a way and he said, 'Jack, do both—people will love you for it.' He thought people would respect me more if I did both and that I mustn't give up photography. I fell for that one, and he talked me into it. Since then, of course, I have done both; I have had pictures to direct or photograph as I went along.

Anyway, photographing *Fanny* was like a holiday after directing. A piece of cake.

JB Had you read Pagnol's original trilogy[15]?

JC Yes, and of course I had also seen the original French film version[16]. But the French version had been black and white, and pretty rough-looking in my opinion. It certainly wasn't a beautiful thing, but it did have these big stars and it had been a very big success. So when Josh Logan comes along, there was an instinctive hostility from the French: 'Here comes Hollywood trying to make something from one of our great masterpieces!' That was their attitude. But the ironic thing was that we had several French actors in our film playing the leads—Maurice Chevalier, Leslie Caron, Charles Boyer[17]

Maurice Chevalier was really more of a Hollywood star than a French star, though. So when the film came out, they said nothing could compare with the original. In actual fact, ours was a very beautiful film.

JB And I would say your film had a better cast than the 1932 Marc Allégret version.

JC It has such a wonderful cast headed by Maurice and Leslie; it was such a well-known cast. With great respect to the original actress (Orane Demazis), I think that Leslie was very beautiful and a marvellous actress. I think it was very sad that Josh Logan's version wasn't acclaimed more than it was in France. It had fairly good success in America and in England.

JB Was Maurice Chevalier good to work with?

JC He was so famous and so very well off that he could really afford to relax. I went to his house and he was a very nice man to know. He had several *fauves*[18] paintings, which today would be worth millions and millions of pounds. He probably had half-a-dozen of the very best *fauves* that I have ever seen—not to mention a collection of Renoirs and many other bits and pieces. So he was pretty well off. He was very quiet and never threw his weight about.

JB And Leslie Caron?

JC She had a natural grace, and was so much better than the original actress. Leslie really fitted the part because she so was so beautiful.

There was also one woman who played the part of the fish seller in the market place. She was such a wonderful character; a great big, fat, raucous woman who was an actress but who also owned a rather down-market dance club on the side. Lionel Jeffries[19], who is a great chum of mine, was in the film, of course, and he and I were invited to go to this club. We went along with our wives, and there were a lot of lesbians dancing there, so I pushed Lionel toward one of these women and made him dance with her. He was furious with me, but then brought her back to our table to talk with us all. Lionel asked the most outrageous questions and it was a wonderful evening.

JB Were you mainly shooting in Marseilles?

JC Yes, we were a long time doing the main shoot in the port at Marseilles, and then we moved to Dinard to get some more shots, and then we went to Paris to do the studio shots.

I think we used Marseilles to great advantage; we actually shot a lot of stuff on the waterfront and it was a very picturesque location. We had some wonderful effects. We shot one sequence from a helicopter where we zoomed in and out of the harbour at Marseilles.

Looking back on it, it was the most pleasant film in the sense that we were on location. Usually you have a pretty dull time of it, but on this film they had what was called 'French Hours', which meant that you didn't have to start until 12 o'clock, midday. So for the actors and actresses, who usually have to be there at 5 am for their hair and make-up, this was a wonderful thing. It meant that they could go to parties and go to bed late, and none of it mattered! That is the horror of working on films for an actor; they have to get up so early in the morning. These 'French Hours' meant that we started at 12 and worked right though without a pause—without lunch

Opposite: Jack Cardiff and Leslie Caron on location, *Fanny* (1960)

because you would have it before you started—and finish at 7.30 at night. That worked beautifully.

JB   You seem to feel that there are plenty of advantages to location work over studio shooting.

JC   Definitely! On location it brings everyone very much closer together, partly because they are forced to spend all of their time together. Locations are often very tough and can be quite horrific, and that is something that you have to go through together. Locations in the main are marvellous—you travel somewhere and you have to work hard. Tourists go back to their hotels at midday to escape from the heat, but film crews have to keep on working right through. It is always worth it.

JB   How were the Paris studio facilities at that time?

JC   Very good. Quite excellent; in fact, they had everything.

JB   How did they compare to, say, Cinecittà in Rome that you had used for *War and Peace*?

JC   Rome was a different ballgame because they had these enormous studios at Cinecittà, but I had the feeling that they didn't really have the facilities to make a series of big pictures, as they often relied on American productions, which came over and hired the studios. But on their own it was a pretty threadbare industry in Rome.

I had always admired the French technicians. Their system was not so hidebound as in England. At this time in England, the unions were very tough, so wherever we went we had to work by the rules very closely; otherwise, we were in deadly trouble. There was the story of a location shoot in Wales where the director wanted a door to be a different colour, and as they were in a hurry, they got the local painter to quickly paint it. When the studios found out, they stopped the production and had the studio painter come out and repaint the door.

It doesn't happen so much now, but it certainly happened a lot in those days. So it was refreshing to be in Paris where, if you had a fairly logical argument why you wanted to take just one camera and an assistant out to shoot something quickly, then you could bend the rules and no one said a word—that's what I liked about it.

JB   The film picked up a raft of award nominations[20] and you were again Academy Award-nominated for your cinematography.

JC   Yes, that was very pleasant. I had been so happy to photograph it because it was wonderful to work on and the net result was that it looked good.

JB   Did you go to the Academy Awards ceremony this time?

JC   No, I have never been to the ceremony when I have been nominated. As always, I was already working on another picture, and I really couldn't afford the time for a long trip.

JB   Did the nomination make you question your decision to be a director?

JC   I don't know; that's an interesting question. Inside me, I wanted to continue to direct, but that all depended on what subjects came up; I was just waiting for another assignment. I suppose I was on a kind of 'sticky wicket' at that time—I hadn't made anything outstanding [as a director] and it wasn't until I had made *Sons and Lovers* that I had more assurance that I would get more directorial jobs.

JB   You did immediately return to directing again after *Fanny*, making *Scent of Mystery* [1960].

JC   The man producing it was Mike Todd Jr, and of course Mike Todd Sr was the big man of the moment. But his son was extremely nice to work with. Again, I'm sure this job would have come through my agent.

JB   You were working with another Korda on this film. You had Vincent as your art director …

Jack Cardiff shooting a car-rig on *Scent of Mystery* (1960)

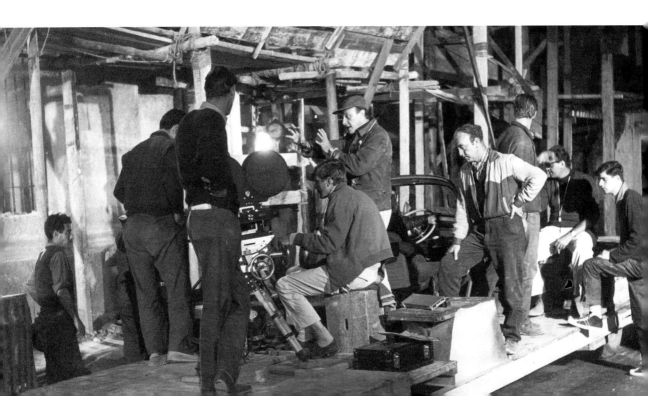

Lighting the exteriors
on *Scent of Mystery*
(1960)

JC Yes, I had forgotten about that. He was a strange man. He was strangely out of character working as an art director, because he was more of a painter or an artist. He made beautiful designs, but he was an expensive art director because usually, if you wanted some paintings for a set, say, the art director would fake something, but Vincent would get the real paintings in. That made him very expensive as an art director. He was also very laconic and critical of everything.

JB You were doing your own cinematography on this?

JC I was supervising and most of it was easy enough. Really just exteriors, as we chased around these wonderful locations. This one was Technicolor.

JB Now *Scent of Mystery* was rather unusual: it was supposed to be released in a format called 'Smell-O-Vision.'[21] What attracted you to a film with such an outlandish gimmick?

JC I was very interested in doing a film that had dramatic smells in it. I had always had this sort of ambition to do something like that; but I had put it away on a shelf. So I really jumped at the chance.

JB Were the smells integral to the plot or simply a gimmick?

JC Well, the script was very well written and it really dramatized the smells. It was a murder mystery and, for instance, perhaps the murderer smoked a pipe, so that when he was hiding in a room and the audience smelled tobacco they would know he was there. It took place in Spain and it was like a gigantic chase. We literally went all over Spain shooting—it was fantastic, just like a giant travelogue.

JB How was the system of smells supposed to work?

JC   The system was that we were shooting on a special wide film that had enough space for a soundtrack and also enough space for a 'smell track'. They would set up under the cinema these vats of odours, things like sea ozone, tobacco, fruit, whatever, and each one was ready to be used. According to the smell track on the film, it would send a 'get ready' message and that would drop a bit of the smell into a groove that then went around the whole cinema. There were pipes along the back of all the seats that had little holes. As the cue came on the film, the smell would be shot out onto the people sitting behind.

JB How were they planning to fit out all of the cinemas?

JC   That's a good point. The trouble is, the cost is enormous.[22]

JB   But no one had really thought about that?

JC   That's the incredible thing: no one seemed to!

JB Had you tested the smells out?

JC   Well, after some weeks of shooting things were going very well, and I suppose I was as guilty as anybody for not asking about the smells, but I took it for granted that they would be okay. The smells were being produced by some professor in Switzerland.[23]

I should, as the director, have asked to see this working; but I didn't. I gathered that the inventor was working away like mad and it would all be ready in time. Before we started work, I should have insisted on having some idea of the smells. But I was told it would be fine …

It was a three-month schedule with a $4 million budget, which was a lot of money then. So we had been working away and I said to Mike Todd Jr, 'Have you actually smelled the effects yourself?' and he said he hadn't, but he was sure it was going to work wonderfully.

JB   So even the film's producer hadn't checked?

JC No, so I suggested he got some samples and he got in touch with Switzerland, and after a couple of weeks, we received a box of samples in little glass tubes. They were all labelled: apricots, sea ozone, whatever. We took a sniff, and everything smelled like a cheap perfume. Nothing like they were supposed to, and nothing like anything but a rather cheap perfume! This was a disaster, so Mike phones the professor, who says not to worry about it because it will all be all right on the night.

So there's nothing else we can do. We have the cast, we have the crew and it's costing $4 million. So we finish the film.

JB **And was it 'all right on the night'?**

Jack Cardiff, Denholm
Elliott and Diana Dors
on location in Spain for
Scent of Mystery
(1960)

JC   No! The first screening for the press was going to be in this specially built cinema in Chicago. On the big night everything smelled like cheap perfume. It was an utter disaster. I never met that bastard, but I wish I had. He was obviously a phoney.

We opened the film up in New York and the critics laughed at it. It was a complete flop because of this idiot who let us all down.

JB   But this was a big film with some big stars …

JC   Well, it was not a bad film at all and yes, a good cast. Liz Taylor was in it; she was married to Mike Todd[24] at the time. She was sort of one of the producers; not a fully-fledged producer, but she was part of the company that was producing the film. So because of that she agreed to appear in the last scene of the picture. That was the mystery: who is this woman? And in the last few moments, you meet her and it turns out to be Liz Taylor.

Peter Lorre[25] was in it, and Denholm Elliott. The two of them are literally running all through the film.

JB   Didn't you almost kill off Peter Lorre with all the running?

JC   Halfway through the picture, I had gone out for dinner and my assistant director came in and said, 'Jack, Peter Lorre's dying.' You can imagine my feelings.

I rushed around to the hotel and there was Peter laid-out on a table and he was gasping for breath, his great big belly going up and down. We were in Córdoba and, as it happened, there was a surgeons' convention going on. So about four or five of them came around and they were all shaking their heads, and they all thought he was going to die within half an hour. Suddenly one of the doctors suggested we try bloodletting. This was like going back two or three hundred years! So as we had nothing to lose, they tried it, and amazingly enough it worked. By 5 o'clock in the morning, he had recovered consciousness.

JB   But you didn't let him do any more running …

JC   No! Because he was now so weak there was no way he could keep doing all of this running. So the company advertised in Madrid for a double and extraordinarily enough they found a man who looked exactly like him. So we just used Peter for the close-ups.

JB   What are the odds of finding a Peter Lorre lookalike in Madrid?

Discussing a scene
with Denholm Elliott
and Peter Lorre for
Scent of Mystery
(1960)

JC   A million to one! But they got one.

JB   But ultimately you didn't get to be the first 'Smelly'?

JC   No, because at the same time some producer character had bought a Japanese film that
he dubbed and he called his film *The First Smelly*. And he opened it a couple of days
before ours came out in New York. All he did was put a couple of buckets full of incense
at the air conditioning intake and flood the cinema with the smell.

JB   And *Scent of Mystery* didn't really work as a story without the smells?

JC   Years later, it did suddenly appear as a film on its own without the smells and it was running at the Coliseum cinema in London[26]. It was really nothing without the smells
because the scenes were geared up for and written for the smells. Tragic.[27]

7 Sons, Lovers, Lions and Motorcycles

- Directing *Sons and Lovers*
- Trevor Howard
- The trouble with censors
- Oscar nominations
- *My Geisha* and Shirley MacLaine
- Never work with children or (wild) animals: *The Lion*
- Fighting on *The Long Ships*
- Walking out on Widmark
- John Ford's boots: directing *Young Cassidy*
- Rod Taylor
- *The Liquidator* and *The Mercenaries*
- Cult classic: *Girl on a Motorcycle*
- Marianne Faithfull
- Stunt rides and Technicolor effects
- The critics

'I have known Jack Cardiff for at least 150 years. I first met him when I was working at Ealing Studios, where Jack was a camera operator; even then, I recognized that he had a magical quality about him. He has used this quality and his enormous personality to promote himself to the very top of his profession. He's not just a great cinematographer, but a wonderful director too. It was true privilege to work with him on *Sons and Lovers*—and I won the Oscar too!'
Freddie Francis—Cinematographer and Director

JB With a few smallish films behind you and one non-smelly disaster, how did *Sons and Lovers*[1] come about?

JC   The big break came about with Jerry Wald.[2] There was this man, Bob Goldstein, who was the manager of the London office of 20th Century Fox; that didn't mean he was a film producer, of course, but he talked films and did contracts and he was the boss.

He said to me that he thought I should do *Sons and Lovers*, but I hadn't read it. So I lied and said that I had read it and loved it and would love to do it; I told him it was a wonderful book! The book rang a bell and I knew it was D H Lawrence, as I had read a bit of his work and knew he was a wonderful writer. I ran around to the nearest bookshop and bought it. I read it and was instantly sold on it. I thought it was a wonderful story and knew it was for me, it had so much drama!

JB   Don't you think you were a funny choice of director?

JC   Yes, well yes, I was. But I certainly wasn't in a position at any stage to say, 'I don't want to do that' or 'I'd rather do that.' I wanted to direct anything.

JB   So you had a pretty big film on your hands and two big producers on your back …

JC   Bob Goldstein was acting like a producer, but then the actual producer was Jerry Wald over in Hollywood. The fact is, he never came to England once during the filming; he stayed in Hollywood. He was such a funny man. He did all the things that big producers do, like sending me letters and telegrams, suggesting things to do. Many of them were very well written and it took me some time to realize that he hadn't written them at all. He had a kind of team of writers and he would just tell them to write to me. He would supervise it, but it wasn't a very personal, intimate approach from a producer.

JB   Did you sense that Jerry Wald had even read the book?

JC   Well, that's an interesting point! He must have done, mustn't he? I wonder if he had?

In fact, one thing happened that was quite unbelievable during the preparation of the film. Jerry wrote to me with some elaborate suggestion about the point of the story and the casting and I read this thing and I thought, 'What the hell?' I realized he had taken one of my points from my letters to him and just sent it back to me! It was a typical trick to take ideas from all sorts of places, but he hadn't realized that in this case the suggestions he was sending me were originally mine—just repeating what I had said!

JB   It's a wonderful method of getting our own way, though …

JC   Yes, it certainly is—quite unbelievable. It is all such a big act in Hollywood. The producer puts on this act of guiding the director and working with the writers and whatever.

JB   How about Goldstein?

JC   I had a love–hate thing for Bob Goldstein. He almost wrecked the picture because he knew nothing about movie-making. There is a scene where they are playing cards and they want the mother to go to bed, but she keeps hanging around and the whole thing is dawdling along and there is tension—will she never go to bed? When Bob saw the rushes of that scene, he phoned me and said, 'Jack, what's happened to your brisk direction? This is a very slow scene!' I said, 'Yeeees, Bob! That's exactly the point!' He just never realized.

I slowly began to understand that Bob Goldstein really had no idea about producing a film, and that his main function was to represent 20th Century Fox from his luxurious wood-lined office in London. I also realized that he was working on a very, very low-budget mentality.

JB   Did his 'low-budget mentality' translate into a low-budget film?

JC   I had had to work very fast and very cheaply on *Intent to Kill*, but with *Sons and Lovers* I thought, 'This is it!' I thought it would be much bigger. But as I began to cast people, he would start to say, 'Jack, no, you can't cast that person, too expensive.' Well, this is something that I hadn't thought about on this picture.

JB   You hadn't really discussed the budget before you signed to the film?

JC   No. In those days you didn't, really. I can't remember what the budget turned out to be, but it was very low. Don't forget that today we talk in terms of millions, but then we talked in terms of hundreds of thousands.

JB   What was your budget, roughly?

JC   Something like £500,000 or £750,000. Maybe it was less than that.

JB   So how did you approach the casting?

JC   I developed a sense of cunning that I didn't know I possessed!

I had my own ideas for the cast and I wanted Trevor Howard. I knew him quite well and also I knew he was a wonderful actor. He had this great humanity on the screen and I knew he could play the part of the father who was rather comical, yet tragic. This relationship was very interesting because his wife was a station above him, far more educated. He was a miner, a very honest man, but truculent and didn't like being put down. It was a wonderful part.

JB   It required subtlety.

JC   Yes, but when I said to Bob that I thought Trevor would be good for the part, he said, 'No, no, no, much too expensive. Out of the question.' So I was still thinking about this for a while, because I wasn't used to this sort of in-fighting.

Trevor's agent was Al Parker, who was a very big London agent and, in broad terms, while I was trying to get Trevor, Bob said, 'Listen Jack, I've got Harry Andrews[3] for the part.' I knew Harry was a good actor, but I still wanted Trevor and wasn't too happy about Harry.

JB   Had you spoken to Trevor Howard about the role?

JC   I had spoken to him before and he had said that he loved the book and would love to do the part. I didn't discuss the money because a director doesn't discuss money with an actor, thank God. I hate talking about money and telling an actor that we can't afford them.

But suddenly, out of the blue, Goldstein said, 'Well, I have Harry Andrews, and I got him for £3,000.' Which wasn't much, even in those days.

Almost immediately, Trevor phoned me to ask what had happened, because he had heard that Goldstein had cast Harry. I think we met to have a drink and discuss it. Because I knew that Trevor wanted £20,000, I explained that Goldstein couldn't afford him on the budget. Trevor said that normally the producer would get in touch with the agent to discuss it and that Al was waiting for Bob to call and he never did. Trevor couldn't understand why there had been no contact at all and I said, 'Well, I don't like it either, there is something funny about all of this.'

I subsequently found out—it's a long time ago, so I can't remember how I did—but I found out that Al Parker had previously tried to get a round-robin petition signed to get Bob Goldstein out from Fox because he thought he was incompetent. So Goldstein no longer wanted anything to do with Parker.

JB   You weren't in a position to negotiate?

JC   Well, I explained the position with Trevor and he told me he would have done the role for half of his usual fee.

This is where I was in luck. The head of Fox in America, the big Buddy Adler[4], was paying a flying visit to London; he just happened to be passing through. I knew that he would be in the London office that morning. so I jumped in a taxi from Kensington, where I was living, and rushed around. I rushed past all of the secretaries and brushed

Jack Cardiff directs scenes from *Sons and Lovers* (1960)

past everyone because I wouldn't take no for an answer and I burst into the office where he was sitting with Bob Goldstein.

I told him that I could get Trevor for £10,000 and Goldstein glared at me and said, 'I told you we have got Harry Andrews for three, for Christ's sakes!' I told them that I thought Trevor was going to be much better for the film and that we really should go for it.

Buddy Adler started pacing up and down and then suddenly said, '£10,000? Get Trevor Howard!' And that was it.

JB Did it get any easier after that?

JC   Well, I had won that battle. But it was still fighting, fighting, fighting.

Then I got a call from Buddy Adler, saying, 'What the hell are you doing? You have an English cast of complete unknowns!' He told me that if I wanted to continue on the picture, I would have to have an American playing the lead. There was no way out of it.

JB What was your reaction?

JC   Quite honestly, that role had been so frustrating to cast because I had wanted Albert Finney, but he wasn't available. Bob Goldstein was making so many ridiculous suggestions for the role. He suggested Sean Connery, but he was too old and not right. Then he suggested Richard Harris. By this time, I was laughing to myself. Even Richard Harris thought the idea was ridiculous. So that's when I ended up with Dean Stockwell[5].

JB What did you ultimately think of his performance?

JC   He wasn't bad, actually. He put on this accent, which if you analyzed it was perhaps a little bit phoney, but in America it went down well because they didn't know the difference.

JB You shot the film in real Lawrence country[6], didn't you?

JC   Yes, we used the actual coalmine that Lawrence's father had worked in; we used the real house and real streets.

Dean Stockwell outside
D H Lawrence's house.
Sons and Lovers (1960)

We started on location with the picture in November. The schedule was murderous. I had Freddie Francis[7] as my cameraman, who was very good and very fast, and thank God for that.

BIRTHPLACE OF
D. H. LAWRENCE
BORN SEPT 11TH 1885
DIED MARCH 2ND 1930

JB   How did you choose Freddie Francis as your cinematographer?

JC   To tell you the truth, I forget. He did have a very high reputation. He was just very right for the film because he had a great quality to his work and he was fast, which was very important. You might have a great cameraman who takes all day to light, and then you are dead! It worked out very well.

But the schedule had been set for the summer, when even in England the sun comes up in the morning and you have some light. We had to shoot in the rain and all kinds of weather. So we were shooting in the winter, but using a summer schedule.

JB   What sort of shortcuts did that require?

JC   Well, for example, I had a long shot of Nottingham left to do, which I felt was essential for the picture, but Bob told me we didn't have the time or money to go and film it. So I caught a dawn train to Nottingham and took my stills camera with me. I climbed some tall building and took some still long shots. I came back about 10 am and had the photographs enlarged and then I filmed the photographs with a bit of cigarette smoke in front of them and it looked marvellous. When Bob saw the rushes, he didn't know what to say or think. He must have assumed I ignored him and had gone off and shot in Nottingham.

I cut the film every night so that when we were finished shooting I had a cut, although not a fine cut.

JB   Were the producers pressuring you at this point?

JC   Bob called me the day after we finished shooting and said, 'Jack I've shown your cut to the British Board of Film Producers here and they have chosen it as the best British film to go to the Cannes Film Festival.' I said, 'That's great, but Cannes is in fourteen days.' We had no music or dubbing or effects, it was just a rough cut. So I promoted the art director to associate producer and told him to go to the labs and check the negative cutting, while I went to Rome to see the musician I wanted.

So I went to Italy and worked with Mario Nascimbene[8] on the music and did it in three days and got the film finished and got it to Cannes.

JB   Were you happy with the results or would you have liked longer? I suppose one always wants longer.

JC   Yes, one always wants longer, but I was happy. I still think it could have been done better if we hadn't had the pressure of Cannes.

JB   Going back a bit, how had you gone about adapting the book? Thomas Clarke[9] seemed an unlikely choice as the writer, given that he was best known for his comedies.

JC   I think he was recommended to me at the time and we met and discussed it. He understood that all it wanted was putting together. The great advantage that a book has is that it can take 20 or 30 pages just building up a character; in a film, you have to achieve the same thing in just a few seconds. If you used every word of a book when you adapted it for film, it would be many, many hours long.

JB   Was Clarke your first choice of writer?

JC   I had also talked to John Osborne[10] about writing the script, but he was too tied up with other things.

JB   How did the studio feel about your choice of writer?

JC   The funny thing was that before this I had gone to Hollywood to make myself known and meet people. I got out there and they gave me three versions of the script to read. I couldn't believe it, they were written by quite well-known writers, but they were just so unlike the story. They were just a Hollywoodized script that had no bearing on the original story at all.

JB   That's always a danger in literary adaptations.

JC   Yes, if a great book comes out and they want to make it into a film, they hire a great writer and pay him a million dollars to write the script. Then he feels obligated and thinks that he can't just copy out the original dialogue and ends up putting in lots of his own. Quite often, it's not as good as the original. I always felt that Lawrence was a great dialogue man and so I changed a lot of the script back to his original lines before we started filming.

So anyway, then I had a meeting with Buddy Adler in this big office and they asked me which script I liked. I told them I didn't like any of them and that I thought they were all terrible. There was a silence and I realized I was stepping into a very dangerous situation because if you say that something is awful, there is a danger that they will simply think you are not the right man for the picture.

Jack Cardiff makes use of the props on *Sons and Lovers* (1960)

But still I told them that I hated the scripts and that Lawrence was a great writer and these scripts were nothing like him. I told Buddy Adler that I would like to go back to England and get an English writer who knows his Lawrence. Lawrence has a real quality and you need that in the script. They agreed.

JB So that's when you got Clarke on board—and again you managed to get your own way.

JC Yes, I suppose directors always have these fights. But I came back to England and worked on the script with Clarke and then I had to take the script back to America. Jerry Wald, who was affable and genial—nothing bothered him—told me that the censors had read the script and wanted to have a meeting. These chaps all turned up their nice suits and ties and the foreman said that there were one or two things that they didn't like. Particularly they disapproved of the scene in the barn where the girl, who is rather cold towards sex, says to the boy, as she does in the book, 'You *shall* have me!' It was in the book, so I put it in the script.

JB That's not too racy, is it?

JC No! But the censor told me that we couldn't say it. Jerry told me not to worry and he showed me the new dialogue: they had changed 'You shall have me!' To 'I do love you.'

They also changed the line, which again was from the book, from the scene when they have made love and he says to her, 'You hated it, didn't you?' They changed it to, 'You would have hated it!' I couldn't believe it.

I flew back to England and during the flight I thought, 'To hell with it. They can only fire me once.' So I used the original lines, faithful to Lawrence.

JB   What were the censors' reactions to your insubordination?

JC   I knew when I flew back to New York to show it to the censors, it was going to be tough. And in they came in their suits and ties and I was with Buddy Adler. We all sat and watched the film and the lights came up and the head of the censors said 'Well, Mr Cardiff, we can see that you didn't take our suggestions very seriously.' But they said that they thought it was done in good taste and they weren't going to touch a frame of it.

We went outside and Buddy was looking very serious. He told me that he thought it was a disaster and that we didn't have a good film. He said that usually he had to fight the censor for weeks before he got what he wanted and because they had passed everything, it meant that we didn't have a good film.

I suggested that we put back in a key scene that we had left out: it was an Oedipus-complex scene. Buddy thought that was a great idea, so I got the cast back and we shot the scene in New York. The scene is that he is washing and she is lying in bed and there is just a hint that while they had been making love, he hadn't been thinking just about her. I did the scene in one day and went back to the hotel to find a telegram from Buddy Adler that said, 'Jack, here are your instructions for this scene: 1—Mary Ure[11] must not be naked in the bed. 2—There must be a minimum of four sheets on the bed. 3—She must not say to him, "Is it me you want or *it*?"' I called him and said that his cable arrived too late and I had already shot it. They did have a bit of a fight over the scene with the censors, but in the end they didn't touch it.

The irony is that when I got back to England I heard the British censors had told Goldstein that if the line, 'Is it me you want or *it*?' were in the film, it would have to have an X certificate. Quite extraordinary.

JB   I can't imagine *Sons and Lovers* with an X certificate.

JC   Well, dear Bob Goldstein took the line out before I could say anything. I had a meeting with the head of the censors here and he realized that it was a mistake to cut the line out and they let it back in. Always these big battles with Goldstein.

JB   How did Clarke react to all these changes to his script?

JC   He laughed at the stupidity of it all. It was a strange thing.

JB   Ultimately you were proven correct in all of this because the press reaction to *Sons and Lovers* could hardly have been better, could it?

JC   I'm not embarrassed to say that the reviews for the film were very good.

When I did *Intent to Kill*, there was an English reporter or reviewer who did a piece with the headline: 'Cardiff Goes Out Front', meaning I was no longer behind the camera, but was directing. Because the press love to label people, which is a form of laziness really, they had previously labelled me, 'Britain's Best Cameraman'. Ridiculous, but I was lucky, I suppose, to have the label.

Anyway, this writer was questioning why someone who was supposed to be the best cameraman would want to become a mediocre director! His advice was I should go back to photography as soon as possible. But when *Sons and Lovers* came out, he wrote a long article saying that he took it all back and that he thought it was a wonderful film.

The reviews really were fantastic. When the film came out in America, it was quite unbelievable and several critics said they thought it was the finest film ever made. That's quite ridiculous because it wasn't, but they said it. At that time, I had a cutting service that would send me all of my reviews. They were really all incredible, but the American ones were probably the best. One review said, 'I urge you to see it!' Another said, 'This film gave me new faith in movies.' I couldn't believe they were talking about my film! It really was an extraordinary thing.

JB   Your faithfulness to Lawrence's novel was also noted.

JC   I think it was the *New York Times* that mentioned that the film's dialogue seemed absolutely right and they said that I had taken a lot of the dialogue from the book. I believed in the book so much that I carried it about with me during filming. As would quite often happen, an actor might say, 'Jack, I'm not happy about this line.' I would say, 'Hang on a minute.' And I would thumb through to the page and there would be the perfect line.

JB   Those reviews combined with the seven Oscar nominations[12] must have been a wonderful vindication after you had been discouraged from directing.

JC   Yes, that's quite true. It really was.

Perhaps with all those fantastic reviews I should have got the Oscar, but what happened was that Billy Wilder's *The Apartment* (1960), which was a wonderful film, won it. It was also an American film … It didn't really sadden me that I didn't win, because at least I had a nomination.

The New York critics have an award and they gave that to me—actually, it was shared with Billy Wilder. I also won a Golden Globe for it and the Film Directors Guild of America gave me the Outstanding Direction Award. So I won plenty of awards for it.

JB   Did you go out to the Oscar ceremony this time?

JC   No, I didn't. It happened the same as with *Black Narcissus*, I was already working on another film.

JB   *My Geisha* (1962) with Shirley MacLaine?

JC   Yes, Shirley MacLaine's husband was a producer[13], not like a real producer, he was quite harmless. But he was married to the star and she was a *big* star then. Of course, her co-star Yves Montand[14] was also a very big star.

JB   You shot on location in Japan.

JC   Yes we did, which was a little awkward at times. We had a Japanese art director who didn't know the Hollywood way of doing things, but it all worked out in the end.

JB   You told me that you thought there was a problem with this film.

JC   I thought it was an extremely good film, but I must say that right from the start of the film I had misgivings about the story structure. The thing that bugged me was that Shirley's character goes incognito as a Geisha and her husband, Yves Montand, is supposed not to recognize her. I thought it stretched credulity that, even with a disguise, a husband wouldn't recognize his own wife.

JB   Did you not trust the make-up?

JC   In point of fact, Shirley's make-up was uncanny and she had these contact lenses, which gave her these dark brown eyes, and she had white make-up and a black wig and you could not recognize her as Shirley. But I felt the audience would still say the same as me and that it stretched credulity.

Shirley MacLaine and Jack Cardiff on location in Japan for *My Geisha* (1962)

When the film opened in London, the critics said, with one voice, that it was an absurd supposition that he couldn't see it was his own wife. It's incredible, all these mistakes that are made in films. It's amazing that they aren't ironed out before you start …

I also questioned the fact that the script was long. But Shirley and the writer didn't agree. By the end of the film, we had some really marvellous stuff and I worked on the editing, and the first cut was something like 2 hours 20 minutes. Then I cut it down to a shade under 2 hours. Paramount thought it was wonderful and I was happy. I went back to England, and then I got a call from my editor to say that the film had gone off to the head of Paramount, who thought it was too long and cut another half an hour out of it. A quarter of my film! I couldn't believe it.

JB You had even more problems to come though?

JC Yes, as a result of us having made the film in Japan, I became the victim of something that the Americans wanted to say. We had had to wait for a long time to clear the Technicolor camera through Japanese customs. It was said that the customs there would often analyze things coming into the country to such a point that they could reproduce it themselves. That may or may not have been true. We then also had a lot of trouble with the studio, which had no heating. So it hadn't been easy making the film in Japan.

At this time, there had been a movement in America to keep production in the country and not shoot abroad or on location.[15] The thing was that these productions were depriving Americans of work in their own studios.

So this was a hot topic at the time and when I got back there was huge pressure from the press to interview me. I was naive and they really led me to say that we had a terrible time working in Japan. The next day in the *Hollywood Reporter* they had a big piece making out that I had an awful time in Japan.

Of course, Shirley and her husband adored Japan and had a house there. They were fanatics about Japan and the reports were a big shock to them. Shirley was very cross with me for innocently saying that it was awful there.

JB We have talked about many different directors. What kind were you?

JC Well, I was not the blustering, screaming type like Hathaway and certainly not the DeMille type. Hitchcock was a fine director and he didn't bluster, but as I said, if he had any fault to find with people he would let the front office handle it. I was different from that; I would have to stand up and say what I thought. But I did find myself developing quite a bit of cunning.

JB Was it Michael Powell whom you had learnt the most from?

JC I think I had a mixture of everybody. I was also very keen on French films at the time. I thought they had a wonderful approach to filmmaking. Everything was so natural and

Yves Montand, Jack Cardiff and Shirley MacLaine on *My Geisha* (1962)

the casting was natural and you believed in these characters. In Britain at the time they were still casting actors from the West End stage, who had these very pretty voices. Very unrealistic.

I also saw a lot of very good, dramatic American pictures. Theatres, too, were much cheaper than today, so I went to many plays just to enjoy the acting.

JB   Your next film, *The Lion* **(1962), was as different again as your last four films as director had been. Were you deliberately trying to mix it up?**

JC   I suppose, looking back, that everyone makes mistakes, and I certainly made them. A really successful director might take his time, if he can afford it, and wait for a *Sons and Lovers* to come along. I was just very happy to take anything that was going, and I would think, 'Well, the script isn't very good, but I'm sure I can do something with it.' And I could in a lot of cases, but it was a very dangerous philosophy, because you can't always do something with it.

The net result was that many of these films were fairly ordinary. They all had good press when they first came out, though.

JB   So, tell me about making *The Lion.*

JC   The story is about a girl who grows up with a lion and she can handle it from the day it is born, but she is the only one who can. It was quite a good little film. We had a lot of bad luck on the film because it rained for weeks in Africa. Bill Holden[16] had a hotel and a huge amount of land there, so we built a stage there.

JB   What about the old maxim, 'never work with children or animals'?

JC   Well, that's the point; we had to be very careful. We had a 'Hollywood lion' sent over, which was a marvellous animal. I have a photograph of myself lying against this lion reading a book, *How to Win Friends and Influence People*.[17]

It was a lovely lion, but you had to be aware of the fact that any lion could suddenly snap. At first, we had to take a piece of the girl's clothing and get it used to that, and then we could bring the girl in and slowly get her closer. Eventually the girl was able to work with the lion.

There are scenes where she is supposed to wrestle in fun with the lion and, of course, we all agreed that this couldn't be done with the girl. As it happened, the lion tamer was a very small man, so he was disguised with a wig and a dress and it worked very well.

JB   But it must have been a constant worry?

JC   There was always this fear that something might happen, and as the director, yes—I was worried all the time about some tragedy happening.

Every scene we did, I had two hunters, one on each side of the camera. They were ready and would follow the lion with their guns and if the lion made a wrong move they would shoot it.

JB   You would shoot it with tranquillizers?

JC   No, no, real bullets. There was no time to argue.

There was another, younger lion in a cage on the set, and the girl was getting rather slaphappy. One day we broke for lunch, and as she passed by, she put her hand through the cage to pat it and the lion leapt at her and clamped its mouth around her arm. It wasn't biting hard, but of course she started to panic and try to pull away, and once that happened, it clamped on to her. I heard this terrible scream and ran over, and we managed to get the lion away. It could have been much worse and the damage wasn't too bad, but obviously it frightened the daylights out of her.

JB   On a happier note, *The Lion* reunited you with Trevor Howard.

Jack Cardiff, producer Samuel Engel and two lion-tamers (plus lion) on *The Lion* (1962)

In conversation with
William Holden during
filming of *The Lion*
(1962)

JC   He was a lovely fellow and terribly professional, but it was during the making of *The Lion* that he was telling us all sorts of wonderful stories about working on *Mutiny on the Bounty*[18] [1962] with Marlon Brando. He told us that Brando would often interfere with the curtain line by refusing to give the right cue. Between takes, Brando used to play with kids on the beach, playing 'guess which hand the stone is in', and the rumour was that the production bribed the local kids to always let him win.

Halfway through the film, Trevor suddenly went cold on us, by which I mean he was bitter, nasty, wouldn't speak to anyone. I asked his wife what she thought the matter was and it turned out that he had just had a letter from the editor of *Bounty* to say that Brando had cut many of his scenes. Of course, Brando was only one of the actors, but he had so much power.

JB   Joseph Kessel,[19] who co-wrote *The Lion* for you, went on to write the classic *Belle de Jour* [1967], didn't he?

JC   Did he really? I didn't realize. That was a very different film. But my one didn't do too badly and was quite successful.

JB **Was your next film,** *The Long Ships* **[1963], inspired by your work on** *The Vikings*?

Jack directs *The Lion* (1962). Note the two large reflectors

JC   That's quite a sordid story, really. I was living in Switzerland at the time and the script was sent to me by post from Columbia Pictures. I didn't even bother reading it; I just sent it back saying I wasn't interested. A funny thing that, because it doesn't sound like me. But I felt instinctively that I had already worked on *The Vikings*, which had been a very successful picture, and it just seemed like an utter waste of time to do another Viking-set picture.

JB **But you relented?**

JC   I'm not sure what happened next. I guess my agent or Columbia Pictures were trying to insist that I do it. I went over to England and read the script. It was an interesting story and I suppose I was led into it. I remember the boss at Columbia in London telling me it was going to be a very big picture, 'The biggest you've ever done!'—that sort of crap. I think I was conned into doing it and I really didn't realize the kind of picture it was going to turn out to be.

JB Were the lead actors, Richard Widmark[20] and Sidney Poitier,[21] already attached to the film?

JC Dick Widmark was going to play the lead and I had a healthy respect for him as a good actor. We also had a script that I thought was very good. So he came over from America and straight away he said that he thought the script was lousy and that he wanted another writer. This was my first experience of the sort of 'Marlon Brando' behaviour. Columbia agreed to his demands and Widmark said that he knew a good writer who he thought would do a great script for us. I felt very dragged into all of this, but I went along to the airport to meet him. Well, he turned up with a sort of white Stetson on like a cowboy. I thought, 'Oh God! Here we go!'

This writer he recommended wrote a script very quickly and it was pure Abbott and Costello. That's when I said very firmly that I didn't want to continue on the picture. That was walk out number one …

JB Did that get you your own way?

JC Well, Dick Widmark said he thought I was absolutely right and the new script was terrible and he didn't know what had gone wrong with this new writer. They got another writer, who wrote us another script, which was OK; it was on a par with the very first one, but I liked the first one anyway.

JB Once the script was agreed, where were you planning to film this? In Norway again?

JC No, we made it in Budapest. This had already been a picture with all kinds of problems because it had been attempted before as far as the preparation had gone. It had been attempted and abandoned by another director, who was also a big star; it was to be his first film as a director. He had to okay this set, which was some 30 kilometres outside Budapest, where they had to build this sort of small town, next to what was supposed to be a Norwegian fjord. The set looked pretty good but I went over to the water and peered in and knew there was something wrong. I took a stick and poked it in, and the water was about 3 inches deep!

Apparently what had happened was that this director had just driven up in his car and said, 'Build it over there', without ever having gotten out of his car!

JB This is something of a problem when you have to sail a Viking long ship down it!

JC   Yes, and I did point that out to them. I told them they would have to dredge a canal down the middle of the river—which they did at quite some expense.

JB   This wasn't the end of your problems by a long way, though …

JC   No. The producer was Irving Allen,[22] who had a reputation for being a nasty piece of work and I had heard that he was apt to re-cutting and even re-shooting directors' work, which is not very nice. Widmark didn't like him anyway.

Day one: It was 8 o'clock in the morning and I was just getting ready to do the first shot with Widmark, and Irving Allen was sitting on a chair on the set watching, which as a producer he had every right to do.

JB   Unusual, though, isn't it?

JC   At 8 o'clock in the morning for a producer, very unusual. But on the beginning of a picture, it is quite normal for a producer to be present.

But Widmark walked over to him and said, 'Mr Allen, I don't want you on the set when I'm working.' And Irving told him to go away and read his contract. I thought, 'Here we go again!' Widmark told Irving he didn't need to read his contract and just walked off.

As I didn't have Widmark, I started to do a few odd shots, which weren't very important. In the meantime, the telephone wires were buzzing with agents talking to agents and heads of studios and, of course, Columbia were in it up to their necks. Finally Widmark's agent told him that the producer had every right to be on the set and there was no way that he could insist that he stayed off. He was told that unless he turned up for work at 8 o'clock the next morning Columbia would stop the picture and sue him for $4 million.

Widmark knew he couldn't possibly win and so agreed to go back to work, but after that he hated everybody and not just Irving Allen. He was then very difficult to work with and he wanted to change the scenes and no longer liked the dialogue. Sidney Poitier caught the bug of dissension and started wanting to change his scenes and his dialogue. I was right in the middle of all of this and you can imagine that I wasn't very happy, but somehow we got through it.

JB   All this must be detrimental to the performances, though?

JC   The ironic thing is that Widmark had, I think, decided he would not be dramatic in the role; he didn't discuss that with me, which you might think he would, he was just mak-

Jack Cardiff sketches
between walkouts on
The Long Ships (1963)

Opposite:
On the set of *The Long
Ships* (1963) with
Rosanna Schiaffino

ing this up as he went along. So he played it sort of for fun, almost like a comedy, and it actually turned out very successfully for him and really lifted his part. Poitier continued to play his role seriously, and that didn't turn out so well for him.

JB How about the way if affected you?

JC I was just striving to get the whole picture finished. But I had an operator working with me, John Drake, who I had known for years, but Irving Allen was looking for an opportunity to get rid of him. One of the scenes turned out to be slightly out of focus, which really wasn't his fault; it was the focus puller's fault. But Irving fired John anyway.

I sent a cable to Irving, who had gone back to London, saying something to the effect of, 'Your intentions are now revealed like a loathsome sore un-bandaged. Why don't you fire me too?' He sent a cable back saying he would get around to it. He never did.

JB Did your relationship with Widmark suffer?

JC   I know that towards the end, on the last few weeks of the picture, we were shooting outside on the lot. It was a set of a palace and I was doing a shot of the girls from the harem peering out through a window, because they weren't supposed to be exposed to public view. Widmark wanted them out on the roof! I refused and Widmark tried to insist, but in a very clumsy way. I just got up quietly and walked off the set. Walk out number two.

That evening, there was a meeting to try and sort it out. I really gave Widmark hell, which shocked him. Columbia said that they understood my position, but we had to be professional and would I finish the picture? The head of Columbia showed me a letter he had from David Lean from the time that he had walked off *Lawrence of Arabia*. He told me how wise Lean had been to go back and how I would be wise to do the same. Finally I agreed.

JB Given your initial misgivings, how do you think the film turned out?

JC   The thing was that when it came out it was really quite successful as a light, slightly comedic kind of thriller. But I was never really happy with it.

JB We have talked about John Ford. How was it stepping into his shoes to direct after he was taken ill making *Young Cassidy* [1964]?

JC   What had happened was that John Ford had collapsed on set and been flown home to Hollywood, so they had no director. I got this cable in Switzerland, asking me to come over at once and finish the picture.

I liked the sound of it and thought it might be interesting, so I flew over and read the script, which was wonderful. They warned me that I might have creative troubles with Rod Taylor[23] because like so many actors he was talking like a producer or a director. There was an incident later when I was working with him on *The Mercenaries* [1967]; the producer told me that when Rod Taylor heard who his co-star was going to be, he said, 'My God, I wonder if I'm going to get a performance out of her?' And the producer said, 'Well, maybe the director will help a bit.'

I think Rod was impervious to sarcasm and he did like to think that he was running the whole show. So when we started on *Young Cassidy*, I just made it clear that I was running things.

JB   Rod Taylor had been something of a protégé of John Ford's, hadn't he?

JC   Yes, exactly. In the same way that he had manufactured John Wayne, he intended to do the same thing with Rod Taylor.

JB   The riot scene in *Young Cassidy* must have been the biggest thing you had directed up until that time.

JC   That sequence was very difficult because it had hundreds of extras—not professional extras, just hundreds of people from Dublin. A huge crowd that I had to control. It was a scene by a river and they were trying to throw this man, along with his horse and cart, into the river. That was a tough one to do. I had three cameras and took two days. It was all done with quick cuts. I have since shown the riot sequence to people when I have been giving talks and it really shakes them up. It's very powerful.

I had a good system of working, where I would go and rehearse in a caravan while the scene was being set. We shot only in real houses and we didn't have any sets. Not having sets has a real advantage, because a studio has a spot rail that you light from, and that can make it very artificial. By shooting in real houses, you have to put lights in through the windows and hide little lamps around the place. It is very effective.

JB   The riot scene that you shot looks very *Battleship Potemkin*.[24]

JC   Yes, well I remembered things that I had seen from *Potemkin*: the woman with her glasses all broken and the fights on the steps. I did all of that sort of thing. I told my assistant

Above: Maggie Smith,
Rod Taylor and Jack
Cardiff (in the wrong
chair) between takes
on *Young Cassidy*
(1964)

to go and get a horse's hoof from the abattoir, which we used for a close-up of a face being trodden on. I shot a lot of very good stuff.

When it opened, it had very good press and several critics said that it had several wonderful scenes that were obviously the work of John Ford. The credits said that it was a John Ford production, directed by Jack Cardiff—which could have meant anything. The riot sequence was singled out and identified as the work of Ford. I included the actual work done by John Ford on the finished film and it totalled four minutes and five seconds out of two hours and ten minutes. I had done all of the rest of the picture, but the damage was done and all of the critics thought that it was largely the work of Ford.

JB **You had a marvellous editor, Anne Coates,[25] who had worked with Lean. Did you discuss your *Battleship Potemkin* influences with her?**

JC   She was wonderful, a really great editor. I didn't really talk to her about that, though.

JB **You also had a young Julie Christie in your cast, just before she shot to fame in *Doctor Zhivago*[26] [1965].**

JC   That's right. In fact, Ford directed very few of the scenes with Julie, only one or two. I did the rest of the scenes with her. She was very nice to work with.

JB **You cast Rod Taylor again in your next film, *The Liquidator* [1965].**

JC   Yes. We got on well together. Rod seemed to like me very much and treated me well. I never had any trouble with him and we never had any arguments.

He wasn't the sort of man to take anything lightly, though, and he would pick a fight with anybody. I remember one of the electricians had said something jokingly to him and Rod just quietly handed me his glass, which I knew meant that he was going to go for this chap. I had to calm him down; he was that sort.

JB   And the rest of your cast?

JC   Trevor Howard was extremely good in it, as was the chap who played the head of MI5, Wilfrid Hyde-White.[27] He was a very interesting character. We had a slight problem with the censors before we even shot a scene, because he has a line to Rod Taylor, 'This thing stinks more than a Turkish wrestler's jock-strap.' That line had to go, but I thought it was wonderful. He had a lot of wonderful lines in it.

JB   Was this an easier shoot than the nightmare of *The Long Ships*?

JC   Well, *The Liquidator* had a producer called Jon Pennington, and I had come onto the film quite late as the director. When I was in the London office doing the preparation, I noticed this young man with red hair and glasses and I asked who he was and they told me not to worry about him, he was just some young chap learning the business. But in fact, his father was very wealthy and he had bought the rights to the story, so he had some sort of say in the film.

After we started the film in France, this boy suddenly came out of the shadows and started saying that he didn't like the way things were being done, and he fired the producer. He got rid of Jon Pennington, so we had no producer.

I was lumbered without a producer and so I worked alone, but then right at the end of the picture, which was a story that aped the James Bond films, they realized they hadn't secured the rights to the story from this boy. He refused. They explained that if he didn't, then they couldn't release it, but still he wouldn't and so they put the film away in a vault for something like three or four years.

JB   Do you think the film suffered as a result of the delay?

JC   If it had come out when we finished the picture, I think it would have been a big success because it was just the right moment for it. But because it was put away for so long before it was released, the flavour had gone, and in the meantime someone else had made a film that was playing on Bond. So it was a disaster.[28]

I never heard of this boy again. For all I know he may have made more films, but let's hope not.

JB   How did the story for *The Mercenaries* come about?

JC   I made a trip to the Congo, and I met reporters who lived through all of the troubles there [following independence in 1960], and they showed me photographs of the real thing—I wish they hadn't. I remember vividly a photograph of a man with his throat cut in the bath; his head was nearly off and the bath was full of blood. The savagery was unbelievable.

JB   *The Mercenaries* is far darker than your previous films. Did you feel that a film like that might be too much?

JC   When I made the film, I thought that it would have been too awful for words to make it like the real violence, but it had to have violence in it.

When the film came out, the critics all thought the violence was so terrible that they couldn't bear to watch it. They were really appalled by its excessive violence. I could only say to those that I met that my film was nothing like the real thing—it was a quarter, a fifth, a sixteenth of the violence that really happened. None the less, it had the reputation as a violent film.

JB   You didn't go back to the Congo to film, did you?

JC   The whole thing takes place on a train and obviously we needed a train to film on, but in the Congo there were no steam trains. Plus we couldn't afford it and it was too remote, so we finally ended up shooting it in the West Indies. We found an enthusiastic amateur there who had his own steam train, so we all traipsed out to the West Indies and made the film there. The jungle all looked very much like the African jungle.

JB   An easier time than the Congo would have afforded …

JC   Except that there was a lot of political unrest there at the time and there was an election, which was causing a lot of fighting. We managed to get over that and film.

JB   It is a very violent film. How do you think it has held up?

JC   The film has stayed the course and still makes it into cinemas from time to time. It is a very violent picture, but very good. Rod Taylor was just the right type for the film; I think it was one of his best films.

JB   **Your love of French film really came to the fore on your next picture, *Girl on a Motorcycle* [1968].**

JC   Yes, and of course the man who wrote the book won the Prix Goncourt for it. It was beautifully written.

Again, I was brought onto the film late, so whereas you can normally ask for two or three months preparation on the film, I suppose I must have had well under a month to talk about where we were going to make it, the money situation, everything.

JB   ***Girl on a Motorcycle* wasn't made for a big studio, so how was it financed?**

JC   It is always difficult to raise the budget for a film, but we had a chap called Drummond whose father had been head of the Drummond Bank chain, and he had been left several million pounds. The money was in trust so that he couldn't spend it all, but he did get permission from the estate to take out perhaps a million or a million and a half. And that's how we started the picture.

JB   **Considering she wasn't really known as an actress, Marianne Faithfull[29] is surprisingly good in the film …**

JC   Marianne was, I guess, pretty good. But before Marianne Faithfull came on the scene, there was another girl who was going to play the part; I think she was either Austrian or German. She was incredibly beautiful and with a wonderful accent—she spoke perfect English, but with a wonderful accent. I know she had been in the centrefold of *Playboy*, so she really was quite something. She was perfect for the part. She was about 19 or 20 and was just so marvellous.

JB   **What happened?**

JC   I went into the office one day just before we were due to start and they said to me, 'Jack, your leading lady is dying of a drug overdose in Germany.' Apparently she had been on drugs the whole time, but I didn't know; I was very naive about these things.

So then Marianne Faithfull was suggested, and all I knew was that she had done some television work where she was singing. It was arranged that I should have lunch with her and she seemed alright. What else could I do? I said 'yes.'

Of course, I didn't know that Marianne was no stranger to drugs either, though not as bad as the other girl, obviously. She was going about with Mick Jagger at that time, and I went around a few times.

JB   **That image of her in her motorbike leathers is really iconic now.**

Jack Cardiff strikes a directorial pose on the steam train used for *The Mercenaries* (1967)

JC   She had this leather outfit, and inside it was lined with a kind of velvet material, really beautiful, and she is naked inside of it.

JB   It has the alternate title *Naked Under Leather*.

JC   *Naked Under Leather*, yes. That was America. Typical!

JB   How did you set up the motorbike shots for her?

JC   We had one of those jeeps with a very low wheelbase. We had a special effects supervisor. who cut out a space in the jeep and fixed the bike to it so that we could tow it. We could get up to 60 or 65 mph. The only problem was that the bike didn't lean properly when we cornered, which was sad as it rather gave the game away sometimes.

JB   She didn't do any riding herself?

JC   Oh no. We had a stunt double [David Watson] to do all of the riding. The double was a smallish man, who also organized the crash scene. She is supposed to being riding along at 100 mph when a truck pulls out; she hits the truck and flies through the air and goes right through the glass of a car coming the other way. We put phoney glass in the car and this double did the whole thing first time. He drove his bike straight at the front right-hand wheel, and just as it stopped, he flew through the air and dived right through this windscreen. It was a wonderful scene. We shot it in an airfield in England. And the last shot is a helicopter shot coming up from it.

JB   You employed some pretty radical visual effects. Were you still trying to upset Technicolor?

JC   I was using solarization for the first time on this film. There was someone who had left Technicolor and who had then invented this box that I called 'the magic box', which could be used for this solarization effect. We would shoot a scene, like the circus scene or a sex scene, where we wanted all the colours to go crazy; you could get away with far more in a sex scene if it is solarized. Then we would develop it and run the negative through this box and on to tape. It allowed us to control what colours went on to the tape during the scene. Later, at the Technicolor lab, we would print back from tape to film.

JB   Is it true that there are two versions?

JC   Yes, I made two versions: one in French, one in English. In Alain Delon's[30] scenes, he just spoke French and later I dubbed him, and the other way around for Marianne Faithfull.

Jack Cardiff directs Mariannne Faithfull on *Girl on a Motorcycle* (1968)

Alain Delon said that he would love to do it, but he was on another picture and only had two weeks. So I told him I would do all of his scenes in two weeks.

JB Which version did you open with?

JC We opened in Paris[31] and it had rave reviews. I thought I had a real success on my hands, but then it came to London and the London critics didn't like it at all. They sneered at it. Strangely, around England it was a big success, but in London they didn't like it.

JB What did they dislike?

JC The whole idea is that she is going on her motorbike on a long journey to go and see her ex-lover. On the journey as she drives, we see her imagining what will happen when she meets her lover again. She imagines that he will take her in his arms, unzip her clothes and say, 'Your body is like a violin in a velvet case.' That was a line that was in the book and I thought it was a hell of a good line. One of the critics picked up on this line and said the dialogue was terrible. He was missing the whole point that Alain Delon doesn't say it; it was in the imagination of this rather stupid young girl.

But even with those criticisms the film was the second highest grosser of the year in England. It made a lot of money.

The end of Marianne
Faithfull in *Girl on a
Motorcycle* (1968)

8 Madmen and Muscles

- *Penny Gold* and *The Mutations*
- *Scalawag*, back with Kirk Douglas
- *Death on the Nile*—Ustinov, Niven and Davis
- *Prince and the Pauper*—Oliver Reed
- The curse of *Avalanche Express*
- *The Fifth Musketeer*
- *The Dogs of War*
- *Ghost Story* and Fred Astaire's feet
- Michael Winner: *The Wicked Lady*
- *The Far Pavilions* and *The Last Days of Pompeii*
- *Conan the Destroyer*
- David Lynch and *Blue Velvet*
- *Rambo: First Blood Part II*—Sylvester Stallone
- *Tai-Pan*

'I worked, some time ago, on the *Rambo* picture, on which Jack was the DP and my function was rather limited. But given the mayhem and elaborate conditions necessary for the creation of these mammoth enterprises, Jack Cardiff somehow stood within the centre of the whirlpool unperturbed, unfazed, and unflustered while chaos reigned supreme and people were being sacked and hired daily all around him. So he seemed to represent something to me, an essentially dignified man with a manner that put the film back on track.'
Steven Berkoff—Actor, Rambo: First Blood Part II

'Jack Cardiff, who has given us some of the most enduring images in film, is one of the few remaining pioneers of colour photography. Not only a pioneer, he is a living, working example of the very highest standards of his art. Jack was never typecast! He shot every kind of film except a Western, some entirely on the stage, others on the most difficult locations imaginable.'
Bill Taylor ASC—Director of Photography, Illusion Art, and Vice Chairman of the Visual Effects Society

JB Your next film as a director, *Penny Gold* [1973], was a much more low-key affair.

JC It was made for a tiny budget at Pinewood Studios. I had known the scriptwriter while I was living in Switzerland and he and I were good friends. It was his own story—all to do with philately—and he wrote the script from that and sold the idea to Pinewood, who gave me the job of directing it. It seemed like it would be fun to come over from Switzerland and make it, so I did.

JB What was your budget?

JC The film took four weeks and cost £98,000. A very low budget and it was a moderate success, and I think it was a jolly good picture actually.

Francesca Annis[1] was in it and she was brilliant. She played herself and her twin, which was fun. She never appeared side by side, it was always separate scenes. The whole thing was fun and made a little bit of a profit. As I recall, it was a quiet time in the British film industry; it was a very low-key time and not a happy and prosperous period.

JB Apart from the obvious limitations, what other difference does working on such a tight budget make?

JC There is something with all of these little low-budget pictures, in that they always run the risk of going unnoticed. As you know, if you are making a fairly big film and you have, say, a budget of $10 million, then you will find that the studios will put in another two or three million for the publicity. If people are told something is big, then it will become big—psychologically that's something of a joke, but that's the way it is. If you make something very small, you run the risk of no-one seeing it.

Something like *The Full Monty*[2] was a small budget, but the subject matter was so hilarious that it became a huge success, mostly through word of mouth.

JB *The Mutations* [1973] is a film that you have described to me as the biggest mistake of your directing life.

JC Oh yes! I had almost forgotten that one. I think I had forgotten it because one doesn't like to remember!

The big mistake I made was this grotesque make-up. This poor actor had to have his face distorted and they had done all these drawings, and I chose one for them to make up. But the problem was that once it was on, it couldn't really be removed. I was stuck with this bloody make-up that took an age to put on. It should have been made out of some medium that allowed it to be taken on and off more easily.

Funnily enough, again abroad, this was quite popular; I always cringe when people say they like it.

JB   You had worked with Donald Pleasance[3] before on *Sons and Lovers* …

JC   Oh, he was a great character. Some people stand out a mile by their character. We don't seem to have the Donald Pleasances and Charles Laughtons today; these people with wonderful faces and mannerisms.

JB   He was an incredibly prolific actor. I would guess he was making around five films a year at this point.

JC   In most of them, he was the villain; he often played the heavy. But played it so wonderfully.

JB   You returned to cinematography with *Scalawag* in 1973. It was directed by Kirk Douglas.

JC   He is the sort of guy that as an actor always knew what he wanted, but I think he always wanted to be a director.

JB   Did he call on you because of your work with him on *The Vikings?*

JC   We always got along together and he had certainly liked what I had done on *The Vikings*. When we started on *The Vikings*, we got on location and it rained and looked like it was going to keep on raining. I had spoken to Dick [Fleischer] and said, 'Look, why don't we just shoot in the rain? They are supposed to be tough Vikings, just get them out in the rain.' They all thought this was a wonderful idea and that's what we did. The funny thing was that rain doesn't always show up on film, so we would add to it with rain effects on the set. The locals all thought we were mad.

Kirk liked me after that, because he was one of the producers on the film and I had saved him a lot of lost time and money.

JB   Did he make a good director?

JC   Kirk occasionally had to impose his will on people. He would really go for them—he wasn't afraid of anybody. I remember him striding up and down this set, making a tirade against one of these actors. He just kept saying, 'You son of a bitch! You do what I tell you.' Or he would walk up and down, growling, 'I'm a mean man! A mean man!' Sometimes he was worse than Hathaway. But it was a very pleasant film to work on.

JB   **It's a little-known film.**

JC   It wasn't a huge success when it came out. I don't know why, perhaps it didn't have very good distribution or something. I thought it was a very good film.

JB   **You were reunited for the first time in 20 years with Dick Fleischer on *The Prince and the Pauper* [1977]. Why had it taken so long to work together again?**

JC   Well, that happens in this industry; things just come up. I still see Dick from time to time and we always just click back into step with each other. We keep in touch.

JB   **Having tackled Kirk Douglas on *The Vikings*, you now had to take on the inimitable Oliver Reed[4] in *The Prince and the Pauper* [1977] …**

JC   Oh God! I shall never forget that. He was quite impossible, really. It was a shame because he was a very good actor. He had a friend with him, who was sort of a stuntman. I remember they were both crazy about rugby and they were always getting involved in some kind of punch-up. It was very disconcerting.

Reed and his chum had an affray in a restaurant: there was a row and then a fight and this man was injured. The police were called in, but I think Ollie got away with it on that occasion. It was a very unpleasant thing. I also remember that we had this big dinner laid out for Mark Lester's[5] birthday where the whole unit sat around this huge table. Oliver turned up with a prostitute as a present for Lester and things all got a bit unpleasant—Ollie jumped on the table and started to smash things up. That broke up the party, of course.

JB   **How did his co-star Raquel Welch react to Reed?**

JC   She was on the production for a short time. I didn't see a great deal of her, so I don't really know.

JB   ***The Prince and the Pauper* was produced by Ilya Salkind.[6] How does his style compare to someone like De Laurentiis?**

JC   He was very quiet and we didn't see too much of him. De Laurentiis was very much more bombastic, but Salkind was very quiet. They were both hugely successful and so, of course, you don't need to be bombastic at all; but those that have that urge to shout, will do it anyway.

JB It's a very lavish adaptation of Mark Twain's book.[7]

JC Oh yes, we found some marvellous locations in Budapest. Around the back of the city, they had houses that were utterly unaltered from the 17th and 18th centuries. All original and quite wonderful settings.

Maurice Jarre[8] provided a wonderful score—I remember it was very good. Music can make such a big difference to a film.

JB How did you approach music on the films that you directed?

JC As we discussed, on *Sons and Lovers* I had very little time for the music because of taking the film to Cannes. I worked with Nascimbene and he did the music in three days. If I had had another few weeks, everything would have been easier and perhaps better.

JB But is the music already in your mind while you are directing a picture?

JC Yes, as it often is with many directors, they see music. The director that I have just worked with in Hollywood [Christopher Coppola] is very keen on music and he says that he always sees it while still directing sequences.

JB *Death on the Nile*[9] [1978] followed *The Prince and the Pauper*. That was something of an epic.

JC That was such a good story.

JB Had you always been a big Agatha Christie fan?

JC Oh yes, and what a good scriptwriter she would have made! The casting was so perfect and Lord Rathbone[10] was a very intelligent producer.

JB It didn't start well for you, though, did it?

Director John Guillerman and Jack Cardiff on location in Egypt for *Death on the Nile* (1978)

JC We got out to Egypt for a recce. There was myself and the director and the production manager. Also, Lord Rathbone's nephew was with us, sort of working in a producers' capacity, not laying down the law, just helping out.

I woke up in the morning at the hotel and I went to wake up the production manager and there was no answer. I tried his door and it was locked. I went downstairs and told them I couldn't wake him. So Rathbone's nephew and I went back up and tried again. Nothing. Then he climbed over the balcony to the room and found him dead—a heart attack in the night. Dead before we had even started shooting the picture. These deaths do seem to follow me around!

JB It was a marvellous ensemble cast that John Guillermin[11] had put together.

JC Yes, the cast was so good. Peter Ustinov was great fun and then there was David Niven; both great raconteurs. Bette Davis was on the film and she was lovely and very professional. She had been trained by Hollywood to be on the set on time and to know her lines. She held anyone less professional rather in contempt.

JB It was one of those 1970s all-star films, which they don't seem to make anymore.

JC That's right. I suppose it must be connected to money. That cast must have cost a packet.

JB It was shot as a combination of location and studio?

JC Yes. Egyptian locations and English studios.

We had a sequence to do on top of the pyramids, which we had to do twice because there was something wrong with the camera. It was also very hot to work there. I remember looking forward to breaking for lunch because as you walked into the hotel you were hit by the cold air.

Then we had some stuff in the studios at Shepperton. We built part of the boat and that was quite difficult to light because they had quite low ceilings. We had one shot where we panned all around the room and I had electricians running around behind me carrying the lamps to light it. There were lots of funny shots.

JB And then more than a decade after you set *The Mercenaries* on a train, you were back on track with *Avalanche Express* [1979].

JC Well, yes, we had to shoot on a real train because you need to see the scenery rushing by. You can do it with rear-projection effects, but that is often very disappointing. I don't remember too much of the film, except that it was shot in Germany and of course the original director, Mark Robson,[12] sadly died during production. He was very nice and very sweet. He died right before the end of the picture and so I had to direct several scenes; nothing important really—just small stuff.

JB   The great Robert Shaw[13] also died during production.

JC   He was a rather difficult man—a very good actor—but strange and certainly not a very happy man at that time. It wasn't really my problem, but I remember he wanted to change the script around, and he certainly wasn't very easy and not the kind of person you could become chums with. Unlike Lee Marvin, who was wonderful and very easy-going indeed.

JB   I think Robert Shaw was already quite ill when he started production on this film.

JC   Possibly. He drank like a fish! He really did. On one occasion, he was almost carried on stage and they put him down at the table to do his shot.

JB   I had read that his work on the film was dubbed afterwards.

JC   That's news to me, but not a surprise because he often slurred his speech because of the drink. Drink is such a big, big problem with so many actors.

Location shoot, *Death on the Nile* (1978)

JB It doesn't sound like the happiest atmosphere to have been working in.

JC   When you make a film and you have four or five actors, it is always a gamble as to whether they are going to get on—it's a strange atmosphere that you are working in, very artificial, and the actors have to gel as a team. I don't think there was any outrageous difference of opinions, but it wasn't an easy film to work on.

Mark Robson was a sweet man, but this picture demanded a really tough director. There was no camaraderie on the picture and I think that they all had their own problems; problems that I wasn't really aware of. It was a sombre picture, and Mark Robson wasn't very strong either physically or mentally at that point.

Checking the light levels with Lee Marvin on *Avalanche Express* (1979)

JB Then it was a return to more swashbuckling with *The Fifth Musketeer* [1979], which was directed by Ken Annakin.[14] Was that a happier experience?

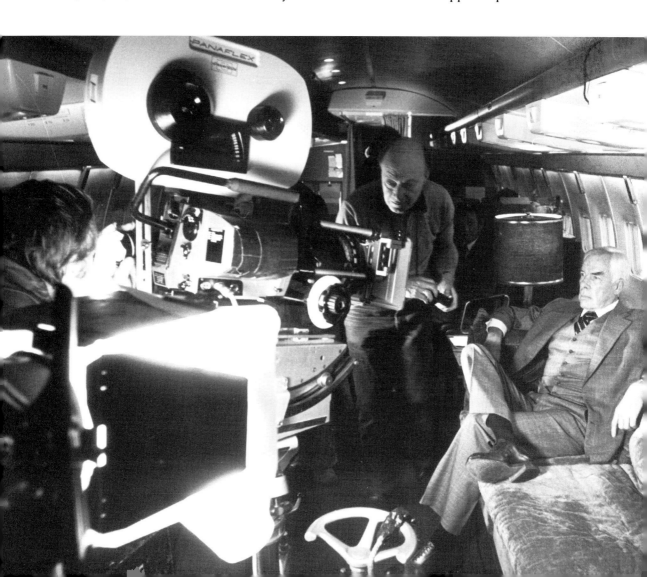

JC That was made in Austria; it was all shot in Vienna, which is such a big, beautiful city. My son, Mason, had a small role in the film—a very small role, just one scene acting with Liz Taylor. Not a bad start!

JB This kind of period action film seems to have cropped up repeatedly in your career. Was it a genre that appealed?

JC You get far more chances to do interesting lighting, certainly. Not just candle light, which I really love doing, but there are the wonderful effects you get from the costumes. So you have all that going for you on a period film. There were a couple of films made around this time with a similar idea too.

JB I have to just ask about the casting of Sylvia Kristel,[15] who was best known for the *Emmanuelle* films.

JC Oh yes! That's right, it all comes back to me now. We had a scene in a huge palace, which is a museum now. We had got permission, God knows how, today I'm sure they would turn it down, but we had permission to set up this bedroom scene. The bed was set in position so that when we looked through the camera we saw this wonderful palace background, but on the other side, just behind the camera, perhaps a few feet away, was this huge curtain hanging down behind which the ordinary tourists and visitors to the museum were walking past. So Sylvia Kristel was just a few feet away from them, stark naked in this bed, and they had no idea …

JB Tell me about *The Dogs of War*[16] (1980) and working with Christopher Walken.

JC He is a great actor, and as is so often the case with actors in dialogue scenes, they don't like looking at people in the eye. They like to look away and look around as if they are gathering their thoughts. He did a lot of that, and the danger for a director is that unless you watch it carefully, you won't be able to cut in the scene to a close-up.

JB Did you call on your experiences from *The Mercenaries* when making it? I would say they are superficially similar films.

Left to right: Lee Marvin, director Mark Robson and Jack Cardiff working on *Avalanche Express* (1979)

JC Yes, we certainly had a lot of fighting and explosions; terrific explosions and lots of night shooting. What terrified me was that in Belize, where we were on location, we were shooting in a real hospital that had been used for torturing people under the old regime.[17] There were all sorts of marks on the wall and lots of strange things there. It felt very weird. Here we were creating a make-believe, and all around us was evidence of a terrible realism.

I was glad when it was over because it was a tough one to work on. It was a very adult film but well made I thought, and again with a very good cast.

JB Wasn't Norman Jewison[18] one of the producers of that?

JC Yes he was, but I don't think he was on the film very much. We travelled around so much. So I have never really worked with him.

JB John Irvin's[19] *Ghost Story* [1981] assembled a grand old cast: Fred Astaire, Melvyn Douglas, Douglas Fairbanks Jr, and John Houseman. That must have been pretty amazing.

JC Wonderful. That was incredible. What a cast!

The director, John Irvin had a lot of very good ideas, but I remember vividly that I thought it had one big mistake: having a ghost is obviously something that is not realistic and should only be slightly manifested, either by a breeze blowing or something. But in this case, the girl who was supposed to be drowned and came back to haunt them was done with a sort of model of the girl that was horrific. But seeing this was as phoney as hell. What you don't see is always the most frightening thing. The model cost a fortune too, but to me it was wrong to show it and it made it farcical and not at all frightening.

JB It's like *The Bad and the Beautiful*[20] [1952], where Kirk Douglas plays the director and they don't have enough money to make the monsters, so they decide it is far more frightening simply not to show them.

JC That was always one of my favourite films. Wonderful. That is so true. Keep the monsters in the dark. The closer you get to horror, the closer you come to ridicule; it can have the reverse of the desired effect.

There is one line in the film, the doctor keeps saying over and over, 'There was no pulse. No pulse.' It became a sort of catchphrase on the film. There is always a line that the crew will latch on to, and on *Ghost Story*, if we were doing a scene that wasn't going well, they would always be saying, 'There's no pulse! No pulse!'

Similarly when I was making *The Lion*, the girl has a line, 'Mornings are best.' After that, when we were working early in the morning, in the cold, someone would always start up with, 'Mornings are best.'

Jack Cardiff takes a light reading from Christopher Walken on the set of *The Dogs of War* (1980)

JB Being a dance fan, it must have been great to meet Fred Astaire.

JC Funnily enough, there is a scene with Fred Astaire in bed, and he was sitting up and I looked at his feet; they looked so rough with terrible bunions and things. I thought that these feet have danced for millions of people and thrilled millions of people. These two ugly feet!

I had a birthday party once in Switzerland and someone asked me if I minded if [Rudolf] Nureyev came along. Of course I said not at all, I really wanted to meet him. We sat and talked for a long time and he was talking about his feet, and to prove a point, he took off his shoes and socks and shoes and showed them to me. They were all gnarled and tough. What dancing does! It *really* punishes your body.

JB *Ghost Story* is deliberately old-fashioned in tone and style.

JC Just the glow of the fires lighting the faces and things. I agree, John Irvin had gotten the right atmosphere for the film, quite old-fashioned.

JB Was there influence from any specific films, Robert Wise's *The Haunting*[21] [1963] perhaps?

JC   No, I don't remember watching anything at that time. I can't recall now where we shot the film.

Jack Cardiff amid the carnage on location in Belize for *The Dogs of War* (1980)

JB   It looks like Vermont or somewhere like that.[22]

JC   That's right, yes. Perhaps the atmosphere came from such a good location.

JB   Lots of snow again?

JC   Yes!

JB   Snow has followed you around quite a bit, hasn't it?

JC   Yes. I should carry my own snow with me.

JB   *Wicked Lady* [1983] was your next picture and Michael Winner your next director. Again, a man with something of a reputation …

JC   My agent suggested me doing a film with Michael Winner and I went to see him in his very grand house in Kensington. Well, he's quite a character! I went into his office and he said, 'Ah! Jack Cardiff—you must be older than God.' Well, this was years ago, so not really. Anyway, he asked me how old I was and I replied, 'You can look it up in *Who's Who*, Michael.' I knew he wasn't in *Who's Who* and I was.

JB   Presumably he knew of your great reputation, though?

JC   He told me that he had heard that I was very slow at lighting and difficult to get along with. So I told him that I had also heard the most terrible things about him. So we started to laugh and that's how the atmosphere continued—we were always sword-fighting. He said that he had worked with an American cameraman who was very fast. Well, I started the picture with him and he's a monster to work with. Always wide angles and nowhere for me to put any lights, so I had to somehow do it. Well, I was very fast, and after the first week or so, we went and had a drink together. I asked him, 'Do you still think I'm slow?' and he said, 'No, Jack, you're the fastest I've ever worked with.' And that is quite something coming from Michael Winner, you know!

JB   So things did improve?

JC   After he realized that he could ask me to do anything and I would do it, we got along just fine. He would get right into the corner of a room and shoot it with the widest possible lens. So where were the lights going to go? Somehow I would get them in somewhere, so he grew to have a certain respect for me. Michael Winner did have this way of working where he rather disregarded everybody else, and I did find myself rather wistfully thinking about working with Michael Powell.

JB   Did he do things like that to be deliberately provocative?

JC   No, but he could be incredibly tough on the set. I remember Denholm Elliott squared up to him on one occasion and he nearly hit him. Denholm was a very good actor and I think that somehow he just never got the right break on a big film, but an awfully good actor. Somehow one endures these things.

JB   This was a Golan and Globus produced film,[23] wasn't it?

JC   Yes, but it was a Michael Winner film and he dominated everything, so even if the producers had been there, you wouldn't have known it. Of course, Michael Winner was so rich he could have financed a film himself anyway—but it is a fact that directors, no matter how rich they are, never finance their own films. Funny that, isn't it?

JB   You mentioned before that Faye Dunaway often carried a mirror with her to check her appearance.

JC   I can understand any woman who is a professional and has to be on the screen looking beautiful being concerned with her appearance, but she was worried stiff about it. She had a make-up man with her all the time and it came to my notice that he had been instructed to check up on the lights. I had a word with him about it and he backed off.

JB   **Was she difficult right from the beginning?**

JC   Yes. I did some tests with her before we started shooting the picture and I really lit it very well with all sorts of soft lighting. We ran the test film in Michael Winner's private theatre and Michael said it was really wonderful and told Faye that she looked beautiful in it, which she did. But then her remark was rather unfortunate. She just turned around and said, 'Now let's see what we can do to improve that.' I rather testily replied, 'Well, I'm afraid there is nothing I can do to improve on that. That is what I would consider very good photography!'

So on the set I used to play games with her. If there was a scene where she was walking outside, there might be no actual sunshine but the sky would be bright and the top light would make shadows under her eyes. So I would have to cover that by putting stretchers [canopies] of cloth and gauze over her wherever she walked. Sometimes when I thought it would further my cause, I would deliberately put a light too high so that when she questioned it, I could move it down and she would be ever so grateful. There were so many games. I just wanted to say, 'Forget how you look. Just act!' But we got through it.

Michael Winner and
Jack Cardiff - *The
Wicked Lady* (1983)

JB   **You worked on the first of two epic TV mini-series next:** *The Far Pavilions* **[1984] first.**

JC The book was so big and it built up its story wonderfully about this boy who was growing up—so beautiful. Right from the beginning, many people wanted it to be a mini-series, but the producers were insisting that it be cut down and released as a film. To me, that would have been a tragedy.

I am told that the director [Peter Duffell] had the choice of two lead actresses, and they were both white! [The character is Indian.] So he chose one [Amy Irving] and she had to be made up with dark make-up, and that is always fatal, I think. It didn't have to be a big star and there were plenty of Asian actresses who could have played the role. When the film came, out one or two critics did remark about it. I do think it ruined the picture.

JB How long were you working on it?

JC Several months, all on location in India, with lots of battle scenes and big sequences. Those who had read the book couldn't believe how much we had had to cut out, though, and M M Kaye, the woman who wrote the book, must have died when she saw it. She came out and saw us on set actually.

John Gielgud heard that I loved my morning newspaper, which unfortunately we couldn't get in India. So he had it sent out to him every day and he would bring it to my room. That was lovely, the great John Gielgud knocking on my door to deliver the paper each day. Not many hotels can boast that level of room service!

JB Do you think it can be a dangerous thing to have writers visit the set?

JC I suppose it can be. I am told that the writer of the novel *Black Narcissus* (Rumer Godden) didn't like the film, although it is loved by so many people.

Enduring the English weather—Jack Cardiff and Michael Winner, *The Wicked Lady* (1983)

JB   **You told me that you often watched rushes sent to you on video during production of *The Far Pavilions*. How else had technology improved location work?**

JC   The technology was all straightforward for filming really. The thing with the rushes was that we weren't really analyzing the quality of the print, which was, in a way, a compliment to me. We were really just looking to see if the acting was all right.

JB   **The other mini-series that you worked on at around the same time was *The Last Days of Pompeii*[24] [1984].**

JC   That was all made at Pinewood, and we had very good sets. We did go to Pompeii, and shot at the amphitheatre there, but it was a predominantly studio-based film.

JB   **This must have been like a reunion party for you—Olivia Hussey, Lesley-Anne Down, Ernest Borgnine, Laurence Olivier—you had worked with all of them before.**

JC   Yes, but that last name is quite sad. I had always so revered Larry as both a great actor and a very nice person. We had worked on several pictures together and he had been so good-looking and strong, with this wonderful voice. They wanted to get him for *The Last Days of Pompeii* and the messages kept coming back saying that he still wasn't very well. Eventually they said he could come, but only at 2 o'clock and only for, say, two hours. This was right near the end of his life and he eventually came down onto the set all made up, and he looked awful! His face looked so different and his hair had gone and his memory had gone, and they had to put up the idiot boards for him—which was such a sad thing to see.

JB   **Happier times working with Dick Fleischer again, this time on *Conan the Destroyer* [1984], which was a sequel to the John Milius film *Conan the Barbarian*[25]...**

JC   I liked Arnold Schwarzenegger's make-up better on *Conan the Barbarian*. He was sort of cleaned up on our picture. I'm not sure how that came about, but on *Barbarian* he was a real barbarian to look at, but on ours Arnold Schwarzenegger was a big film star and they cleaned him up to be a better-looking star.

JB   **How was he to work with?**

JC   He was very good and I liked him very much. I didn't work with him again, but he would send messages on my birthdays and things. He was a very amicable person.

Schwarzenegger has lost a bit of weight since that time. He used to carry his training equipment all over the place. He would have his suite in the hotel and then he would have another suite and they would take all of the furniture out to put his heavy equipment in. I had a go on the training equipment for about 30 seconds and that was enough.

JB   So you worked out with Schwarzenegger?

JC   Yes, I worked out with Schwarzenegger!

JB   Weren't you due to do _Blue Velvet_ [1986] for David Lynch[26] at this time?

JC   I had been standing by to do _Blue Velvet_ and I had worked on a couple of tests with David Lynch, the director, and it had gone very well. But we couldn't start straight away and while I was waiting I had a call from Dino begging me to please help them because their cameraman on _Conan_ was ill. They wanted me to go over to Mexico and take over.

So I agreed, but then I found out that their cameraman wasn't ill. In fact, their first cameraman had seen the horror of the shoot—it was in the jungle with lots of heat and insects and snakes—and he had given up after one day. He just left a note on his pillow saying, 'By the time you read this, I shall be back home.'

Then another guy came in. I know he had a few day-for-night scenes to do and he had got the wrong exposure on them. All completely 'NG'. He was fired.

That's when they got me over.

JB   Do you regret making it at the expense of shooting _Blue Velvet_?

JC   Well, I think it would have been interesting, but on the other hand I know I wasn't completely in tune with David Lynch. Perhaps I could have done some good work on it.

I liked him and we were good friends, but he was crazy with effects, he was abstract. He had this abstract way of going about things that was far worse than any director I had ever worked with. I felt that I wouldn't get in on the act at all. That was my main fear because you have to feel that you can contribute and create yourself. So I wasn't particularly disappointed.[27]

JB   And from one muscle man to another, Sylvester Stallone on _Rambo: First Blood, Part II_ [1985]. Another sequel too, come to think of it.

JC   Again, quite honestly I think the first one was better.[28] It was more down to earth with its idea. By this time it was a success story and they had lost the roughness with it. Stallone had written the script for this one.

JB   You sound like you enjoyed working with Stallone less than Schwarzenegger.

JC   Stallone was someone who you couldn't really take seriously, although he was a very serious person. He didn't have a particularly happy personality. He was always very quiet and reserved, but just like Schwarzenegger he would train, spending an hour or more every morning doing his exercises before he came on set.

He would go to his trailer to get made up and when he came out he would have his own make-up man, hairdresser, costume expert, secretary and a hood [bodyguard]. A whole train would come out of this huge trailer. He would come on and do one take and go over to the television set next to the camera, where they would play it back for him. He would just say, 'Let's do it again.' His word was law; it was like God.

He had no animation in his face, he was always deadpan. He didn't throw his weight about, but he would just quietly demand. It was more like a gangster's threat.

JB   Did you have problems with him directly?

JC   I know on one occasion I was lighting a scene and he said to me, 'Shouldn't that key light go a bit higher?' And I told him it was fine. That evening we saw the rushes, which were good, and I went up to him afterwards and said, 'Look, don't ever tell me where to put the lights'. And he never mentioned it after that. Give him an inch and he'll take a mile.

JB   Squaring up to Stallone was probably a result of working out with Schwarzenegger.

JC   Yes!

JB   Physical endurance sounds essential for a film like this …

JC   It was a terrible physical situation to shoot in. I used to take half a dozen shirts with me every morning, because once I started work, within twenty minutes the shirt would be wet through from the humidity and you would have to change. It was so hot and humid. Added to this, there was a big battle being shot for most of the film, so they had gun-fire and tanks and a lot of burning tyres that are used to make black smoke. This would go on all day so we were always breathing in this dreadful black smoke. Between that

Jack Cardiff takes a light reading on the set of *The Far Pavilions* (1984)

and the heat, it was really quite something. Somehow we survived. It wasn't very pleasant.

JB **This one had even more explosions than** *Dogs of War*. **There's the famous exploding waterfall for a start …**

JC We shot that scene and then we went on to another location while the special effects team were clearing up. The top of the waterfall was probably a hundred or so feet. One of the stunt guys [Cliff Wenger Jr] got too near the edge, slipped and fell down. He was killed. I remember we got the news when we were in the assistant director's cabin and Stallone came in and mumbled, 'I think we should go back to work.' He was one of those.

JB **More globetrotting followed. Off to China for Daryl Duke's adaptation of James Clavell's novel** *Tai-Pan* **[1986].**

JC That was another sad one because sometime earlier, I was living in London when Dick Fleischer came to town and told me that he was about to direct a very big film called *Tai-Pan*. He asked me if I would photograph it and of course I said yes. Then something happened with the contracts and the project faded and Dick was no longer on it. Then the actor who was supposed to be in it, Steve McQueen, insisted that although the film really needed to be shot in China, he would only do it if it could all be done in America. Some people have said in retrospect that perhaps he already knew that he had cancer and he didn't want to travel so far away from home. It's certainly a possibility. So that all faded and I thought, 'Well, that's it!'

But then Dino De Laurentiis announced that he was going to be making it with Sean Connery. He would have been perfect, because in the book he was supposed to be around 60 and Connery was certainly over 50 by that time, and he also had to be a Scot. But again it all went wrong and Connery was out and in came the Australian actor Bryan Brown.[29]

JB **Were you still officially connected to the project after all this time?**

JC No, I wasn't asked to photograph it. The new director, Daryl Duke, had already made quite a famous television series[30] and he had asked for his own cameraman to work on *Tai-Pan*. I was rather disappointed, but then I heard that the cameraman, who was rather old—even older than I was at the time—announced that he couldn't face the heat and how tough the filming was going to be. That's when Dino De Laurentiis asked me to do it. I went out to meet them and Raffaella, his daughter, was producing it.

JB **How did Raffaella De Laurentiis[31] compare to Dino?**

JC   She was a first-class producer, no doubt about that. I had worked on *Conan* with her and she did a wonderful job on that, but on *Tai-Pan* she really had no chance of succeeding with that setup. It was a very difficult picture to make.

JB   What made it so problematic?

JC   For a start, when I started work on the picture it became apparent to me that Bryan Brown was alright, but nothing special. Of course, Brown was an Australian and not a Scot, and then they hired someone to play a London Cockney who really was a Scot. It was such a mess of all the wrong people and the wrong nationalities and accents. To top it off, they had a man brought over from Hollywood to act as the dialogue coach and he really didn't have a clue about Scottish or Cockney accents.

It was a hard picture to make in China, lots of travelling by little boats, and often we had to stay away from filming near the water because of all these tourist boats. Just things like that. We staggered through the picture and eventually I was in Hollywood when they had a test screening and it really wasn't very successful. It came out and played for maybe a couple of weeks and then was taken off and never heard of again, which is really tragic as people had worked on that film for years, on and off.

Again, this should have probably been a mini-series and not a film, because the book was something like 1000 pages. A great novel made into a reasonable two hours.

9 'If you don't like it …'

- *Million Dollar Mystery*
- Showscan—*Call From Space*
- Classical Music Videos
- Lifetime Academy Award
- Going digital

> 'Jack Cardiff is one of the greatest visual artists ever to work in film. His work is pure, visionary and timeless. He has given us some of the most enduring images in motion picture history.'
> *Robert Rehme—President (2001) The Academy of Motion Picture Arts and Science*

JB In 1987, you made your final feature film with Dick Fleischer, *Million Dollar Mystery*.

JC They offered a prize, supposedly a million dollars, to anyone who could find the correct solution to their mystery. As far as I know, they must have paid it out to somebody by now.

JB You didn't find out in the film?

JC I was just thinking that! No. In theory I should have known and I could have written in for the prize or told someone else to! It was probably all a huge publicity gimmick.

The stuntman, Dar Robinson,[1] was tragically killed on that film. So sad, because he wasn't even doing a stunt when it happened—he just got too near to the edge on his motorbike and was killed. It's funny how stuntmen get kind of cocky and take things for granted, just like on Rambo when the other stuntman was killed at the waterfall. Very sad.

JB You did also make *Call from Space* [1989] with Fleischer, but that wasn't a normal feature film.

JC No, it was done with this big screen process.[2] It was very tough because it was all a set in a studio in Hollywood. Also, the problem with these special cameras was that they needed a lot of light because the negative was so large and the lens set-up demanded a lot of light to expose it. But my God, on screen it was so exciting to see. The problem was that you had to custom-build all of the cinemas to screen it, which would have been prohibitive. The cameras weren't easy to move either—you certainly couldn't have handheld.

JB   Were there other technical limitations?

JC   Yes. When you are photographing an actor 10 feet away and another 4 feet away, you want them all sharp and at f/2 they aren't all sharp—it's as simple as that! But this process, because it was such a large area of film to expose, meant that I was shooting at something like f11. That's a lot! An *enormous* amount of light.

JB   But you were still attracted to working with the system?

JC   Yes, because when I first saw the rushes, I thought it was wonderful and I could just imagine doing the Battle of Trafalgar with Nelson's armada. You really felt you were there, and when we did some things with boats, you really did feel you were out at sea. It extended beyond your line of vision.

The finished films were very good, and it was great to see Dick again. When you know someone like I know Dick, it really works very well. It becomes a great joy to work on a film; it's like working with family.

JB   How did the chance to direct the two classical music videos, *Delius* [1989] and *The Four Seasons* [1991], come about?

JC   That was a whole new ball game for me. There was a man in Japan who wanted these films to be made. I had the job of writing the script and directing it, and I had a crew of just four on the film. That was delightful because I didn't have to worry about anything. I could say, 'Let's just wait for the sun to come around a bit.' Time didn't matter with four people; there were no overheads in waiting.

JB   Were these big budget?

JC   The videos were made at a fairly good budget, not huge, about £22,000. That makes you inventive, because you can't just sit on your arse and say you want a camera crane.

Before I started *The Four Seasons*, I told them that I wanted to film snow in Venice for the winter section. This is asking the impossible because it hardly ever snows in Venice, so I asked EMI to just be ready to let us go over at a moment's notice if it did suddenly snow there. I had a guy in Venice who was going to help when I was there, and he called me and told me it was due to snow the next day. So I got in touch with EMI and they said I couldn't because the contracts weren't ready yet. I went anyway.

We flew over there and the snow had arrived and was already melting. So I was furious with EMI's delaying tactics. I found a photographer who had taken pictures when the snow had still been on the ground. There were about ten of these pictures and I think it cost me around £500 to buy them from him.

The problem with them was that they were of snow on the ground and not of snow actually falling down. What I did was I went into my back garden and fixed up a bit of black velvet in front of my 16mm camera. I bought some artificial snow and fixed up a ladder, and my wife and son went up and shook the snow down. In order to slow it all down, I filmed it at 64 frames per second instead of the usual 24 frames; it looked marvellous. We superimposed the film over these photographs of Venice and moved the camera a bit from side to side to make it look like it was shot from a boat. It was great fun doing all of this, as you could really go to town.

It worked very well, and I was able to try a lot of tricky stuff without people telling me it would never work. I could just do what I liked.

JB   Was this only shot on 16mm film or combined with 35mm?

JC   This was mostly 16mm because it was all going onto tape in the end anyway

JB   Tell me about receiving your Honorary Academy Award.

JC   I had this telephone call and this strange American voice said, 'Mr Cardiff, I'm talking from the Academy and we have decided to give you a special award.' I thought this was a gag and I nearly said, 'Oh yeah? Come on, who is it?' But it turned out to be true. It was a wonderful surprise.

The great thing is, if you have worked on a film and you have done well, then perhaps you get nominated, but that doesn't mean you have won the Oscar. In this case, they were just giving it to me!

We went and had a wonderful time. They asked me to write a speech that you have to submit to them.

JB   Really?

JC   Oh yes, I suppose in case you have something up your sleeve that you are planning on saying. Brando played that trick.[3] So anyway, I sent my script and they thought it was fine.

They originally said if I wanted any help with my script, they could give me a writer to work on it with me. That's so Hollywood, isn't it?

JB   And the whole thing is rehearsed too, right?

JC   The day before the big night, we had the rehearsal and I met Dustin Hoffman, who was presenting me with the award. Something about him reminded me of Errol Flynn, he had a devilment about him. He told me not to worry about my speech and that I should just go out there and tell them I was trying to set up a film and did any of them have any spare cash.

On the big night, I had to hide behind a big wooden statuette, about 25 feet high. And this sounds very primitive, but I had to watch the side wings for a man to flash a torch at me. When the torch flickers, I'm supposed to make my entrance. The arrangement was I was supposed to go on, shake Dustin's hand, he would hand me my Oscar and then he would walk off to the side while I made my speech.

There were, by the official count, 5250 people in the audience that night, and you can add to that a couple of billion from the TV audience. So I was a little nervous. The torch flashes and I'm on the stage in the glare of the lights with all these people applauding. I get to Hoffman and he shakes my hand and goes to the side, but … he takes my Oscar with him!

Strangely, it was a wonderful feeling of relief. I no longer felt nervous and I just said, 'Hey! What about my Oscar?' Everyone roared with laughter and it really cooled me down.

JB   This, I think was the first ever lifetime achievement Oscar to go to the technical side of filmmaking.

JC That's true, and only the third Englishman, with Larry Olivier and Charlie Chaplin before me.

JB Now, quite unexpectedly, you have just had to rush off to America to work!

JC It was quite out of the blue that I had this call from Hollywood. Christopher Coppola[4] said he was a fan of Michael Powell and a fan of mine and he loved *The Red Shoes*—all of that stuff. He said that he had a sequence to do for his film [*Bloodhead*] and he wondered if I would mind coming out and doing it. I was absolutely stunned.

When I got out there, I found I was working on stage 11 at MGM, which was where they had shot *Gone With the Wind* [1939] and Orson Welles's *The Magnificent Ambersons* [1942]. So that alone was an amazing thing. I even had my own trailer with my name on it—quite unbelievable!

JB This was a digital shoot and you had never worked with that technology, had you?

JC No I hadn't, and of course this was all on digital and that was so exciting for me because I had always wanted to do something on digital. I couldn't help reflecting that I had now worked on the whole range from the first silent films, to the first talkies and then the first colour and now one of the first digital features.

JB What exactly were you shooting?

JC: It was a montage sequence. But then, to my great joy, they asked me if I would do the editing on it while they were still finishing the picture. I worked with a young cutter who was brilliant and who showed me how it all worked. It is amazing and the great advantage is that you have instant rushes; you could watch them in the lavatory if you wanted to!

JB How did you find digital editing?

JC When you are editing the old way, you have to print the film and cut it up and stick it together, and it takes weeks or months and you collect all these cans of films that need to be labelled. Then, when it's finally cut, it needs to be printed exactly right by Technicolor or whoever, and then you have to make another 50 prints or more for all the cinemas. Can you imagine the amount of film involved and the cost of it all?

Putting them on planes and sending them all over the world. With digital, you can do it all in one, tiny room, pushing a few buttons. Hit a button and the film has gone to India—boom!

JB   What about the image quality? Does that hold up against traditional film in your opinion?

JC   It's excellent! I must say that what I saw in Hollywood, if they had told me it was normal film I would have believed it. There are certain things that you are warned against; for example, backlight can cause some problems, and black can be difficult to get right on digital—but they are getting better and better all the time. It has only just started and I think that in a year's time they will have the filters that will solve these issues. These are not insurmountable problems and this is only the beginning.

JB   Do you think that celluloid is dead?

JC   I think it will still be used for some things, but as far as motion pictures are concerned, I think it will be. There are some costs that have to be dealt with initially for digital, but it is just a question of time.

JB   It doesn't sadden you that film will die?

JC   Film has been my whole life and so I might be sad if I never saw it again, but at the same time, when I was working in the 1930s I could have said that I would be sad not to see much black and white any more. You know, there was an assistant that I used to work with, Ted Scaife, and he used to say, 'Well, you know the rules: if you don't like it, you shouldn't have joined!' If you don't like it you shouldn't have joined!

The Milestone Films

Wings of the Morning (1936)
Director: Harold Schuster

Wings of the Morning was the first Technicolor film to be produced in Europe, the result of the corporation's decision to expand its growing empire to encompass Britain. Jack Cardiff was chosen, from among the camera operators working for Alexander Korda at the time, to join Technicolor and work on their British features. Natalie Kalmus, the wife of Technicolor founder Herbert Kalmus, had worked with the corporation as a 'colour consultant' almost from its inception and came to England to supervise personally the production of *Wings of the Morning* and subsequent UK films.

The film was shot on location in England and Ireland, and it is clear from the outset that the plot (based on a story by Brian Oswald Donn-Byrne) is secondary to the vividly colourful set pieces. The narrative follows a young girl, Maria (played by Annabella), who escapes the Spanish Civil War disguised as a boy and falls in love with Kerry (Henry Fonda). Far more important than the gossamer-thin narrative is the multi-coloured background against which the action is set: gaudy, romanticized gypsies, campfire revelries, and, of course, the carnival atmosphere of the climactic Derby horserace—all designed to showcase Technicolor in its full glory.

Adding to the sense that *Wings of the Morning* was more of an 'event' than a mere film are the cameo appearances by Irish tenor John McCormack (who sings in the predictably lavish ball scenes) and champion jockey Steve Donaghue, playing himself.

Western Approaches (1942)
Director: Pat Jackson

An exemplary piece of wartime documentary propaganda—easily comparable to the best work of Humphrey Jennings (with whom Jackson had worked on *The First Days*)—*Western Approaches* was produced under the auspices of the Crown Film Unit for the Ministry of Information. It celebrates the bravery of the Merchant Navy, which was charged with maintaining the Atlantic lifeline between Britain and North America during World War II.

Director Pat Jackson, cinematographer Jack Cardiff, and their cast of non-professional actors (drawn from the ranks of the real Merchant Navy) spent almost two-and-a-half years filming in conditions almost as hazardous as those faced on active duty. The docudrama, which was co-written by Jackson and Gerry Bryant, follows a group of seamen adrift in their lifeboat after their ship is sunk; they are faced with a dilemma when they suspect that the U-Boat responsible for their plight may still be tailing them, waiting to strike at potential rescuers.

Western Approaches was one of only four Technicolor feature films released in Britain during World War II. The others were: *This Happy Breed* (David Lean, 1944), *Henry V* (Laurence Olivier, 1944) and *Blithe Spirit* (David Lean, 1945). *Western Approaches* premiered in London on 8 December 1944.

A Matter of Life and Death (1946)
Directors: Michael Powell and Emeric Pressburger

'This is the universe,' booms a celestial voice at the beginning of *A Matter of Life and Death*. 'Big, isn't it?'

This was the first of three sublime collaborations between Jack Cardiff and the post-war powerhouse of Michael Powell and Emeric Pressburger's Archers production company. Commissioned by Jack Beddington of the Film Division of the Ministry of Information, *A Matter of Life and Death* was intended to be a regular propaganda film aimed at strengthening Anglo-American relationships. In the hands of Michael Powell, it became a timeless love story, which retains its resonance and humanity to this day.

Returning from a bombing mission, Peter Carter is forced to bail out of his damaged plane, but not before he has fallen in love with the radio voice of June (Kim Hunter), a young American working for the RAF, who Peter believes will be the last person he will ever speak to. Peter should indeed have died, but due to a celestial mix-up he is temporarily spared while heaven convenes a court to hear his case and decide his fate.

With a typical Powell touch, the scenes in heaven are rendered in shimmering monochrome, while earth bathes in glorious Technicolor. Cardiff's stunning cinematography brilliantly illuminates the extravagant sets designed by the inimitable Alfred Junge, combining to produce a vision that has never been equalled. The vast heavenly court scene alone employed almost 5500 extras, many of them either real RAF crews or nurses of the British Red Cross.

In 1999, *A Matter of Life and Death* was voted number 20 by members of the British Film Institute in their Best British Film poll.

Black Narcissus (1947)
Directors: Michael Powell and Emeric Pressburger

Powell and Pressburger's decision to film their Himalayan-set story entirely in English studios (with the exception of two brief English location scenes) put the onus of success or failure squarely on the shoulders of cinematographer Jack Cardiff, production designer Alfred Junge and effects maestro William Percy 'Poppa' Day. It was a challenge they rose to, surpassing all expectations and creating a living mountain environment completely believable in every detail.

The film, based on the novel by Rumer Godden, follows the emotional, as much as physical, journey of a group of Anglican nuns as they attempt to establish a remote convent among the high ruins of an abandoned Himalayan harem. Powell and Pressburger again seemed to be courting deliberate controversy in their exploration of faith and repressed sexual tension. The acting is exemplary, particularly from Kathleen Byron as Sister Ruth and Deborah Kerr as Sister Clodagh, and a further dash of the 'exotic' is added through the casting of Sabu and the luminescent Jean Simmons. The smouldering tensions build palpably towards an inevitable and unavoidable conclusion, heightened by a stirring score from composer Brian Easdale.

Black Narcissus is perhaps Jack Cardiff's finest hour and the film in which his love of the great painters is most evident (every shot resembles a living Vermeer); he was justly honoured with his first Academy Award for the work.

The Red Shoes (1948)
Directors: Michael Powell and Emeric Pressburger

Jack Cardiff's third and final film with Powell and Pressburger was every bit as magically productive as their preceding endeavours.

Under the guidance of charismatic impresario Lermontov (Anton Walbrook), his protégé Victoria Page (Moira Shearer) is, perhaps, able to realize her full potential as a dancer, but only through utter devotion to her art by forsaking the man she loves. *The Red Shoes* can be seen as a companion piece to *Black Narcissus*, sharing many of its themes of obsession, desire and doomed ambition; but here Powell and Pressburger add a near Faustian twist that seals the fate of the young dancer. At the centre of the film is a fifteen-minute ballet sequence based on the Hans Christian Andersen fairy tale of the title, and it is here that both the director and Cardiff are at their most creative. Mixing stop-motion with high speed and slow speed filming, employing shimmering shafts of light and powerful follow-spots, and creating a dance sequence the likes of which has not been seen on film subsequently.

The film was showered with awards and nominations on its release. These included: Academy Award wins for Art Direction (Hein Heckroth and Arthur Lawson) and Best Music (Brian Easdale); Academy Award nominations for Editing (Reginald Mills), Best Picture (Michael Powell and Emeric Pressburger) and Best Writing (Emeric Pressburger). It additionally won a Golden Globe for the music and was nominated for the Best British Film BAFTA.

The Red Shoes was voted number 9 by members of the British Film Institute in their Best British Film poll (1999).

Scott of the Antarctic (1948)
Director: Charles Frend

Charles Frend had already proven himself a dependable director of heroic drama with his 1943 film *San Demetrio, London* before he turned his attention in 1948 to *Scott of the Antarctic*. The script by Walter Meade and Ivor Montagu (with additional dialogue by Mary Hayley Bell) drew heavily on Scott's recovered diaries and followed the ill-fated British team's race to the South Pole. It is,

in many ways, an intensely British story of stiff upper lips, unimaginable endurance, self-sacrifice and heroic failure.

Before Jack Cardiff joined the production, cinematographer Osmand Borrodaile had already been dispatched to the Antarctic to film location sequences. In addition, Geoff Unsworth had shot extensive long shots in both Norway and Switzerland—it was Cardiff's unenviable task to draw together the disparate elements (with wildly varying colour balances) and match the exteriors to the interiors, shot on a small soundstage at Ealing Studios.

John Mills, who had established a reputation for playing the level-headed British hero, was perfectly cast as Robert Falcon Scott and he was suitably supported by Kenneth More as Lieutenant Evans, Harold Warrender as Wilson, Derek Bond as Oates, Reginald Beckwith as Bowers and James Robertson Justice as Petty Officer Evans. An outstandingly atmospheric score by Ralph Vaughan Williams (which went on to form the basis of the composer's 7th Symphony) deepens the pathos of the film, and the superb art direction by Arne Akermark adds a detailed level of authenticity.

On its release, *Scott of the Antarctic* was nominated for the Best British Film BAFTA and also earned director Charles Frend a Golden Lion nomination at the Venice Film Festival. It was selected as the Royal Command Performance, but ultimately performed poorly at the box office.

The African Queen (1951)
Director: John Huston

At the outbreak of World War I, Charlie Allnut (Humphrey Bogart) is ferrying supplies to villages in East Africa on his old steamboat, *The African Queen*. When Reverend Sayer (Robert Morley) is killed by German troops, Allnut reluctantly agrees to transport his spinster sister Rose (Katharine Hepburn) back to 'civilization'. In typical 'odd couple' fashion, the two slowly fall for each other's irascible charms and Allnut is ultimately persuaded to take a stand against the German forces.

The location shoot for *The African Queen* was almost certainly the toughest of Jack Cardiff's career. It was initially slated to shoot in Uganda, but Huston found locations he preferred in the Belgian Congo, several days drive outside Stanleyville. Here the cast and crew endured soldier ants, malaria, bilharzia, extreme humidity and dysentery; only Huston and Bogart are said to have been spared the latter because of their preference for drinking whisky rather than water. It has been widely and erroneously reported that sections of the film were shot on location in Dalyan, Turkey. In fact, the sequences—in which Bogart and Hepburn have to drag the boat through reed beds— were shot in studios in England because of fears of waterborne disease.

Humphrey Bogart won the Academy Award for his performance and Katharine Hepburn was also nominated. John Huston was nominated as both Best Director and for his screenplay (a nomination shared with co-writer John Agee).

In 1990, Clint Eastwood directed and starred in *White Hunter, Black Heart*, a fictionalized account of the trials of production on *The African Queen* and the director's obsession with 'bagging' big game animals while on location in Africa.

The Barefoot Contessa (1954)
Director: Joseph L Mankiewicz

Written and directed by Mankiewicz, *The Barefoot Contessa* is every bit as sharp as that combination would suggest. Similar in construct and theme to Vincente Minnelli's *The Bad and the Beautiful* (released two years

previously), Mankiewicz's film follows washed-up director Harry Dawes (Humphrey Bogart), who gets a second chance to prove himself when hired to write and direct a film, set to star dancer Maria Vargas (Ava Gardner). Perhaps not as acerbic as Minnelli's searing indictment of the Hollywood machine, *The Barefoot Contessa* is still a hugely entertaining look at the workings of the film industry, and enormous fun is to be had trying to see through the director's thinly veiled portrayals of real-life Hollywood players.

This was Jack Cardiff's only film with Mankiewicz, but it was as rewarding personally as it was professionally; Mankiewicz actively encouraged Cardiff not to give up his directorial dreams after the failure of his *William Tell* project.

The Barefoot Contessa won both an Academy Award and a Golden Globe for co-star Edmond O'Brien and an Academy nomination for Mankiewicz's screenplay.

War and Peace (1956)
Director: King Vidor

King Vidor's adaptation of Leo Tolstoy's tale of a Russian family during the 1812 war is epic in every sense. The fact that more than half-a-dozen writers are credited with struggling to distil the novel's essence into some 200 minutes perhaps tells its own story—although the results are as lucid as could be expected. Often accused of being miscast (the stars include Audrey Hepburn, Henry Fonda and Mel Ferrer), the film is nonetheless a hugely enjoyable piece of grandiose filmmaking, not least because of the contributions from extrovert producer Dino De Laurentiis.

It was shot predominantly at Rome's famed Cinecittà studios, where Jack Cardiff again masterfully matched set-bound sequences, such as the famous duel, with sweeping location work. His efforts were rewarded with another Academy Award nomination and a Best Cinematography Award from the British Society of Cinematographers. Costume designer Maria De Matteis was also nominated for an Oscar, as was Vidor as Best Director.

The Prince and the Showgirl (1957)
Director: Laurence Olivier

The Prince and the Showgirl, set in the early 20th century, follows the fortunes of an American actress, Elsie Marina (Marilyn Monroe) who, through chance, meets the Prince of Carpathia (Laurence Olivier). A 'will they, won't they?' romance ensues, as both must learn to accept their differences and overcome their wildly different backgrounds.

It is perhaps fitting, given the story's premise, that such an unlikely pairing as Monroe and Olivier should be cast opposite each other—but it was a combination that proved to be highly volatile. Olivier appears to have shown little patience with Monroe's temperamental antics (more often than not a result of her extreme nerves and her uncertainty in her abilities), and for her part, Monroe seems, on occasion, to have deliberately provoked her co-star and director's wrath. The situation was compounded by the frequent presence on set of Vivian Leigh; not only was she the then-wife of Olivier and an actress whom Monroe greatly admired, but she had also played the lead role in Terence Rattigan's stage play, *The Sleeping Prince*, upon which the film was based.

Despite the obvious production difficulties, *The Prince and the Showgirl* remains a charming romantic comedy, sumptuously realized through a combination of great art direction, cinematography and costume design. The film was honoured with no fewer than five BAFTA nominations: Best British Actor (Laurence Olivier), Best British Screenplay (Terence Rattigan), Best British Film, Best Film from any Source, and Best Foreign Actress (Marilyn Monroe).

The Vikings (1958)
Director: Richard Fleischer

The first of five films that Jack Cardiff and Richard Fleischer made together—the later ones being: *Crossed Swords* (1978), *Conan the Destroyer* (1984), *Million Dollar Mystery* (1987) and *Call from Space* (1989). Cardiff is often erroneously credited with shooting Fleischer's 1983 film *Amityville 3-D*.

The story, based on a novel by Edison Marshall and adapted by Dale Wasserman, follows two Viking half-brothers, Einar (Kirk Douglas) and Eric (Tony Curtis), who compete to capture the throne of Northumbria, each unaware of the other's identity. The film is a lusty tale of rape and pillage with a heavy dose of bloodletting, revenge and near Shakespearian family feuding. The cast is fleshed out with fine performances from Ernest Borgnine as Ragnar, Janet Leigh as the object of warring affections, Morgana, and Frank Thring (later to play Pontius Pilate in William Wyler's 1959 *Ben-Hur*) as the villainous Aella.

The production was troubled to an extent, both by the tough Norwegian exterior locations and by the complexity of having Kirk Douglas both star in and produce the film. But what lifts *The Vikings* above its more pedestrian action-adventure cousins andwhat made it one of the top-grossing films of the year is its fine attention to period detail (with full credit to production designer Harper Goff) and its unflinching portrayal of the period's brutality. The film was scored by Italian composer Mario Nascimbene, who would later collaborate with Jack Cardiff on both *Scent of Mystery* (1960) and *Sons and Lovers* (1960).

Intent to Kill (1958) and Beyond This Place (1959)
Director: Jack Cardiff

After the failure of the Jack Cardiff and Errol Flynn project *William Tell* in 1953, Cardiff was finally able to cut his directorial teeth on two low-key (and low-budget) melodramas.

The first, *Intent to Kill*, based on a novel by Michael Bryan and adapted for the screen by Jimmy Sangster, follows a Montreal doctor, Bob McLaurin (Richard Todd), who is in love with his colleague, Dr Nancy Ferguson (Betsy Drake), despite being married to Margaret (Catherine Boyle.) The plot—not to mention the relationships—are complicated when McLaurin is called upon to operate on a South American president (Herbert Lom), who in turn is marked for assassination. The film and its direction are routine enough, but the chill Canadian locations and the stark black-and-white cinematography by Desmond Dickinson add a sense of bleak menace.

Cardiff followed up with *Beyond This Place*, adapted from the novel by A J Cronin and loosely based on the true-life story of Oscar Slater, who was wrongly accused and imprisoned for murder in 1908. Returning to his native Liverpool after two decades in America, Paul Mathry (Van Johnson) discovers that the father he thought to have died in the war is, in fact, incarcerated for murder. Believing his father to be innocent, he sets out to solve the mystery. Vera Miles, playing Lena Anderson, makes a pre-*Psycho* (1960) appearance.

Again Cardiff chose to shoot in black and white, this time employing cinematographer Wilkie Cooper and, as with *Intent to Kill*, the film received a number of solid reviews.

Fanny (1960)
Director: Joshua Logan

Jack Cardiff, despite having already realized the beginnings of his directorial ambitions with *Intent to Kill* (1958) and *Beyond This Place* (1959), was lured back to cinematography by Joshua Logan, the director best known for *Bus Stop* (1956) and *South Pacific* (1958).

Based in part on Marcel Pagnol's 'Marseille trilogy'—*Marius, Fanny* and *César*—and on Logan's own Broadway adaptation, *Fanny* is a light romantic comedy following the relationship between Marius (Horst Buchholz) who longs for a life at sea, and Fanny (Leslie Caron) who longs for Marius. Despite the fine line-up of French talent involved in the film—Leslie Caron, Maurice Chevalier, Charles Boyer—there was a degree of hostility to the project in France, in part because of the earlier success of a 1932 version, directed by Marc Allégret and starring Orane Demazis as the eponymous Fanny.

Regardless, the film was a commercial and critical success, attracting Academy Award nominations for Charles Boyer (Best Actor), William Reynolds (Best Film Editing), Morris Stoloff and Harry Sukman (Best Music, Dramatic or Comedy Picture), Joshua Logan (Best Film) and Jack Cardiff (Best Cinematography, Colour.)

Sons and Lovers (1960)
Director: Jack Cardiff

Sons and Lovers was Jack Cardiff's big break and undoubtedly his finest film as a director. He was chosen by producers Jerry Wald and Bob Goldstein at 20th Century Fox to bring D H Lawrence's semi-autobiographical novel to the screen, despite never having read the book (he lied and told them he had). Thomas Clarke, although best known for his comedies such as *Passport to Pimlico* (1949) and *The Lavender Hill Mob* (1951), was finally chosen to adapt the work for the screen, wisely electing to retain much of Lawrence's original dialogue.

The casting proved problematic, with Cardiff and the Fox executives often butting heads over differing opinions. Harry Andrews was the studio's first choice for the role of Walter Morel, although the part eventually went to Cardiff's contender, Trevor Howard. Similarly, Cardiff had wanted Albert Finney to play Paul Morel, but when he proved unavailable, the studio made numerous (unlikely) suggestions including Sean Connery and Richard Harris, before finally offering the role to Dean Stockwell.

Sons and Lovers was shot on location in Nottingham and the surrounding Midlands areas, making much use of Lawrence's real childhood haunts. Despite its tight budget, the film is a visual masterpiece, thanks in no small part to the outstanding cinematography of Freddie Francis, and was showered with critical praise on its release, receiving seven Academy Award nominations for: T E B Clarke and Gavin Lambert (Best Screenplay Based on Material from Another Medium), Jerry Wald (Best Picture), Mary Ure (Best Supporting Actress), Trevor Howard (Best Actor), Lionel Couch and Thomas Morahan (Best Art Direction, Black and White), Freddie Francis (Best Cinematography, Black and White) and Jack Cardiff (Best Director). Of the seven, only Francis won for his cinematography.

Young Cassidy (1964)
Director: Jack Cardiff

Young Cassidy is based on the life of Dublin writer Sean O'Casey and draws largely on his autobiography, which was published as six individual volumes beginning in 1939

and later collectively as *Mirror in My House* in 1956. The film follows his poverty stricken early life, through the political troubles that shaped much of his work, and culminates in the opening of his third play *The Plough and the Stars* (its name taken from the banner of the Irish Citizen Army), which was dedicated to his mother: 'To the gay laugh of my mother at the gate of the grave.' Rod Taylor, in what is often regarded as the best performance of his life, plays the O'Casey character, John Cassidy, with sterling support from Flora Robson as Mrs Cassidy, Maggie Smith as Nora, Michael Redgrave as Yeats and a revelatory turn from a young Julie Christie as Daisy.

Jack Cardiff was called in to take up the directorial reins after the original director, John Ford, was taken ill during production. As a result, the two are often erroneously credited as co-directors, and upon its release critics often, unfairly, attributed many of the film's finest scenes to Ford; Cardiff himself calculates that no more than four minutes of the finished screen running time were directed by Ford.

The fine period detail and the authentic look of *Young Cassidy* are a credit to Edward Scaife's cinematography, Michael Stringer's art direction and Margaret Furse's costume design, which was nominated for a BAFTA. The film was edited by Anne Coates, fresh from her Academy Award-winning work on David Lean's *Lawrence of Arabia* (1962).

Girl on a Motorcycle (1968)
Director: Jack Cardiff

Girl on a Motorcycle was Jack Cardiff's last great film as a director, his two films of the early 1970s, *Penny Gold* and *The Mutations* (both 1973) passing largely unnoticed.

Girl on a Motorcycle, based on the novel *La Motocyclette* by André Pieyre De

Mandiargue and adapted by Ronald Duncan and Gillian Freeman, follows Rebecca (Marianne Faithfull) as she leaves her husband, Raymond (Roger Mutton), and heads out on the open road to revisit her lover, played by Alain Delon. The psychedelic road movie is pure late-1960s zeitgeist, which still retains a cult following among audiences. Cardiff both directed and photographed the film, adding hypnotic 'solarization' techniques to his Technicolor cinematography, which acted to both heighten the sense of the decade's drug-culture obsessions and more prosaically to help obscure certain scenes that may otherwise have proved problematic with the censors.

Two versions were released: one in French, opening on 21 June 1968, in Paris and the other in English, opening on 12 September 1968 in London. The film was extremely well received by the critics, with the exception of the London press, who inexplicably pilloried it. Regardless, *Girl on a Motorcycle* went on to be one of the top grossing films of the year.

Filmography

My Son (1918)
Cast: Stewart Rome, Violet Hopson, Jack Cardiff

Billy's Rose (1922)
Writer: George R Sims (poem)
Cast: Jack Cardiff, Jack's mother and father

The Loves of Mary Queen of Scots (1922)
Director: Denison Clift
Writer: Denison Clift
Cast: Fay Compton (Mary Stuart), Gerald Ames (Bothwell), Harvey Braban (Ruthven), Irene Rooke (Catherine de Medici), Ellen Compton (Queen Elizabeth), Basil Rathbone (uncredited), Jack Cardiff

Tip Toes (1927)
Director: Herbert Wilcox
Writer: Guy Bolton, Fred Thompson (novel)
Cast: Dorothy Gish (Tiptoes Kaye), Will Rogers (Uncle Hen Kaye), Denis Hoey, Nelson Keys, John Manners, Jack Cardiff

The Informer (1928)
Director: Arthur Robison
Writers: Benn W Levy, Rolf E Vanloo, Liam O'Flaherty (play)
Cinematographers: Werner Brandes, Theodor Sparkuhl
Production runner: Jack Cardiff
Cast: Lya De Putti (Katie Fox), Lars Hanson (Gypo Nolan), Warwick Ward (Dan Gallagher), Carl Harbord (Francis McPhillip), Janice Adair (Bessie), Ray Milland (uncredited)

The American Prisoner (1928)
Director: Thomas Bentley
Writers: Eliot Stannard, Garnett Weston
Cinematographer: René Guissart
Clapper boy: Jack Cardiff
Cast: Charles Ashton (Carberry), Cecil Barry (Peter Norcutt), Carl Brisson (Lt Stark), Madeleine Carroll (Grace Malherb), A Bromley Davenport (Squire Malherb), Robert English (Col Governor)

The Hate Ship (1929)
Director: Norman Walker
Writers: Monckton Hoffe, Eliot Stannard, Bruce Graeme (novel)
Cinematographer: René Guissart
Assistant Camera: Jack Cardiff
Cast: Randle Ayrton (Captain MacDarrell), Jean Colin (Sylvia Paget), Syd Crossley (Rigby), Edna Davies (Lisette), Ivo Dawson (Col Paget), Charles Dormer (Nigel Menzies)

Harmony Heaven (1930)
Director: Thomas Bentley
Writers: Randall Faye, Frank Launder, Arthur Wimperis
Cinematographer: Theodor Sparkuhl
Clapper boy: Jack Cardiff
Cast: Trilby Clark (Lady Violet Mistley), Aubrey Fitzgerald (Suggs), Stuart Hall (Bob Farrell), Philip Hewland (Beasley Cutting), Jack Raine (Stuart), Gus Sharland (Stage Manager)

Loose Ends (1930)
Director: Norman Walker
Writers: Norman Walker, Dion Titheradge (play)
Editor: Emile DeAuelle
Cinematographer: Claude Friese-Greene
Camera assistant: Jack Cardiff
Cast: Miles Mander (Raymond Carteret), Edna Best (Nina Grant), Adrianne Allen (Brenda Fallon), Donald Calthrop (Winton Penner), Edna Davies (Deborah Price), Gerard Lyley (Cyril Gayling)

The Flame of Love (AKA The Road to Dishonour) (1930)
Directors: Richard Eichberg, Walter Summers (additional footage)
Producer: Richard Eichberg
Writers: Monckton Hoffe, Adolf Lantz, Walter Summers, Ludwig Wolff
Editor: Emile de Ruelle
Cinematographers: Otto Baecker, Heinrich Gärtner, Bruno Mondi, Willi Herrmann, Werner Schlichting
Camera assistant: Jack Cardiff
Cast: Anna May Wong (Hai Tang), John Longden

(Lt Boris), Mona Goya (Yvette), Percy Standing (Col Moravjev), Louis Lerch, Alexander Granach

1931–33

Employed on various 'British Quota Quickie' films, titles now unknown. Directors included Tom Walls and Ralph Lynn.

The Ghost Train (1931)

Director: Walter Forde
Producers: Michael Balcon, Phil C Samuel
Writers: Lajos Biró, Sidney Gilliat, Angus MacPhail, Arnold Ridley (play)
Editor: Ian Dalrymple
Cinematographer: Leslie Rowson
Art Director: Walter W Murton
Camera Assistant: Jack Cardiff
Cast: Jack Hulbert (Teddy Deakin), Cicely Courtneidge (Miss Bourne), Donald Calthrop (Saul Hodgkin), Angela Baddeley (Julia Price), Cyril Raymond (Richard Winthrop), Ann Todd (Peggy Murdock)

The Skin Game (1931)

Director: Alfred Hitchcock
Producer: John Maxwell
Writers: Alfred Hitchcock, Alma Reville, John Galsworthy (play)
Editors: A R Gobbett, Rene Marrison
Cinematographer: J J Cox
Art Director: J B Maxwell
Clapper Boy: Jack Cardiff
Cast: Edmund Gwenn (Mr Hornblower), Helen Haye (Amy Hillcrest), C V France (Squire John Hillcrest), Jill Esmond (Jill Hillcrest), Phyllis Konstam (Chloe Hornblower), John Longden (Charles Hornblower)

Diamond Cut Diamond (1932)

Directors: Fred Niblo, Maurice Elvey
Producer: Eric Hakim, Sol Lesser
Writer: Viscount Castlerosse
Assistant Camera: Jack Cardiff
Cast: Adolphe Menjou (Dan McQueen), Claud Allister (Joe Fragson), Benita Hume (Marda Blackett), Kenneth Kove (Reggie Dean), Desmond Jeans (Blackett)

Brewster's Millions (1935)

Director: Thornton Freeland
Producer: Herbert Wilcox
Writers: Douglas Furber, Paul Gangelin, Clifford Grey, George Barr McCutcheon (play)
Cinematographer: Barney McGill
Camera Operator: Jack Cardiff
Music: Ray Noble
Cast: Jack Buchanan (Jack Brewster), Lili Damita (Rosalie), Nancy O'Neil (Cynthia), Sydney Fairbrother (Miss Plimsole), Ian Maclean (McLeod), Fred Emney (Freddy)

The Ghost Goes West (1935)

Director: René Clair
Producer: Alexander Korda
Writers: Robert E Sherwood, René Clair, Geoffrey Kerr
Editors: Harold Earle-Fishbacher, Henry Cornelius
Cinematographer: Harold Rosson
Camera Operator: Jack Cardiff
Music: Michael Spolianski
Set Designer: Vincent Korda
Special Effects: Ned Mann, W Percy Day (matte paintings)
Cast: Robert Donat (Murdoch Donald Glourie), Jean Parker (Peggy Martin), Eugene Pallette (Joe Martin), Elsa Lanchester (Lady Shepperton), Ralph Bunker (Ed Bigelow), Patricia Hilliard (Shepherdess)

Honeymoon for Three (1935)

Director: Leo Mittler
Producer: Stanley Lupino
Writers: Frank Miller, Stanley Lupino
Cinematographer: George Stretton
Camera Operator: Jack Cardiff
Cast: Stanley Lupino (Jack Denver), Aileen Marson (Yvonne Daumery), Jack Melford (Raymond Dirk), Robert English (Herbert Denver), Dennis Hoey (M Daumery), Arty Ash (Herbert Jones)

As You Like It (1936)

Director: Paul Czinner
Producer: Paul Czinner
Writers: James M Barrie, Robert Cullen, William Shakespeare (play)
Editor: David Lean
Cinematographer: Harold Rosson, Jack Cardiff

Music: William Walton

Art Director: Lazare Meerson

Cast: Elisabeth Bergner (Rosalind), Laurence Olivier (Orlando), Sophie Stewart (Celia), Henry Ainley (Exiled Duke), Leon Quartermaine (Jacques), Mackenzie Ward (Touchstone)

Things to Come (1936)

Director: William Cameron Menzies

Producer: Alexander Korda

Writers: Lajos Biró, H G Wells (novel)

Editors: Charles Crichton, Francis D Lyon

Cinematographer: Georges Périnal

Camera Operator: Jack Cardiff

Music: Arthur Bliss

Art Director: Vincent Korda

Special Effects: Ned Mann, W Percy Day (matte paintings)

Cast: Raymond Massey (John Cabal/Oswald Cabal), Edward Chapman (Pippa Passworthy/Raymond Passworthy), Ralph Richardson (The Boss), Margaretta Scott (Roxana Rowena), Cedric Hardwicke (Theotocopulos), Maurice Braddell (Dr Harding)

The Man Who Could Work Miracles (1936)

Director: Lothar Mendes

Producer: Alexander Korda

Writer: Lajos Biró, H G Wells (novel)

Editors: William Hornbeck, Philip Charlot

Cinematographer: Harold Rosson

Camera Operator: Jack Cardiff

Music: Michael Spoliansky

Special Effects: Ned Mann, W Percy Day (matte paintings)

Cast: Roland Young (George McWhirter Fotheringay), Ralph Richardson (Col Winstanley), Edward Chapman (Major Grigsby), Ernest Thesiger (Mr Maydig), Joan Gardner (Ada Price), Sophie Stewart (Maggie Hooper)

Coronation of King George VI (Documentary)

Camera operator: Jack Cardiff

Wings of the Morning (1937)

Director: Harold Schuster

Producer: Robert T Kane

Writer: Tom Geraghty, Brian Oswald Donn-Byrne

Editor: James B Clark

Cinematographers: Ray Rennahan, Henry Imus

Camera Operator: Jack Cardiff

Music: Arthur Benjamin

Cast: Annabella (Marie), Leslie Banks (Lord Clontarf), Henry Fonda (Kerry), D J Williams (Marik), Philip Frost (Valentine), Stewart Rome (Sir Valentine), Irene Vanbrugh (Marie)

1937–40

Jack Cardiff filmed numerous travelogues in the *World Windows* series, produced by Count von Keller.

Dark Journey (1937)

Director: Victor Saville

Producer: Alexander Korda, Victor Saville

Writer: Arthur Wimperis, Lajos Biró (play)

Editors: William Hornbeck, Hugh Stewart, Lionel Hoare

Cinematographers: Georges Périnal, Harry Stradling

Camera Operator: Jack Cardiff

Music: Richard Addinsell

Special Effects: Ned Mann

Cast: Conrad Veidt (Baron Karl von Marwitz), Vivien Leigh (Madeleine Godard), Joan Gardner (Lupita), Anthony Bushell (Bob Carter), Ursula Jeans (Gertrude), Eliot Makeham (Anatole Bergen)

Knight Without Armour (1937)

Director: Jacques Feyder

Producer: Alexander Korda

Writers: Lajos Biró, Arthur Wimperis, Frances Marion, James Hilton (novel)

Editors: William Hornbeck, A W Watkins

Cinematographers: Harry Stradling, Bernard Browne

Camera Operator: Jack Cardiff

Music: Miklós Rózsa

Special Effects: Ned Mann, W Percy Day (matte paintings)

Cast: Marlene Dietrich (Alexandra Vladinoff), Robert Donat (Ainsley Fothergill), Irene Vanbrugh (Duchess of Zorin), Herbert Lomas (Gen Gregor Vladinoff), Austin Trevor (Col Adraxine), Basil Gill (Axelstein)

Paris on Parade (1938)

Director: James Fitzpatrick

Producer: James Fitzpatrick

Music: Jack Shilkret

Cinematographer: Jack Cardif
Cast: James Fitzpatrick (narrator)

The Four Feathers (1939)

Director: Zoltan Korda
Producer: Alexander Korda
Writer: R C Sherriff, Lajos Biró, Arthur Wimperis, A E W Mason (novel)
Editor: William Hornbeck, Henry Cornelius
Cinematographers: Georges Périnal, Osmond Borradaile
Camera Operator: Jack Cardiff
Music: Miklós Rózsa
Cast: John Clements (Harry Faversham), Ralph Richardson (Capt John Durrance), C Aubrey Smith (Gen Burroughs), June Duprez (Ethne Burroughs), Allan Jeays (Gen Faversham), Jack Allen (Lt Willoughby), Georges Périnal, Osmond Borradaile (Narrators)

Main Street of Paris (1939)

Director: Jean Bernard
Cinematographer: Jack Cardiff

Cadburys commercial (1939)

Camera Operator: Jack Cardiff

Peasant Island (1940)

Director: Ralph Keene
Cinematographer: Jack Cardiff

Green Girdle (1941)

Director: Ralph Keetie
Producer: Basil Wright
Cinematographer: Jack Cardiff
Music: Richard Addinsell
Cast: Bruce Belfrage (Commentary), Robert MacDermot (Commentary)

Queen Cotton (1941)

Director: Cecil Musk
Cinematographer: Jack Cardiff

Plastic Surgery in Wartime (1941)

Director: Frank Sainsbury
Producer: John Taylor
Cinematographer: Jack Cardiff

Western Isles (1941)

Director: Terence Bishop
Cinematographer: Jack Cardiff

Music: William Alwyn
Cast: Jospeh Macleod (Commentary)

Border Weave (1942)

Director: John Lewis Curthoys
Producer: George E Turner
Cinematographer: Jack Cardiff

Colour In Clay (1942)

Director: Catling
Cinematographer: Jack Cardiff

The Great Mr Handel (1942)

Director: Norman Walker
Producer: James B Sloan
Writers: Gerald Elliot, Victor MacLure, L du Garde Peach
Editor: Sam Simmonds
Cinematographers: Jack Cardiff, Claude Friese-Green
Cast: Wilfred Lawson (George Frederic Handel), Elizabeth Allan (Mrs Cibber), Allan Malcolm (Lord Chesterfield), Max Kirby (Prince of Wales)

Out of the Box (1942)

Director: Terence Bishop
Cinematographer: Jack Cardiff

This is Colour (1942)

Director: Jack Ellitt
Producer: Basil Wright
Cinematographer: Jack Cardiff
Cast: Richard Addinsell, Dylan Thomas, Marjorie Fielding (Commentary)

Western Approaches (1942)

Director: Pat Jackson
Producer: Ian Dalrymple
Writer: Pat Jackson, Gerry Bryant
Editor: Jocelyn Jackson
Cinematographer: Jack Cardiff
Music: Clifton Parker
Art Director: Edward Carrick
Cast: Burt Wadham (Wireless Officer on Leander), Chief Engineer Russell (Lifeboat Chief Engineer), Eric Baskeyfield (Chief Officer on Leander), Chief Petty Officer Hills (Gunner on Leander), Captain P J Pyecraft (Lifeboat Captain)

Scottish Mazurka (1943)

Director: Hans Nieter
Cinematographer: Jack Cardiff

The Life and Death of Colonel Blimp (1943)

Directors: Michael Powell, Emeric Pressburger
Producers: Michael Powell, Emeric Pressburger
Writers: Michael Powell, Emeric Pressburger
Editor: John Seabourne
Cinematographer: Georges Périnal
Second-unit (photographed and lit inserts): Jack Cardiff
Music: Allan Gray
Production Designer: Alfred Junge
Special Effects: W Percy Day
Cast: Roger Livesey (Clive Candy), Deborah Kerr (Edith Hunter/Barbara Wynne/Johnny Cannon), Anton Walbrook (Theo Kretschmar-Schuldorff), Roland Culver (Col Betteridge), James McKechnie (Spud Wilson), Albert Lieven (Von Ritter)

Steel (1945)

Director: Ronald Riley
Producer: Ronald Riley
Cinematography: Jack Cardiff

Caesar and Cleopatra (1945)

Director: Gabriel Pascal
Producers: Gabriel Pascal, J Arthur Rank
Writer: George Bernard Shaw
Editor: Frederick Wilson
Cinematographer: Freddie Young
Second-unit Egypt (exteriors only): Jack Cardiff
Music: Georges Auric
Art Director: John Bryan
Cast: Claude Rains (Julius Caesar), Vivien Leigh (Cleopatra), Stewart Granger (Apollodorus), Flora Robson (Ftatateeta), Francis L Sullivan (Pothinus)

A Matter of Life and Death (AKA Stairway to Heaven) (1946)

Directors: Michael Powell, Emeric Pressburger
Producers: Michael Powell, Emeric Pressburger
Writers: Michael Powell, Emeric Pressburger
Editor: Reginald Mills
Cinematographer: Jack Cardiff
Music: Reginald Mills
Production Designer: Alfred Junge
Cast: David Niven (Squadron Leader Peter D Carter), Kim Hunter (June), Roger Livesey (Dr Reeves), Marius Goring (Conductor 71), Raymond Massey (Abraham Farlan), Kathleen Byron (An Angel), Richard Attenborough (English Pilot)

Black Narcissus (1947)

Directors: Michael Powell, Emeric Pressburger
Producers: Michael Powell, Emeric Pressburger
Writers: Michael Powell, Emeric Pressburger
Editor: Reginald Mills
Cinematographer: Jack Cardiff
Music: Brian Easdale
Production Designer: Alfred Junge
Special Effects: W Percy Day (matte paintings)
Cast: Deborah Kerr (Sister Clodagh), Kathleen Byron (Sister Ruth), Flora Robson (Sister Philippa), David Farrar (Mr Dean), Sabu (Dilip Rai), Jean Simmons (Kanchi), Edmond Knight (Gen Toda Rai)

The Red Shoes (1948)

Directors: Michael Powell, Emeric Pressburger
Producers: Michael Powell, Emeric Pressburger
Writers: Michael Powell, Emeric Pressburger, Keith Winter, Hans Christian Andersen (novel)
Editor: Reginald Mills
Cinematographer: Jack Cardiff
Music: Brian Easdale
Music Director: Sir Thomas Beecham
Choreography: Robert Helpmann
Production Designers: Hein Heckroth, Arthur Lawson
Cast: Anton Walbrook (Boris Lermontov), Moira Shearer (Victoria Page), Marius Goring (Julian Craster), Léonide Massine (Grischa Ljubov), Robert Helpmann (Ivan Boleslawsky), Albert Basserman (Sergei Ratov), Edmond Knight (Livy)

Scott of the Antarctic (1948)

Director: Charles Frend
Producer: Michael Balcon
Writers: Walter Meade, Ivor Montagu, Mary Hayley Bell
Editor: Peter Tanner
Cinematographer: Jack Cardiff
Additional Photography: Osmond Borradaile, Geoffrey Unsworth
Music: Ralph Vaughan Williams
Music Director: Ernest Irving
Production Designers: Arne Akermark, Jim Morahan
Cast: John Mills (Captain Robert Falcon Scott), Derek Bond (Captain L E G Oates), Harold Warrender (Dr E A Wilson), James Robertson

Justice (Petty Officer Taffy Evans), Reginald Beckwith (Lt H R Bowers), Kenneth More (Lt Teddy Evans)

Under Capricorn (1949)

Director: Alfred Hitchcock
Producers: Sidney Bernstein, Alfred Hitchcock
Writers: Hume Cronyn, James Bridie, Helen Simpson (novel), John Colton (play), Margaret Linden (play)
Editor: A S Bates
Cinematographer: Jack Cardiff
Music: Richard Addinsell
Production Designer: Thomas Morahan
Cast: Ingrid Bergman (Henrietta Flusky), Joseph Cotten (Sam Flusky), Michael Wilding (Charles Adare), Margaret Leighton (Milly), Jack Watling (Winter), Alfred Hitchcock (Man at Governor's reception - uncredited)

Montmartre/Montmartre Nocturne (AKA Paris) (1950)

Director: Jack Cardiff
Producer: Jean Bernard
Cinematographer: Jack Cardiff

The Black Rose (1950)

Director: Henry Hathaway
Producer: Louis D Lighton
Writers: Talbot Jennings, Thomas B Costain (novel)
Editor: Manuel del Campo
Cinematographer: Jack Cardiff
Music: Richard Addinsell
Production Designers: William C Andrews, Paul Sheriff
Special effects: W Percy Day
Cast: Tyrone Power (Walter of Gurnie), Orson Welles (Bayan), Cécile Aubry (Maryam), Jack Hawkins (Tristram Griffin), Michael Rennie (King Edward), Finlay Currie (Alfgar)

Pandora and the Flying Dutchman (1951)

Director: Albert Lewin
Producers: Albert Lewin, Joseph Kaufman
Writer: Albert Lewin
Editor: Ralph Kemplen
Cinematographer: Jack Cardiff
Music: Alan Rawsthorne
Production Designer: John Bryan
Cast: James Mason (Hendrick van der Zee), Ava Gardner (Pandora Reynolds), Nigel Patrick (Stephen Cameron), Sheila Sim (Janet Fielding), Harold Warrender (Geoffrey Fielding), Mario Cabre (Juan Mantalvo), John Laurie (Angus)

The African Queen (1951)

Director: John Huston
Producers: Sam Spiegel, John Woolf
Writers: James Agee, John Huston, C S Forester (novel)
Editor: Ralph Kemplen
Cinematographer: Jack Cardiff
Music: Allan Gray
Production designer: Wilfred Shingleton
Cast: Humphrey Bogart (Charlie Allnut), Katharine Hepburn (Rose Sayer), Robert Morley (Rev Samuel Sayer), Peter Bull (Captain of Louisa)

The Magic Box (1951)

Director: John Boulting
Producer: Ronald Neame
Writer: Eric Ambler, Ray Allister (biography, *Friese-Greene: Close-Up of an Inventor*)
Editor: Richard Best
Cinematographer: Jack Cardiff
Music: William Alwyn
Production Designer: John Bryan
Cast: Renée Asherson (Miss Tagg), Richard Attenborough (Jack Carter), Robert Beatty (Lord Beaverbrook), John Charlesworth (Graham Friese-Greene), John Howard Davies (Maurice Friese-Greene), Robert Donat (William Friese-Greene), Mary Ellis (Mrs Collings)

It Started in Paradise (1952)

Director: Compton Bennett
Producers: Sergei Nolbandov, Leslie Parkyn
Writer: Marghanita Laski
Editor: Alan Osbiston
Cinematographer: Jack Cardiff
Music: Malcolm Arnold
Production Designer: Edward Carrick
Cast: Martita Hunt (Mme Alice), Jane Hylton (Martha Watkins), Muriel Pavlow (Alison), Ilan Hunter (Arthur Turner), Brian Worth (Michael)

The Master of Ballantrae (1953)

Director: William Keighley
Writers: Herb Meadow, Harold Medford, Robert Louis Stevenson (novel)
Editor: Jack Harris

Cinematographer: Jack Cardiff
Music: William Alwyn
Music Director: Muir Mathieson
Art Director: Ralph W Brinton
Cast: Errol Flynn (James Durrisdeer), Roger Livesey (Col Francis Burke), Anthony Steel (Henry Durrisdeer), Beatrice Campbell (Lady Alison), Yvonne Furneaux (Jessie Brown), Jacques Berthier (Arnaud), Felix Aylmer (Lord Durrisdeer), Mervyn Johns (MacKellar)

William Tell (unfinished project) (1953)
Director: Jack Cardiff
Cast: Errol Flynn (William Tell), Antonella Lualdi, Bruce Cabot, Waltraut Haas

Il Maestro di Don Giovanni (AKA Crossed Swords) (1953)
Directors: Milton Krims, Vittorio Vassarotti
Producers: J Barret Mahon, Vittorio Vassarotti
Writer: Milton Krims
Cinematographer: Jack Cardiff
Art Director: Arrigo Equin
Cast: Errol Flynn (Renzo), Gina Lollobrigida (Francesca), Cesare Danova (Raniero), Nadia Gray (Fulvia), Paola Mori (Tomasina), Roldano Lupi (Pavoncello)

The Barefoot Contessa (1954)
Director: Joseph L Mankiewicz
Producer: Joseph L Mankiewicz
Writer: Joseph L. Mankiewicz
Editor: William Hornbeck
Cinematographer: Jack Cardiff
Music: Mario Nascimbene
Cast: Humphrey Bogart (Harry Dawes), Ava Gardner (Maria Vargas), Edmond O'Brien (Oscar Muldoon), Marius Goring (Alberto Bravano), Valentina Cortese (Eleanora Torlato-Favrini)

The Brave One (1954)
Director: Irving Rapper
Producers: Maurice King, Frank King
Writers: Dalton Trumbo, Harry S Franklin, Merrill G White
Editor: Merrill White
Cinematographer: Jack Cardiff
Cast: Michel Ray (Leonardo), Rodolfo Hoyos (Rafael Rosillo), Elsa Cardenas (Maria), Carlos Navarro (Don Alejandro), Joi Lansing (Marion Randall)

War and Peace (1956)
Director: King Vidor
Producer: Dino de Laurentiis
Writers: Bridget Boland, Robert Westerby, King Vidor, Mario Camerini, Ennio de Concini, Ivo Perilli, Irwin Shaw, Leo Tolstoy (novel)
Editors: Stuart Gilmore, Leo Catozzo
Cinematographer: Jack Cardiff
Music: Nino Rota
Art Director: Mario Chiari
Cast: Audrey Hepburn (Natasha Rostov), Henry Fonda (Pierre Bezukhov), Mel Ferrer (Prince Andrei Bolkonsky), Vittorio Gassman (Anatole Kuragin), John Mills (Platon Karatayev), Herbert Lom (Napoleon)

The Big Money (1956)
Director: John Paddy Carstairs
Writer: John Baines
Editor: Alfred Roome
Cinematographer: Jack Cardiff
Music: Van Phillips
Cast: Ian Carmichael (Willie Frith), Belinda Lee (Gloria), Kathleen Harrison (Mrs Frith), Robert Helpmann (Reverend)

Legend of the Lost (1957)
Director: Henry Hathaway
Producer: Henry Hathaway
Writers: Ben Hecht, Robert Presnell Jnr
Editor: Bert Bates
Cinematographer: Jack Cardiff
Music: Angelo Francesco Lavagnino
Art Director: Alfred Ybarra
Cast: John Wayne (Joe January), Sophia Loren (Dita), Rossano Brazzi (Paul Bonnard), Kurt Kasznar (Prefect Dukas), Sonia Moser (Girl), Angela Portaluri (Girl), Ibrahim El Hadish (Galli Galli)

The Prince and the Showgirl (1957)
Director: Laurence Olivier
Producer: Laurence Olivier
Writer: Terence Rattigan (plus play, *The Sleeping Prince*)
Editor: Jack Harris
Cinematographer: Jack Cardiff
Music: Richard Addinsell
Production Designer: Roger Furse
Cast: Marilyn Monroe (Elsie Marina), Laurence Olivier (Charles), Sybil Thorndike (Queen

Dowager), Richard Wattis (Northbrooke), Jeremy Spenser (King Nicholas), Edmond Knight (Hoffman)

The Diary of Anne Frank (1958)
Director: George Stevens
Producer: George Stevens
Writers: Frances Goodrich, Albert Hackett, Anne Frank (diary)
Editors: Robert Swink, William Mace, David Brotherton
Cinematographer: William Mellor
Location Cinematographer: Jack Cardiff
Music: Alfred Newman
Art Directors: Stuart A Reiss, Walter M Scott
Cast: Millie Perkins (Anne Frank), Joseph Schildkraut (Otto Frank), Shelley Winters (Mrs Van Daan), Richard Beymer (Peter Van Daan), Gusti Huber (Edith Frank), Lou Jacobi (Mr Van Daan), Diane Baker (Margot Frank)

The Vikings (1958)
Director: Richard Fleischer
Producer: Jerry Bresler
Writers: Dale Wasserman, Calder Willingham, Edison Marshall (novel)
Editor: Elmo Williams
Cinematographer: Jack Cardiff
Music: Mario Nascimbene
Production Designer: Harper Goff
Cast: Kirk Douglas (Einar), Tony Curtis (Eric), Ernest Borgnine (King Ragnar), Janet Leigh (Princess Morgana), James Donald (Lord Egbert), Orson Welles (Narrator)

Intent to Kill (1958)
Director: Jack Cardiff
Producer: Adrian D Worker
Writer: Jimmy Sangster
Editor: Tom Simpson
Cinematographer: Desmond Dickinson
Music Director: Muir Mathieson
Music: Ken Jones
Art Director: Allan Harris
Cast: Richard Todd (Dr Bob McLaurin), Betsy Drake (Dr Nancy Ferguson), Herbert Lom (Juan Menda), Warren Stevens (Finch), Carlo Justini (Francisco Flores)

Beyond This Place (1959)
Director: Jack Cardiff

Producers: Maxwell Setton, John R. Sloan
Writers: Kenneth Taylor, A J Cronin (novel)
Editor: Ernest Walter
Cinematographer: Wilkie Cooper
Music: Douglas Gamley
Cast: Van Johnson (Paul Mathry), Jameson Clark (Swann), Michael Collins (Detective Sergeant Trevor), Vera Miles (Lena Anderson), Rosalie Crutchley (Ella Mathry), John Glyn-Jones (Magistrate), Danny Green (Roach), Joyce Heron (Lady Catherine Sprott)

Fanny (1960)
Director: Joshua Logan
Producer: Joshua Logan
Writer: Julius J Epstein, S N Behrman (play), Joshua Logan (play), Marcel Pagnol (original trilogy)
Editor: William H Reynolds
Cinematographer: Jack Cardiff
Music: Harold Rome
Art Director: Rino Mondellini
Cast: Leslie Caron (Fanny), Maurice Chevalier (Panisse), Charles Boyer (Cesar), Horst Buchholz (Marius), Salvatore Baccaloni (Escartifique), Lionel Jeffries (Monsieur Brun)

Scent of Mystery (1960)
Director: Jack Cardiff
Producer: Michael Todd Jnr
Writers: Gerald Kersh, Kelley Roos, William Rose
Editor: James E Newcom
Cinematographer: John von Kotze
Art Director: Vincent Korda
Production Designer: Vincent Korda
Music: Harold Adamson, Mario Nascimbene, Jordan Ramin
Costume: Charles Simminger
Cast: Mary Laura Wood (Margharita), Peter Arne (Robert Fleming), Beverly Bentley (Decoy Sally), Diana Dors (Winifred Jordan), Denholm Elliott (Oliver Larker), Peter Lorre (Smiley), Elizabeth Taylor (uncredited)

Sons and Lovers (1960)
Director: Jack Cardiff
Producer: Jerry Wald
Writers: Gavin Lambert, T E B (Thomas) Clarke
Cinematographer: Freddie Francis
Music: Mario Nascimbene
Art Director: Lionel Couch
Cast: Trevor Howard (Walter Morel), Dean

Stockwell (Paul Morel), Wendy Hiller (Mrs Morel), Mary Ure (Clara Dawes), Heather Sears (Miriam Lievers), William Lucas (William), Conrad Phillips (Baxter Dawes), Donald Pleasance (Pappleworth)

My Geisha (1962)
Director: Jack Cardiff
Producer: Steve Parker
Writer: Norman Krasna
Editor: Archie Marshek
Cinematographer: Shunichiro Nakao
Music: Franz Waxman
Art Directors: Hal Pereira, Arthur Lonergan, Makoto Kikuchi
Costumes: Edith Head
Cast: Shirley MacLaine (Lucy Dell Yoko Mori), Yves Montand (Paul Robaix), Edward G Robinson (Sam Lewis), Robert Cummings (Bob Moore), Yoko Tani (Kazumi Ito)

The Lion (1962)
Director: Jack Cardiff
Producer: Samuel G Engel
Writers: Irene Kamp, Louis Kamp, Joseph Kessel
Editor: Russell Lloyd
Cinematographer: Edward Scaife
Art Directors: John Hoesli, Alan Withy
Music: Malcolm Arnold
Cast: William Holden (Robert Hayward), Trevor Howard (John Bullit), Capucine (Christine), Pamela Franklin (Tina), Samuel Obiero Romboh (Kihero), Christopher Agunda (Elder of Masai), Paul Oduor (Orlunga)

The Long Ships (1963)
Director: Jack Cardiff
Producer: Irving Allen
Writers: Frans G Bengtsson, Beverley Cross, Berkely Mather
Editor: Geoffrey Foot
Cinematographer: Christopher Challis
Music: Dusan Radic
Production Designers: Vlastimir Gavrik, Zoran Zorcic
Cast: Richard Widmark (Rolfe), Sidney Poitier (Aly Mansuh), Rosanna Schiaffino (Aminah), Russ Tamblyn (Orm), Oskar Homolka (Krok), Lionel Jeffries (Aziz)

Young Cassidy (1964)
Directors: Jack Cardiff (John Ford additional footage)
Producers: Robert D Graff, Robert Emmett Ginna
Writer: John Whiting, Sean O'Casey (autobiography, *Mirror in My House*)
Editor: Anne V Coates
Cinematographer: Ted Scaife
Music: Sean O'Riada
Cast: Rod Taylor (John Cassidy), Flora Robson (Mrs Cassidy), Jack MacGowran (Archie), Siân Phillips (Ella), T P McKenna (Tom), Julie Ross (Sara), Robin Sumner (Michael), Philip O'Flynn (Mick Mullen), Maggie Smith (Nora), Julie Christie (Daisy Battles), Michael Redgrave (William Butler Yeats)

The Liquidator (1965)
Director: Jack Cardiff
Producer: Jon Penington
Writer: Peter Yeldham, John Gardner (novel)
Editor: Ernest Walter
Cinematographer: Ted Scaife
Music: Lalo Schifrin
Cast: Rod Taylor (Boysie Oakes), Trevor Howard (Col Mostyn), Jill St John (Iris MacIntosh), Wilfrid Hyde-White (Chief), David Tomlinson (Quadrant), Eric Sykes (Griffen)

The Mercenaries (AKA Dark of the Sun) (1967)
Director: Jack Cardiff
Producer: George Englund
Writers: Quentin Werty, Adrian Spies, Wilbur Smith (novel)
Editor: Ernest Walter
Cinematographers: Ted Scaife, Jack Cardiff
Music: Jacques Loussier
Cast: Rod Taylor (Captain Bruce Curry), Yvette Mimieux (Claire), Jim Brown (Ruffo), Kenneth More (Dr Reid), Peter Carsten (Henlein), Olivier Despax (Surrier)

Girl on a Motorcycle (1968)
Director: Jack Cardiff
Producer: William Sassoon
Writers: Ronald Duncan, Gillian Freeman, André Pieyre De Mandiargues (novel)
Editor: Peter Musgrave
Cinematographer: Jack Cardiff
Music: Les Reed

Art Directors: Jean d'Eaubonne, Russell Hagg
Cast: Alain Delon (Daniel), Marianne Faithfull (Rebecca), Roger Mutton (Raymond), Marius Goring (Rebecca's Father), Catherine Jourdan (Catherine), Jean Leduc (Jean)

Penny Gold (1973)
Director: Jack Cardiff
Cast: James Booth, Penelope Keith, Joss Ackland, Francesca Annis, Nicky Henson

The Mutations (1973)
Director: Jack Cardiff
Producer: Robert D Weinbach
Writers: Edward Mann, Robert D Weinbach
Editor: John Trumper
Cinematographer: Paul Beeson
Music: Basil Kirchin
Art Director: Herbert Smith
Cast: Donald Pleasance (Professor Nolter), Tom Baker (Lynch), Brad Harris (Brian), Julie Ege (Hedi), Michael Dunn (Burns), Jill Haworth (Lauren)

Scalawag (1973)
Directors: Kirk Douglas
Producer: Anne Douglas
Writers: Sid Fleischman, Albert Maltz, Robert Louis Stevenson (novel)
Editor: John C Howard
Cinematographer: Jack Cardiff
Music: John Cameron
Cast: Kirk Douglas (Peg), Mark Lester (Jamie), Neville Brand (Brimstone/Mudhook), George Eastman (Don Aragon), Don Stroud (Velvet), Lesley-Anne Down (Lucy-Ann)

Ride a Wild Pony (1976)
Director: Don Chaffey
Producer: Jerome Courtland
Writer: Rosemary Anne Sisson, James Aldridge (novel)
Editor: Mike Campbell
Cinematographer: Jack Cardiff
Music: John Addison
Art Director: Robert Hilditch
Costumes: Judith Dorsman
Cast: Michael Craig (James Ellison), John Meillon (Charles E Quayle), Robert Bettles (Scotty Pirie), Eva Griffith (Josie Ellison), Graham Rouse (Bluey Waters), Alfred Bell (Angus Pirie)

Prince and the Pauper (1977)
Director: Richard Fleischer
Producers: Ilya Salkind, Pierre Spengler
Writers: Berta Domínguez, George MacDonald Fraser, Pierre Spengler, Mark Twain (novel)
Editor: Ernest Walter
Cinematographer: Jack Cardiff
Music: Maurice Jarre
Production Designer: Anthony Pratt
Costumes: Judy Moorcroft
Cast: Oliver Reed (Miles Hendon), Raquel Welch (Edith), Mark Lester (Edward/Tom), Ernest Borgnine (John Canty), George C Scott (The Ruffler), Rex Harrison (Duke of Norfolk), David Hemmings (Hugh Hendon)

Death on the Nile (1978)
Director: John Guillermin
Producers: John Brabourne, Richard Goodwin
Writer: Anthony Shaffer, Agatha Christie (novel)
Editor: Malcolm Cooke
Cinematographer: Jack Cardiff
Music: Nino Rota
Production Designer: Peter Murton
Art Design: Brian Ackland, Terry Ackland-Snow
Cast: Peter Ustinov (Hercule Poirot), Jane Birkin (Louise Bourget), Bette Davis (Mrs Van Schuyler), Mia Farrow (Jacqueline de Bellefort), Olivia Hussey (Rosalie Otterbourne), George Kennedy (Andrew Pennington), Angela Lansbury (Mrs Salome Otterbourne), Simon MacCorkindale (Simon Doyle), David Niven (Colonel Rice), Maggie Smith (Miss Bowers), Sam Wanamaker (Rockford)

Avalanche Express (1979)
Director: Mark Robson (Jack Cardiff: additional footage)
Producers: Lynn Guthrie, Mark Robson
Writer: Abraham Polonsky, Colin Forbes (novel)
Editor: Garth Craven
Cinematographer: Jack Cardiff
Music: Allyn Ferguson
Costumes: Mickey Sherrard
Cast: Lee Marvin (Col Harry Wargrave), Robert Shaw (General Marenkov), Linda Evans (Elsa Lang), Maximilian Schell (Nikolai Bunin), Joe Namath (Leroy)

A Man, a Woman and a Bank (1979)

Director: Noel Black
Producers: Peter Samuelson, John B Bennett
Writers: Raynold Gideon, Bruce A Evans, Stuart Margolin
Editor: Carl Kress
Cinematographer: Jack Cardiff
Music: Bill Conti
Production Designer: Anne Pritchard
Cast: Donald Sutherland (Reese), Brooke Adams (Stacey), Paul Mazursky (Norman), Allen Magicovsky (Peter), Leigh Hamilton (Marie)

The Fifth Musketeer (1979)

Director: Ken Annakin
Producer: Ted Richmond
Writer: David Ambrose, Alexandre Dumas (novel)
Cinematographer: Jack Cardiff
Music: Riz Ortolani
Art Director: Theo Harisch
Cast: Beau Bridges (King Louis), Sylvia Kristel (Marie-Therese), Ursula Andress (Mme de la Valliere), Cornel Wilde (D'Artagnan), Ian McShane (Fourquet), Lloyd Bridges (Aramis), Olivia de Havilland (Queen Anne), Rex Harrison (Colbert)

The Awakening (1980)

Director: Mike Newell
Producer: Robert Solo
Writers: Clive Exton, Chris Bryant, Allan Scott, Bram Stoker (novel)
Cinematographer: Jack Cardiff
Music: Claude Bolling
Production Designer: Michael Stringer
Cast: Charlton Heston (Matthew Corbeck), Susannah York (Jane Turner), Jill Townsend (Anne Corbeck), Stephanie Zimbalist (Margaret Corbeck)

The Dogs of War (1980)

Director: John Irvin
Producer: Larry De Waay
Writers: Gary DeVore, George Malko, Frederick Forsyth (novel)
Editor: Anthony Gibbs
Cinematographer: Jack Cardiff
Music: Geoffrey Burgon
Production Designer: Peter Mullins
Art Director: John Siddall, Bert Davey

Cast: Christopher Walken (Shannon), Tom Berenger (Drew), Colin Blakely (North), Hugh Millais (Endean), Paul Freeman (Derek), Jean-François (Stevenin Michel), JoBeth Williams (Jessie)

Ghost Story (1981)

Director: John Irvin
Producer: Burt Weissbourd
Writer: Larry Cohen, Peter Straub (novel)
Editor: Tom Rolf
Cinematographer: Jack Cardiff
Music: Philippe Sarde
Production Designer: Norman Newberry
Cast: Fred Astaire (Ricky Hawthorne), Melvyn Douglas (John Jeffrey), Douglas Fairbanks Jnr (Edward Wanderly), John Houseman (Sears James), Craig Wasson (Don David), Alice Krige (Alma Eva)

Scandalous (1983)

Director: Rob Cohen
Producers: Arlene Sellers, Alex Winitsky
Writers: John Byrum, Larry Cohen, Rob Cohen
Editor: Michael Bradsel
Cinematographer: Jack Cardiff
Music: Dave Grusin
Production Designer: Brian Ackland-Snow
Cast: Jim Dale (Anthony Crisp), John Gielgud (Uncle Willie), Robert Hays (Frank Swedlin), Pamela Stephenson (Fiona Maxwell Sayle), M Emmet Walsh (Simon Reynolds)

The Wicked Lady (1983)

Director: Michael Winner
Producers: Yoram Globus, Menahem Golan
Writers: Leslie Arliss, Michael Winner, Magdalen King-Hall (novel)
Editors: Arnold Crust Jnr, Michael Winner
Cinematographer: Jack Cardiff
Music: Tony Banks
Production Designer: John Blezard
Cast: Faye Dunaway (Lady Barbara Skelton), Alan Bates (Jerry Jackson), John Gielgud (Hogarth), Denholm Elliott (Sir Ralph Skelton), Prunella Scales (Lady Kingsclere), Oliver Tobias (Kit Locksby)

The Far Pavilions (1984)

Director: Peter Duffell
Producer: Geoffrey Reeve
Writers: Julian Bond, M M Kaye (novel)

Editors: Peter Boita, John Jympson
Cinematographer: Jack Cardiff
Music: Carl Davis
Production Designer: Robert W Laing
Cast: Ben Cross (Ashton 'Ash' Pelham-Martyn),
Amy Irving (Princess Anjuli), Christopher Lee
(Kaka-ji Rao), Benedict Taylor (Wally), Rossano
Brazzi (Rana of Bhitour), Saeed Jaffrey (Biju
Ram), Robert Hardy (Commandant)

The Last Days of Pompeii (1984)
Directors: Peter H Hunt, Peter R Hunt
Writer: Carmen Culver, Edward George Bulwer-
Lytton (novel)
Cinematographer: Jack Cardiff
Music: Trevor Jones
Art Director: John Roberts
Cast: Lesley-Anne Down (Chloe), Olivia
Hussey (Ione), Laurence Olivier (Gaius),
Anthony Quayle (Quintus), Tony Anholt
(Lepidus), Ned Beatty (Diomed), Brian Blessed
(Olinthus), Ernest Borgnine (Marcus), Donald
Pleasance

Conan the Destroyer (1984)
Director: Richard Fleischer
Producer: Raffaella De Laurentiis
Writer: Stanley Mann
Cinematographer: Jack Cardiff
Music: Basil Poledouris
Production Designer: Pier Luigi Basile
Cast: Arnold Schwarzenegger (Conan), Grace
Jones (Zula), Wilt Chamberlain (Bombaata),
Tracey Walter (Malak), Olivia d'Abo (Princess
Jehnna), André the Giant (Dagoth)

Cat's Eye (1985)
Director: Lewis Teague
Producer: Martha J. Schumacher
Writer: Stephen King
Cinematographer: Jack Cardiff
Music: Alan Silvestri
Art Director: Jeffrey Ginn
Cast: Drew Barrymore (Our Girl), James Woods
(Morrison), Alan King (Dr Donatti), Kenneth
McMillan (Creszner), Robert Hays (Norris),
Candy Clark (Sally Ann)

Rambo: First Blood, Part II (1985)
Director: George P Cosmatos
Producer: Buzz Feitshans
Writers: Kevin Jarre, James Cameron, Sylvester
Stallone
Cinematographer: Jack Cardiff
Music: Jerry Goldsmith
Production Designer: Bill Kenney
Cast: Sylvester Stallone (Rambo), Richard Crenna
(Trautman), Charles Napier (Murdock), Steven
Berkoff (Podovsky)

Tai-Pan (1986)
Director: Daryl Duke
Producer: Raffaella De Laurentiis
Writers: John Briley, Herbert Wright, James
Clavell (novel)
Art Director: Benjamín Fernández
Cinematographer: Jack Cardiff
Music: Maurice Jarre
Production Designer: Anthony Masters
Cast: Bryan Brown (Dirk Struan), Joan Chen
(May-May), Tim Guinee (Culum Struan), Bill
Leadbitter (Gorth Brock), Norman Rodway
(Aristotle Quance), Kyra Sedgwick (Tess
Brock)

Million Dollar Mystery (AKA Money Mania) (1987)
Director: Richard Fleischer
Producer: Stephen F Kesten
Writers: Rudy De Luca, Tim Metcalfe, Miguel
Tejada-Flores
Cinematographer: Jack Cardiff
Music: Paul Sabu
Cast: Jaime Alcroft (Bob), Royce D Applegate
(Tugger), Penny Baker (Charity), Tom Bosley
(Sidney Preston), Eddie Deezen (Rollie), Mack
Dryden (Fred)

Call From Space (Showscan presentation) (1988)
Director: Richard Fleischer
Producers: Peter Beale, Roger Wielgus
Writers: Chris Langham, Sarah Paris
Editor: Walter Murch
Cinematographer: Jack Cardiff
Music: Herb Pilhofer
Production Designer: William J Creber
Cast: Bill Campbell (Young Man), Richard
Brestoff (Movie Director), J P Burns
(Counsellor), Charlton Heston (Alien Voice),
James Coburn

The Magic Balloon (Showscan presentation) (1989)
Director: Ronald Neame
Producer: Peter Beale
Writers: Peter Beale, Ronald Neame, Sarah Paris
Editor: Bill Butler
Cinematographer: Jack Cardiff
Production Designer: William J Creber
Cast: Henry Gibson, Lynn Kim, Frank Langella, Mari Yoshino

Delius (Music video for Toshiba/EMI) (1989)
Director: Jack Cardiff

Vivaldi's Four Seasons (Music video for Toshiba/EMI) (1991)
Director: Jack Cardiff

The Dance of Shiva (1998)
Director: Jamie Payne
Producers: Stephanie Crawford, Thomas Delfs, Jamie Payne
Writer: Joseph Miller
Editor: Peter Beston
Cinematographer: Jack Cardiff
Music: Nitin Sawhney
Production Designer: Luke Smith
Cast: Sanjeev Bhaskar (Sergeant Bakshi), Kenneth Branagh (Colonel Evans), Julian Glover (General Willis), Paul McGann (Captain Greville), Samuel West (Lieutenant Davis), Malcom Ridley (Lieutenant Frewer)

The Suicidal Dog (2000)
Director: Paul Merton
Producer: Jill Robertson
Writers: John Irwin, Paul Merton, Sarah Parkinson
Cinematographer: Jack Cardiff
Cast: Steve Steen (Steve), Tilly Vosburgh (Tilly), Richard Vranch (Balloon vendor), Stephen Frost (Philip)

Untitled (2002)
Director: Christopher Coppola
Cinematographer: Jack Cardiff
Digital Editing Supervisor: Jack Cardiff

Awards and Nominations

Academy Award (nominations)

1962 Best Cinematography, Colour for *Fanny*, 1961 Best Director for *Sons and Lovers*, 1957 Best Cinematography, Colour for *War and Peace*

Academy Award (awards)

2001 Honorary Award, 1948 Best Cinematography, Colour for *Black Narcissus*

American Society of Cinematographers

1993 International Award Lifetime Achievement

British Academy of Film and Television Arts (nominations)

1985 Best Film Cameraman for *The Far Pavilions*

British Academy of Film and Television Arts (awards)

2001 Lifetime Achievement Award

British Society of Cinematographers (BSC)

1994 BSC Lifetime Achievement Award, 1956 Best Cinematography Award for *War and Peace*

Cinematographie de Vichy (France)

1951 *Pandora andthe Flying Dutchman*

Coup de Soir Award

1951 *Pandora and the Flying Dutchman*

Directors Guild of America

1961 Outstanding Directorial Achievement

for *Sons and Lovers*

Golden Globes

1961 Best Motion Picture Director: *Sons and Lovers*, 1948 Best Cinematography for *Black Narcissus*

Laurel Awards

1962 3rd Place Cinematography, Colour for *Fanny*

London Critics Circle Film Award

1997 Lifetime Achievement Award

London Film Circle

1997 Lifetime Achievement Award

LOOK award for Film Achievement

Royal Photographic Society

1999 Lumiere Award for Services to Cinematography

National Board of Review

1960 Best Director for *Sons and Lovers*

New York Film Critics Circle Awards

1960 Best Director for *Sons and Lovers*

Salon Eurotechnica Award (Italy)

1951 *The Magic Box*

Technicolor Award

Award for Special Achievement for Colour Photography

Honours:

Fellow of the British Film Institute, 2002
OBE (Officer of the Order of the British
Empire), 2000
Honorary Doctor of Art, Royal College of
Art, 2000
Honorary Doctor of Art, University of
Rome, 1953
Honorary Doctor of Letters, Bradford
University, 1996
Honorary Member, French Association of
Cameramen

Technical Glossary

2k lamp 2000-watt light.

2-reeler A 2-reeler film consists of two reels of film equalling around 22 minutes of footage. A 4-reeler doubles that at 44 minutes, etc.

10x8 Camera A large-format stills camera with a 10 by 8 inch photographic plate onto which the image is exposed. The large negative size provides fine detail.

Arc Lights High intensity lamps that use an electric current (arc) passed between two conductors. The light from such lamps is white, strong and extremely hot.

Art Director The art director, also known as the production designer, is responsible for translating the director's vision through the use of costume, settings, architecture, props and the like. The creative 'look' of the film is the responsibility of the art director, who must work closely with the costume designers, cinematographer, builders, special effects crews and the other creative artists involved in production.

Assistant Director Also called the AD, or first assistant director. Responsible for coordinating the production schedule, ensuring that the right actors are available for upcoming scenes, etc.

Back Light The light used to add a feeling of depth and space to a scene.

Blimp A large camera housing used to prevent the sound from the camera being heard on set.

Camera Operator Under the guidance of the director and the cinematographer, responsible for the physical movements of the camera. Occasionally the director or cinematographer may operate their own camera, although this is now rare.

CinemaScope The proprietary name given to the wide-screen presentation format introduced by 20th Century Fox, from the pioneering work of Henri Chrétien. The system involves an anamorphic camera lens that 'squeezes' the horizontal axis of the scene in order for it to be exposed onto the relatively narrow width of film. A corresponding anamorphic lens must be employed on the projection system in order to 'unpack' the image back to its original dimensions. The first film to be released using the system was Henry Koster's 1953 epic, *The Robe*, starring Richard Burton, Jean Simmons and Victor Mature. CinemaScope began life with a width-to-height ratio of 2.66:1, with the sound on a separate reel. When it became necessary to transfer the sound to the film print, CinemaScope adopted a new ratio of 2.55:1, ultimately settling at 2.35:1.

Curtain Line A theatrical term meaning a dramatic line of dialogue that often marks a turning point in the action. Its origins come from the fact that it was often the line spoken immediately before the curtain fell at the end of an act.

Dailies See Rushes.

Depth of Field In practical terms, this relates to the distance between the nearest and furthest objects from the camera lens that can remain in sharp focus simultaneously.

Dimmer Shutters A device placed in front of a light to decrease physically the amount of illumination that is emitted from the maximum level that the light produces. Used when a variable power supply to the light, which would have the same effect, cannot be employed.

Eastman Color A proprietary colour film system introduced by the Eastman Kodak Corporation in 1950. In 1952, the company was awarded a special Oscar for its technical innovations.

Filler Light Usually positioned close to the camera, the filler lights are generally very soft and used to eliminate shadows without creating shadows of their own or adversely affecting the overall exposure of the shot.

Focus Puller The primary job of the focus puller is to change (pull) the focus of the camera from one predetermined distance to another during a single take. Each focus point is calculated during the camera rehearsal and the position to which the cameras lens must be adjusted is marked on a (generally) side-mounted dial.

Fog Filter A diffusion filter placed over the lens of the camera, which slightly reduces both contrast and sharpness to create a 'softer' image.

Foot-candle The foot-candle is a unit of illumination that derives its name from the amount of light delivered by a 'standard candle' placed one foot away from an object. In technical, contemporary terms, one foot-candle is the equivalent of approximately 10.8 lux.

F-stops The f-Stop (or f-Number) indicates the size of the lens opening: the larger the f-stop, the smaller the lens opening. Technically it is the ratio of the focal length of the lens to the diameter of its aperture.

Geared Head The mounting between the camera and tripod, which can be raised and lowered by a crank handle.

Guide Track A tape of completed film music that is played back 'live' on the set or location to allow the actors, director, etc. to respond appropriately, in scenes where exact co-ordination of action and soundtrack is needed. Also called 'playback'.

Grading The process of ensuring that all of the disparate elements of film are printed at the same levels of brightness and contrast.

Hairs in the Gate The camera gate is the aperture assembly where the film is exposed. Tiny particles (sometimes hairs) can become trapped in the mechanism and are often apparent only when the film is processed. The camera gate would normally be checked after each shot to ensure that it is clear of such debris.

Head The mounting between the camera and the tripod. See: Geared Head.

Idiot Boards Large boards placed behind/beside the camera, on which an actor's lines are written.

Incandescent Lights Small, unobtrusive lights, often using standard bulb filaments.

Key Light As the name implies, this is the main light used to define the appearance of a scene.

Kicker Lights A light placed between the backlight (the light used to add space and 'dimension' to a scene) and the filler light (the soft light used to eliminate harsh shadows). Sometimes used to simulate window light from behind a character.

Klieg Lights Carbon-based arc lamps named after their inventors, John and Anton Kliegl, German immigrants to the United States, who founded a successful lighting production company in the nascent Hollywood climate. For unknown reasons, the final 'l' of the brothers' name was dropped from the lights named after them.

Magazine Reel of film ready to load onto the camera.

Monopack The patent for the Monopack process, which greatly improved on

Technicolor's 'Three-Strip Process' because of its use of a single, multi-layered film, was granted to Dr Leonard J Troland (of Technicolor) in 1931. The Monopack system was not fully introduced until a decade later, with the first feature, *Thunderhead, Son of Flicka* (directed by Louis King), appearing in 1944.

Numbers Boy The numbers boy is in charge of writing the scene and take numbers on the clapperboard, which is filmed before each shot. Now often called a clapper-loader with the combined responsibility of operating the clapperboard and loading film stock into the camera's magazines. On a small production, the assistant cameraman may perform all of these duties and more.

Panavision A trademark name for numerous wide-screen technologies developed by the Panavision Company.

Post-production All work subsequent to the main shooting of the film: editing, music scoring, dubbing, special optical effects, etc.

Pre-production All work done prior to the start of filming: casting, script editing, storyboarding, etc.

Rear-projection The rear-projection effect was largely used for simulating the background motion for scenes set in cars, trains, etc. It utilized a semi-transparent screen onto which was projected the pre-shot exterior backgrounds, while the camera recorded the live action performed in front of it. The method has largely been replaced by digital effects where a brightly lit screen (usually green) is replaced in post-production with the required imagery.

Reflectors Simple reflective surfaces that are used to bounce light (often natural sunlight) back on to the performers.

Rushes The first print of shot footage, usually viewed on a daily basis (hence the alternative phrase, 'dailies'), used to judge the quality of work to date.

Second Unit A small film crew employed to shoot (generally) less important sequences, such as exterior establishing shots, close-ups of set detail, etc. A second unit may also be specialist, such as those responsible for complex stunt sequences or aerial photography.

Snoot A cylindrical metal tube, which can be placed in front of a light to create a very concentrated, narrow beam.

Solarization In non-technical terms, for the purposes of *Girl on a Motorcycle*, solarization involved the replacement of certain colours on the film, and the enhancement or suppression of other colours, to produce a hypnotic, hallucinogenic effect. The 'fantasy colour consultant' on the film was Laurie Atkin.

Spot Rail A lighting gantry, from which lamps are hung.

Notes

Chapter 1

1. *My Fair Lady* opened in March 1956, starring Rex Harrison and Julie Andrews. It ran for more than nine years and some 2700 performances. Clearly, Jack Cardiff is using this simply as an example of a successful musical, not as one in which his parents actually performed.

2. They appeared together on stage in Fred Karno's *Mumming Birds* revue.

3. St Margaret's Studios, Twickenham (close to London) was founded by Ralph Jupp, the owner of the London Film Company and Provincial Cinematograph Theatres. It was opened in 1912 on the site of a former roller-skating rink.

4. The Technicolor Motion Picture Corporation was established in 1915, an expansion (following an advance of $10,000 from a Boston corporate lawyer, William Coolidge) of the industrial research company Kalmus, Comstock & Wescott. The leading light of the company was Herbert Thomas Kalmus, who had studied physics and chemistry at the Massachusetts Institute of Technology before receiving his doctorate from the University of Zurich. The company pioneered colour motion film in all its forms, constantly developing radical new cameras, films and processing systems.

5. Although born in San Francisco, Hopson found her fame and fortune in the early British silent cinema, epitomizing the vulnerable English heroine in films such as Frank Wilson's *The Vicar of Wakefield* (1913) and Cecil Hepworth's *A Moment of Darkness* (1915). She later headed her own production company with producer-director Walter West, often specializing in equestrian-themed melodramas.

6. The Elstree studios were founded in 1914 by filmmakers Percy Nash and John East. Their reason for selecting the location was simple: it was close enough to London to provide easy access, yet far enough away to avoid the terrible smog that still blighted the city.

7. Richard Fleischer (born 1916) is the son of the animation legend Max Fleischer (*Betty Boop*, etc.) He joined RKO-Pathé's newsreel department in 1942, before moving to Hollywood and directing a series of thrillers, such as *Trapped* (1949) and *Armored Car Robbery* (1950)—the latter film a clear inspiration for Quentin Tarantino's *Reservoir Dogs* (1992). Following the success of *20,000 Leagues Under the Sea* in 1954, he directed a number of 'epic' movies, including *The Vikings* (1958), *Fantastic Voyage* (1966) and *Tora! Tora! Tora!* (1970). He also directed the cult classics *The Boston Strangler* (1968) and *Soylent Green* (1973).

8. Frank HArris (1856-1931) made his name as a journalist and author, becoming a key figure in the literary and political scene of the late 19th and early 20th centuries. His circle of associates boasted Oscar Wilde, George Bernard Shaw, Winston Churchill and the infamous Aleister Crowley. The first volume of his autobiography was published in Paris in 1922.

9. The first issue of *The Magnet*, entitled *The Making of Harry Wharton*, was actually published in February 1908. One of its most enduring characters was Frank Richard's Billy Bunter. *The Magnet* made its final appearance (*The Shadow of the Sack*) in May 1940.

10. Ted Moore (1914–87) later became a highly respected cinematographer, winning the 1967 Best Cinematography (Colour) Oscar for *A Man for all Seasons*.

11. In 1908, André Debrie's firm introduced its 'Parvo' series of robust, compact cameras, and set the standards for future camera technology.

12. Richard Albert Eichberg (1888–1953) was the German-born director of more than 80 films, from *Vom Spielteufel Befreit* in 1915 to *Die Reise nach Marrakesch* in 1949. Eichberg's foray into English-language film, *The Flame of Love*, starred Anna May Wong, whom he also cast in *Schmutziges Geld* (also known as *Show Life* and *Song*, 1928) and *Großstadtschmetterling* (also known as *City Butterfly*, 1929).

13. Carl Brisson (1893–1958) was a Danish-born actor, who made his debut in A W Sandberg's *De Mystiske Fodspor* (1918). His son, Frederick Brisson, was a producer whose work included *The Pajama Game* (1957).

14. Madeleine Carroll (1906–87) was born Marie-Madeleine Bernadette O'Carroll. She was a 'classic British blonde,' who came to fame playing heroines in two early Hitchcock films: *The 39 Steps* (1935) and *Secret Agent* (1936). She moved to Hollywood following the success of the latter and enjoyed a career of moderate success in the early 1940s.

15. Chris Challis was born in 1919 and began his career as a news cameraman. His most notable work includes *Ill Met by Moonlight* (1957), *Arabesque* (1966), *Chitty Chitty Bang Bang* (1968) and *The Deep* (1977).

16. Freddie Young (1902–98) was one of the world's most renowned cinematographers. He enjoyed a career that spanned almost 70 years from his first break at the age of 15, to his final role on Joseph Brooks's *Invitation to the Wedding* (1985). His early work included *Limelight* (1936) and *Goodbye, Mr Chips* (1939) but the most celebrated association in his life was with director David Lean. He was Oscar-nominated for *Ivanhoe* (1952) and *Nicholas and Alexandra*

(1971) and won three Oscars on Lean films: *Lawrence of Arabia* (1962), *Doctor Zhivago* (1965) and *Ryan's Daughter* (1970). He was awarded an OBE (Officer of the Order of the British Empire) in 1970.

17. The British and Dominion Film Corporation (B&D) was founded by Herbert Wilcox (1892–1977), who had begun work in the British film industry in 1919, quickly establishing a solid reputation for himself by importing Hollywood and European stars. He co-founded British National Pictures at the new Elstree Studios with J D Williams and W Schlesinger, before a series of financial disagreements divided the company. In 1928, Wilcox founded the British and Dominion Film Corporation with Nelson Keys, again at the Elstree Studios.

18. Sir Alexander Korda (1893–1956) was a canny and flamboyant film entrepreneur and one of the key figures in the history of British film production. Born in Hungary, Korda came to film directing via publishing and journalism, making numerous films in his homeland as well as Germany and Austria. He tried his luck in America, working for both First National and 20th Century Fox. He disliked the climate in Hollywood and settled in England (after a brief period in France) in 1931. The following year, he founded London Films, which saw its first success with 1933's *The Private Life of Henry VIII*. Korda was naturalized a British subject in 1936 and knighted for services to the film industry in 1942 by King George VI; he was the first person from the film profession to be so honoured.

19. In 1927, the Cinematograph Films Act was introduced in order to force studios and distributors to supply a certain quota of British films to the exhibitors. Additionally it required those exhibitors to screen that quota in their annual programmes. The act demanded that at least 20 per cent of the films screened in British cinemas by the mid-1930s should be of British origin. A complex definition of 'British' was employed and many studios simply turned out inexpensive 'quickies' to fulfil the demands of the act.

20. Denham Studios were established in 1936 by Alexander Korda after he purchased a house and country estate on the site for £15,000. It was, at the time, the largest studios in England. The original Alexander Korda building still remains today, having been listed as being of 'Special Architectural or Historic Interest.'

21. René Clair (1898–1981) was an early master of French film comedies He worked in both England and America directing a succession of slight, whimsical films, including *Under the Roofs of Paris* (1930), *The Ghost Goes West* (1935) and *It Happened Tomorrow* (1944).

22. Sam Spiegel (1903–85) was a legendary producer whose work earned him four Oscars: *On the Waterfront* in 1955, *Bridge on the River Kwai* in 1958, *Lawrence of Arabia* in 1964, and the Irving G Thalberg Memorial Award Oscar in 1964. He was further nominated for his work on *Nicholas and Alexandra* in 1972.

23. William Cameron Menzies (1896–1956) was one of the most renowned designers, producers and directors of his generation. He started his career in set design at United Artists with some of his most daring work created for the 1924 version of *The Thief of Bagdad*; he was awarded the first ever Academy Award for set design for *The Dove* (1927).

24. Ned Mann (1893–1967) was a one-time stage actor, who turned to a highly successful career in film special effects. His most notable works included *Things to Come* (1936), *The Man Who Could Work Miracles* (1936) and *Fire Over England* (1937).

25. Based on the book by H G Wells, *The Man Who Could Work Miracles* was directed in 1936 by Lothar Mendes and starred Roland Young and Ralph Richardson.

26. Hal Rosson (1895–1988) was a tough talking, New York-born cinematographer whose most famous work includes *The Wizard of Oz* (1939), *The Asphalt Jungle* (1950), *Singin' in the Rain* (1952) and *El Dorado* (1967).

27. Writer and director Jacques Feyder (1885–1948) was born in Brabant, Belgium. He co-directed (with Gaston Ravel) his first film, *Des Pieds et des Mains*, in 1915, and in 1926 wrote and directed *Carmen*, featuring a young Luis Buñuel (three years before Buñuel's surrealist masterpiece *Un Chien Andalou* was released).

28. Harry Strandling (1901–70) enjoyed a career as a cinematographer spanning some 50 years from *The Devil's Garden* (1920) to *The Owl and The Pussycat* (1970). He was nominated for an incredible fourteen Oscars; he won two of those, the first in 1945 for *The Picture of Dorian Gray* (Best Cinematography, Black and White) and the second twenty years later for *My Fair Lady* (Best Cinematography, Colour).

29. Josef von Sternberg (1893–1969) began his distinguished film career as a lowly cleaner and repairer of film prints. He became an apprentice filmmaker and found some success with *The Salvation Hunters* in 1925, before making his big break with *Underworld* two years later. In 1930, he cast the then-unknown Marlene Dietrich in *The Blue Angel* and in so doing, created a screen icon.

Chapter 2

1. Directed in 1937 by Harold D Schuster and starring Annabella, Henry Fonda and Leslie Banks; it was the first Technicolor film to be produced in Europe. See appendix:

the Milestone Films.

2. Annabella (1904–96) was born Suzanne Georgette Charpentier in France. She appeared in Abel Gance's classic *Napoleon* (1927) and a decade later made the move to Hollywood, where she met and married Tyrone Power.

3. Ray Rennahan (1896–1980) worked on Cecil B DeMille's 1923 epic *The Ten Commandments* before carving out a career as one of the greatest cinematographers in the world. He won his first Oscar in 1939 for *Gone with the Wind* (shared with Ernest Haller) and his second in 1941 for *Blood and Sand*. He is one of only four cinematographers to have a star on the 'Hollywood Walk of Fame' (the others are J Peverell Marley, Hal Mohr and Leon Shamroy).

4. Head of Technicolor's camera department in Britain.

5. A small, often foldaway, third seat in the back of a two-seater car.

6. The ancient city of Petra, in modern-day Jordan, was from the 4th century BC to the 1st century AD the capital of the ancient Nabataeans, who carved their monumental city from the living rock. Petra was 'lost' until the Swiss traveller Johann Burckhardt rediscovered it in 1812.

7. The Khasnet (or Treasury), an enormous, classical-style temple, which featured as the final resting place of the Holy Grail in Steven Spielberg's film *Indiana Jones and the Last Crusade* (1989).

8. *Petra* by Dean Burgen.

9. First published in 1926, *The Seven Pillars of Wisdom* is T E Lawrence's own account of his involvement in the Arab Revolt and the campaign against the Turks during World War I.

10. British born cinematographer Geoffrey Unsworth (1914–78), won his first Oscar for *Cabaret* in 1972. His second, for Roman Polanski's *Tess* (shared with Ghislain Cloquet) was awarded posthumously in 1981. He also won numerous BAFTAs (British Association of Film and Television Arts awards) including Best Cinematography for *2001: A Space Odyssey* (1968), *Cabaret* and *A Bridge Too Far* (1977).

11. Claude Friese-Greene's father, William (1855–1921) was a well-known portrait photographer with studios in London's West End. He dabbled endlessly with various moving-image inventions in addition to working on colour-film emulsions, stereo (3-D) images and the application of sound to film.

12. Prior to working on *Western Approaches*, Pat Jackson (born in London in 1916) had worked with the great documentary filmmaker Humphrey Jennings on *The First Days* (1939). During the 1950s, he directed numerous feature films, including *Shadow on the Wall* (1950), *The*

Feminine Touch (1957) and *Virgin Island* (1958). Jackson undertook an increasing amount of television work during the 1960s, including contributions to *The Saint*, *Danger Man* and *The Prisoner*.

13. Situated some 20 miles west of London, the original Victorian house and grounds (Heatherden Hall) was sold in 1934 to Charles Boot, who subsequently formed a partnership with J Arthur Rank and began construction of the new studio facilities. Once these were completed in 1936, the first production was Herbert Wilcox's *London Melody*. Three years later, they took over control of Denham Studios hence the 'D and P' ('Denham and Pinewood') logo that adorned their films of the period. Pinewood remains a thriving studio today, although it is now effectively a 'four-wall' (for hire) facility.

Chapter 3

1. Michael Powell (1905–90) spent his early years working in banking before taking on various film jobs at the thriving Pinewood and Denham Studios. He was employed on numerous 'British Quota Quickies' before forming one of the most successful and celebrated partnerships in British film history when he established a production company called The Archers with the Hungarian émigré Emeric Pressburger. Together they wrote, produced and directed some of the most influential and critically acclaimed films of the 1940s and 50s. He and Pressburger received three Oscar nominations, two in 1943 for *One of our Aircraft is Missing* and *The 49th Parallel* and one in 1949 for *The Red Shoes*. After Powell and Pressburger parted company, neither man found great solo success. In 1960, Powell released *Peeping Tom* (often referred to as 'the English *Psycho*') which, although now recognized as a masterful cult classic, was vilified by the press of the day, effectively ending Powell's career. The work of Powell and Pressburger was 'rediscovered' and re-evaluated in the late 1980s, when their work was championed by Francis Ford Coppola and Martin Scorsese.

2. Emeric Pressburger (1902–88), born in Hungary, was educated in Prague and Stuttgart and found early employment as a journalist in both Germany and Hungary, later working as an author and scriptwriter in Germany and France. He finally settled in London, where he formed the hugely successful partnership with Michael Powell, producing films under their Archers banner. His writing style was unique and his ability to perfectly portray British idiosyncrasies was the skill upon which he most prided himself. In addition to the three Oscar nominations that he shared with Michael Powell, he won

the 1943 Oscar for Best Writing (Original Story) for *The 49th Parallel*.

3. French cinematographer Georges Périnal (1897–1965) worked on almost 70 films between *La Justicière* (1925) for director Maurice Gleize and *Once More, With Feeling* for Stanley Donen in 1960. During his illustrious career, his services were called upon by directors as prominent as William Cameron Menzies, Zoltan Korda, Michael Powell and Carol Reed. He received an Academy Award nomination in 1940 for *The Four Feathers* and won the award the following year for his work on *The Thief of Bagdad*.

4. *A Life in Movies*, published in 1987.

5. Outstanding art director and set designer Alfred Junge (1886–1964) was born in Gorlitz, Germany. He began his career as a scenic artist for the Berlin State Opera and State Theatre Studios. He worked on ten Michael Powell films between 1934 (*The Fire Raisers*) and 1947 (*Black Narcissus*). He was awarded an Oscar for *Black Narcissus* and received a second Oscar nomination for Richard Thorpe's *Knights of the Round Table* in 1954.

6. Douglas Slocombe, born in 1913, began his career as a newsreel cameraman during World War II. He joined Ealing Studios as a director of photography in 1948, where he worked on classics such as *The Lavender Hill Mob* and *The Man in the White Suit* (both 1951) and *The Titfield Thunderbolt* (1953). Later he collaborated with Spielberg on all three *Indiana Jones* films.

7. Marius Goring (1912–98) was born in England, yet studied variously in Frankfurt, Vienna and Paris before returning to London to study drama. His first stage appearance was in 1925 in Cambridge and two years later he followed it with his London debut, later touring Europe with numerous stage productions. He played small, uncredited screen roles in *The Amateur Gentleman* (Thornton Freeland, 1936) and *Rembrandt* (Alexander Korda, 1936), but slowly his star began to rise. Goring made four films with Michael Powell and Emeric Pressburger: *The Spy in Black* (1939), *A Matter of Life and Death* (1946), *The Red Shoes* (1948) and *Ill Met by Moonlight* (1957).

8. The story was commissioned by Jack Beddington from the Film Division of the Ministry of Information, to help improve Anglo-American relations.

9. As the film was originally set to star Laurence Olivier, then on active war service, the cooperation of both the Ministry of Information and the Ministry of War was required. Both ministries turned the project down. Churchill himself was said to think the film was in poor taste and was actively obstructive in the film's production

and, once it was completed, attempted to prevent its export.

10. Powell and Pressburger's production company, The Archers, featured a target logo, into which arrows thudded.

11. Thelma Schoonmaker is Martin Scorsese's long-time editing collaborator. She was nominated for her first Oscar in 1970 for *Woodstock* (directed by Michael Wadleigh), won an Oscar ten years later for Scorsese's *Raging Bull* and received a further nomination in 1990 for *Goodfellas*. Additionally she won BAFTAs for both *Raging Bull* and *Goodfellas* and was nominated for her work on *The King of Comedy* (1983) and *Cape Fear* (1991).

12. The huge escalator, which was supposed to link heaven and earth, was nicknamed 'Ethel' by the engineers at the London Passenger Transport Board, who designed and built it. 'Ethel' had 106 steps, each 20 feet wide, and took the firm three months to construct.

13. Bernardo Bertolucci's 1993 film *Little Buddha* starred Keanu Reeves and was shot largely on location in the Himalayan landscapes of Bhutan and Nepal.

14. The Leonardslee Gardens, near Horsham, West Sussex, were owned and maintained by Sir Giles Loder, an enthusiastic expert on, and collector of, exotic flora.

15. Walter Percy Day (1878–1965), known simply as 'Poppa' or 'Pop', initially served a three-year photographic apprenticeship before studying at the Royal Academy of Art in London. He found initial success as a fine-art painter, before being hired in 1919 by Ideal Films at Elstree Studios for their special effects department. Day pioneered the 'glass shot' effect, which allowed filmmakers to shoot live action sequences while masking unwanted surroundings (such as lighting gantries) and later replace these areas with 'painted in' scenery. Day's 'glass shot' was used for the first time in Henry Roussel's *Les Opprimés* (1923), and the basic principle of the system remained unchanged for decades, although he continued to pioneer a succession of other special effect techniques. Day was awarded an OBE (Officer of the Order of the British Empire) in 1948 for his services to British cinema.

16. German-born Hein Heckroth (1897 1970) worked as a set and costume designer for the German National Ballet before moving to England, where he successfully applied his considerable talents to film work. He won the Best Costume Design Oscar for *The Red Shoes* and was nominated in both the Best Costume Design and Best Art Direction/Set Decoration categories at the 1952 Oscars for *The Tales of Hoffman*.

17. Sabu Dastagir (1924–63), known simply as Sabu, first came to public attention in Robert Flaherty's *Elephant Boy*

(1937). But it was the eponymous role in *The Thief of Bagdad* (1940) and his portrayal of Mowgli in Zoltan Korda's *The Jungle Book* (1942) that brought Sabu his greatest fame. He died from a heart attack shortly before his fortieth birthday.

18. Composer Brian Easdale (1909–95) was born in Manchester and studied at the Royal College of Music. Although officially serving with the Royal Artillery during World War II, Easdale spent the majority of his service seconded to work composing music for various training and propaganda films. His most memorable film work was in conjunction with Michael Powell—from the haunting beauty of *The Red Shoes* and *Black Narcissus* scores to the near-deranged accompaniment to 1960's *Peeping Tom*, via *The Small Black Room* (1949), *The Elusive Pimpernel* (1950), *Gone to Earth* (1950) and *The Battle of the River Plate* (1956).

19. Sir Frederick Ashton's masterpiece *Symphonic Variations* premiered at Covent Garden on 24 April 1946. The original cast were: Margot Fonteyn, Pamela May, Moira Shearer, Michael Somes, Henry Danton and Brian Shaw.

20. Merle Oberon was born and raised in India. At the age of 17, she settled in London and began to take small parts in film. Her breakthrough came with *The Private Life of Henry VIII* (1933) for Korda, who subsequently groomed her for stardom. Korda sold a share of her contract to Sam Goldwyn in 1935, allowing Oberon to become a success in the UK and US simultaneously.

21. Sir William Russell Flint (1880–1970) studied at the Royal Institution School of Art in Edinburgh. He achieved international fame as a watercolour artist and was knighted in 1947.

22. Léonide Massine (1895–1979) studied at the Moscow Bolshoi School, graduated in 1912 and joined the Bolshoi Ballet. He then moved to the Ballet Russes in 1914, choreographing his first ballet for them in 1915. A prolific choreographer, he created more than fifty ballets, including *La Boutique Fantasque* (1919).

23. Lee Garmes (1898–1978) began his career as a camera operator in 1918 and went on to become one of the greatest cinematographers of the 1920s and 1930s, earning his first Academy Award nomination in 1931 for Josef von Sternberg's *Morocco* and his first (and only) win the following year for *Shanghai Express*. He was later nominated for John Cromwell's *Since You Went Away* (1944) and Frank Borzage's *The Big Fisherman* (1959).

Chapter 4

1. Charles Frend (1909–77) began his film career as an editor, including cutting three films for Alfred Hitchcock: *The Secret Agent* (1936), *Sabotage* (1936) and *Young and Innocent* (1937). He moved to Ealing Studios in the early 1940s and began work as a director; his most famous works there were *Scott of the Antarctic* (1948) and *The Cruel Sea* (1953).

2. Canadian cinematographer Osmond Borradaile (1898–1999) had worked extensively with Zoltan Korda (*Sanders of the River* in 1935 and *The Four Feathers* in 1939, among others) before his aborted work on *Scott of the Antarctic*.

3. All additional 'exteriors' were shot inside on a small soundstage at Ealing Studios.

4. Hitchcock's 1948 fictionalization of the Leopold and Loeb murder case was filmed as if in one continuous shot, though actually a series of cleverly edited eight-minute takes.

5. Originally a stage actor and critic, Joseph Cotten (1905–94) became involved in film through his friendship with Orson Welles from his days with the Federal Theater and the Mercury Company. He starred in Welles's *Citizen Kane* (1941) and *The Magnificent Ambersons* (1942) and in Carol Reed's *The Third Man* (1949).

6. The Everyman's Library, launched in 1906 with the intention of bringing the world's classic books to the masses at affordable prices.

7. rving Grant Thalberg (1899–1936) became an executive at Universal Studios by the age of twenty and within five years became Louis B Mayer's number two at Metro-Goldwyn-Mayer. His wunderkind career was plagued by ill health and he died at just 37.

8. Starring Gary Cooper, *The Lives of a Bengal Lancer* (1935) was nominated for Oscars for Best Art Direction, Best Director, Best Film Editing, Best Picture, Best Screenplay, Best Sound, and Best Assistant Director. Paul Wing and Clem Beauchamp won the Oscar in the latter category.

9. Cecil B DeMille was the archetypal Hollywood producer-director. He came from a theatrical family and his showmanship was his defining quality. He enrolled in the Academy of Dramatic Arts in New York and in 1913 formed the Jesse L Lasky Feature Play Co. (the nascent Paramount Pictures) with Jesse Lasky and Samuel Goldwyn. DeMille was one of the 36 founders of the Academy of Motion Picture Arts and Sciences.

10. The various positions in which an actor must stop during a scene are often marked on the floor in either chalk or with tape. An actor is required to stop exactly on these marks to ensure he or she is in focus (all the

focusing points of a scene having been pre-calculated)—hence the term 'hitting the mark.'

11. Tyrone Power (1914–58) was the son of a silent screen star, also called Tyrone, and by the time he was in his teens he was following in the family footsteps and making regular stage appearances. His own screen debut came in 1932 (the year after his father's death) in William Wyler's melodrama *Tom Brown of Culver*. Finally Power was offered a full contract at 20th Century Fox, where he quickly established his star credentials. His heyday at Fox came during the 1930s and early 1940s, when he scored hit after hit with films such as *Suez* (Allan Dwan, 1938), *Johnny Apollo* (Henry Hathaway, 1940), *Blood and Sand* (Rouben Mamoulian, 1941) and *The Black Swan* (Henry King, 1942). After completing *Witness for the Prosecution* for Billy Wilder in 1957, Power began working on King Vidor's *Solomon and Sheba*, but collapsed and died from a heart attack following the filming of a duel sequence.

12. Welles's landmark first feature, *Citizen Kane* (1941), encountered strong opposition largely because of its thinly veiled depiction of multi-millionaire tycoon William Randolph Hearst.

13. Welles's second feature, an adaptation of Booth Tarkington's novel. RKO removed more than 50 minutes of the film (destroying the footage) and added a happier, 'Hollywood' ending while the director was out of the country. Welles described the result as looking like it had been 'edited by a lawnmower'.

14. The Latin name of Odysseus the hero of Homer's classic *Odyssey*.

15. Welles's odd homage to magic and forgery, presented in pseudo-documentary style. It is the film that probably best demonstrates Welles's sense of mischief and illusion.

16. Welles was obsessive about bringing Cervantes's epic *Don Quixote* to the screen. The project was started and abandoned on a number of occasions, taxing the director for more than thirty years.

17. Gregg Toland (1904–48) began his career as a camera operator in the silent era. His most revolutionary work came with Welles on *Citizen Kane*, but he is also known for his association with John Ford, with whom he made *The Grapes of Wrath* (1940), *The Long Voyage Home* (1940) and *December 7th* (1943). He was nominated for a total of six Oscars, winning in 1940 for *Wuthering Heights*.

18. James A Fitzpatrick (1902–80) was a prolific American producer and director of documentaries, with close to 100 films to his credit. After working as a journalist, Fitzpatrick moved into the moving image, producing and directing his own films from the mid-1920s and specializing in (often exotic) travelogues, later marked out by their vibrant use of Technicolor. The titles of his films were perfectly self-explanatory—*Songs of the British Isles* (1925), *Visiting St Louis* (1944), *Night in Mexico City* (1944)—and were often distributed under a series of titles such as *Fitzpatrick Traveltalks* and *Vistavision Visits*.

19. Al Lewin (1894–1968) was associate producer on, among other films, the 1935 Frank Lloyd version of *Mutiny on the Bounty*, starring Charles Laughton and Clark Gable.

20. John Bryan (1911–69) was nominated for the Best Art Direction Oscar for *Caesar and Cleopatra* (1945), won the Oscar for his work on David Lean's *Great Expectations* the following year, and was again nominated in 1964 for *Becket*, a film for which he won the BAFTA for Best British Art Direction.

21. In fact, Gardner (1922–90) was born in Grabton, North Carolina.

22. John Boulting (1913–85) was the twin brother of the writer-director Roy Boulting (1913–2001). They shared directing credits on two films: *Crest of the Wave* (1954) and *Suspect* (1960). During the 1950s, they became famous for their social comedies *Lucky Jim* (1957), *Brothers in Law* (1957) and *I'm All Right Jack* (1959).

Chapter 5

1. ohn Woolf (1913–99) was Oscar-nominated for Jack Clayton's *Room at the Top* (1959) and won the Best Picture Oscar for Carol Reed's *Oliver!* in 1968.

2. Howard Hawks's 1944 masterpiece, which first teamed Bogart and Bacall. The coruscating exchanges of dialogue between the two leads are legendary: 'You know how to whistle, don't you, Steve? You just put your lips together and blow.'

3. Clint Eastwood's 1990 fictionalization of the filming of *The African Queen*. Eastwood himself took on the Huston character for the film.

4. TV mini-series directed by Peter Duffell and starring Ben Cross, Amy Irving, Christopher Lee and Saeed Jaffrey.

5. William Keighley (1889–1984) came from a stage-acting and directing background before his move to Hollywood fortuitously coincided with the advent of sound, providing him with work as a dialogue director at Warner Brothers. He made his first film as director, *The Match King*, in 1932 and his work on films like *'G' Men* (1935), *Special Agent* (1935) and *Bullets or Ballots* (1936) quickly helped Warner Brothers to establish their gritty gangster house style. Although he later turned his hand with some success to comedy—*No Time for Comedy* (1940) and *The Man Who Came to Dinner* (1942) for example—his popularity as a director, and therefore his output, slowly declined. He retired from filmmaking after completing *The Master of*

Ballantrae in 1953.

6. Roger Livesey (1906–76) was the son of actor Sam Livesey, who had appeared in Harold Schuster's *Wings of the Morning* (1937); both of his brothers were also actors and by 1917 he was making his own stage debut. He toured extensively with stage productions during the 1920s and 1930s, making only the occasional foray into film before being offered the lead role by Michael Powell in *The Life and Death of Colonel Blimp* (1943). Their collaboration continued with *I Know Where I'm Going!* (1945) and *A Matter of Life and Death* (1946).

7. *The Octoroon* (1859) was written by Dion Boucicault as an adaptation of Mayne Reid's 1856 novel *The Quadroon*. Several versions of the play have been performed with different endings.

8. Also known as *Il Maestro di Don Giovanni*, directed in 1953 by Milton Krims.

9. Barry Mahon (1921–99) was the producer of *Crossed Swords*. In addition to producing, Mahon also directed a raft of curious 1960s exploitation films, including *Music to Strip by* (1965), *Sin in the City* (1966) and *Fanny Hill Meets Lady Chatterley* (1967).

10. Her husband was Milko Skofic.

11. John Dighton (1909–89) worked at Gaumont-British in the early 1930s before moving to Warners and ultimately to Ealing Studios in 1939, where his most famous work included *Kind Hearts and Coronets* (1949) and *The Man in the White Suit* (1951).

12. Situated on the Italian side of Mont Blanc.

13. Joseph L Mankiewicz (1909–93) is widely regarded as one of America's most urbane writers and directors. He worked first in Europe, translating caption cards for silent films, before heading for Hollywood in the early 1920s. He wrote many of the period's finest filmscripts, before taking to directing in 1946 with *Dragonwyck*. He received a total of ten Oscar nominations; his first for *Skippy* in 1931 and his last in 1973 for *Sleuth*. In 1950, he won two Oscars for *A Letter to Three Wives* (Best Writing and Best Director) and he earned a second 'double' the following year for *All About Eve*.

14. Born in 1919, Dino De Laurentiis attended film school before taking a number of minor positions in the film industry to develop his understanding of the business. He served in the Italian army during World War II, returning to film at its conclusion and scoring his first major success with *Bitter Rice* in 1949. He formed a business partnership with Carlo Ponti and later established his own studio facilities, Dinocittà. After the failure of the venture, he moved his operations to America and opened a new outfit, DEG Studios in North Carolina. That, too,

ultimately failed, as did much of De Laurentiis's US output, although in 2001 he received the Irving G Thalberg Memorial Academy Award.

15. Sam Goldwyn (1882–1974) formed the Jesse L Lasky Feature Play Company in 1913 with Lasky (his brother-in-law) and Cecil B DeMille. Three years later, the company was merged with Adolph Zukor's Famous Players Film Company. Over the following years, Goldwyn was responsible for the 'discovery' and development of numerous silent-era stars. He was a ruthless businessman and a showman almost on a par with DeMille, yet equally remembered for his (in)famous quotations (or 'Goldwynisms'), such as 'What we need now is some new, fresh clichés' and 'A verbal contract isn't worth the paper it's written on.'

16. Leo Tolstoy devoted five years of his life to creating his key work, *War and Peace*. It was published between 1865 and 1869 and its sprawling narrative, set against the Napoleonic invasion of Russia, includes almost 600 characters.

17. King Vidor (1894–1982) was a Texan-born writer, producer, and director whose career covered almost 50 years. As a director, he received five Oscar nominations for *The Crowd* (1929), *Hallelujah* (1930), *The Champ* (1932), *The Citadel* (1939) and *War and Peace* (1957). In 1979, he was awarded an Honorary Academy Award for his achievements and innovations.

18. The famed Cinecittà studios in Rome were founded in 1937. Immediately the studios became closely connected with the Istituto Luce, which was largely producing propaganda newsreels and documentaries. Production, though limited, continued throughout the war at Cinecittà, and in the post-war years large numbers of American productions began to make use of the impressive facilities (and relatively cheap costs), dubbing the studios 'Hollywood on the Tiber'. Melvyn LeRoy's *Quo Vadis?* (1951), Jean Negulesco's *Three Coins in the Fountain* (1954) and William Wyler's *Ben-Hur* (1959) all utilized Cinecittà's epically proportioned sound stages. In addition to American productions, the majority of Federico Fellini's films were shot at Cinecittà.

19. The Battle of Borodino took place on 7 September 1812; it was one of the most significant encounters of the Napoleonic campaigns and is one of *War and Peace*'s grandest set-pieces.

20. The 1968 version of *War and Peace* was directed by Sergei Bondarchuk. Among other achievements, he shot the Battle of Borodino sequences on the site of the original encounter.

21. Ben Hecht (1894–1964) worked on scripts for almost

150 films, including *Stagecoach* (1939), *Gone with the Wind* (1939), *Spellbound* (1945) and *Monkey Business* (1952). He was nominated for six Oscars, winning one for *Underworld* in 1929 and a second in 1936 for *The Scoundrel*. In 1981, he was posthumously awarded the Laurel Award for Screen Writing Achievement by the Writers Guild of America.

22. Italian actor Rossano Brazzi (1916–94) played Paul Bonnard in *Legend of the Lost* (1957).

23. Wayne played the role opposite Susan Hayward in Dick Powell's 1956 film, *The Conqueror*.

24. Playwright Arthur Miller was married to Monroe between June 1956 and January 1961.

25. A made-for-television, mini-series directed by Peter Hunt and starring Lesley-Anne Down, Olivia Hussey and Laurence Olivier.

26. Monroe's last complete film, directed by John Huston and co-starring Clark Gable and Montgomery Clift.

27. American baseball legend and briefly (January –October 1954) Monroe's second husband.

Chapter 6

1. Writer, producer, director and cinematographer George Stevens (1904–75) was born in Oakland, California, the son of a jobbing actor familiar in both the silent and early 'talkie' periods. His first employment in the film industry was at the Hal Roach studio in the 1920s, where he worked as a cameraman on numerous comedy shorts. By 1930 he was directing his own shorts, and by 1933 he broke into features with *The Cohens and Kellys in Trouble*. A renowned perfectionist, Stevens was nominated no fewer than eleven times for the Academy Award, winning his first in 1952 for *A Place in the Sun*, his second in 1954 (the Irving G Thalberg Memorial Award) and his third in 1957 for *Giant*.

2. Forced into hiding to escape the persecution of the Jews in Amsterdam, Anne Frank kept her diary from 12 June 1942 to 1 August 1944. After she and her family were betrayed and arrested, Anne was taken to the Bergen-Belsen concentration camp, where she died, aged fifteen, in March 1945. Her father, Otto, who survived, discovered her diary and it was first published (as The *Diary of a Young Girl*) in 1947. The book has been translated into some 67 languages and has sold more than 31 million copies worldwide.

3. The most common wide-screen aspect ratio is 1.85:1, often just termed '185'. The image of a 185 film is recorded onto the whole of the 35mm frame, which has an aspect ratio of 1.33:1—also called 'Academy Aperture' or 'Academy Ratio' and is approximately the same as a standard television broadcast. When a 185 film

is projected, the top and bottom are simply masked out by the projector in order to deliver a wide-screen image at a ratio of 1.85:1.

4. Mike Todd (1909–58) was one of the 1950s' greatest exponents of 'cinema as spectacle'. He worked on technical innovations such as Cinerama and numerous other large-format systems as well as surround-sound and multi-screens. He developed the Todd-AO system, which combined many of these elements and which was designed to run at 30 frames per second (instead of the usual 24).

5. Curtis and Leigh were married for eleven years, between 1951 and 1962. Their daughter is Jamie Lee Curtis, who first came to prominence in a series of horror films in the late 1970s and early 1980s.

6. Ernest Borgnine was born in Connecticut in 1917. At eighteen he joined the American Navy, serving with them for a decade before enrolling at the Randall School of Drama in Hartford. Learning his craft on the stage (including a stint on Broadway), Borgnine moved to Hollywood in 1951 and made his debut on film in Robert Siodmak's *The Whistle at Eaton Falls* in the same year. Two years later, his role as 'Fatso' Judson in Fred Zinnemann's *From Here to Eternity* brought him to a wider audience, and in 1955 Delbert Mann's *Marty* made him a star in addition to earning him the Oscar, the BAFTA and almost every other major award of the year.

7. English cinematographer Desmond Dickinson (1902–86) enjoyed a career that spanned more than 40 years, and which encompassed Anthony Asquith's *The Importance of Being Earnest* (1952) and Robert Parrish's *Fire Down Below* (1957). He became inextricably linked with horror films during the last twenty years of his career, working on oddities such as John Lemont's *Konga* (1961), Jim O'Connolly's *Berserk!* (1968) and Freddie Francis's *Trog* (1970).

8. Richard Todd (born in Ireland in 1919) began his career on stage, founding the Dundee Repertory Theatre in 1939. After the war, he returned to the stage, appearing in John Patrick's *The Hasty Heart*, the film version of which, directed by Vincent Sherman in 1949, won Todd the Golden Globe for Most Promising Newcomer in addition to an Oscar nomination. He later appeared in a string of semi-swashbucklers such as Ken Annakin's *The Story of Robin Hood and his Merrie Men* (1952) and Harold French's *Rob Roy, The Highland Rogue* (1953). He also drew on his military experience and appeared in numerous heroic war roles, including his portrayal of Wing Commander Guy Gibson in Michael Anderson's *The Dam Busters* (1954).

9. Betsy Drake was born in Paris in 1923. She appeared in less than a dozen films and is probably best remembered for appearing opposite Jayne Mansfield in Frank Tashlin's *Will Success Spoil Rock Hunter?* (1957).

10. In December 1908, the battered body of Marion Gilchrist was discovered. The police arrested Oscar Slater; he was found guilty at his trial and sentenced to death. Ultimately, the entire affair was proven to be an incredible miscarriage of justice and Slater was released and finally compensated for his imprisonment. Among Slater's most prominent supporters was Sir Arthur Conan Doyle.

11. Van Johnson was born 1916 and came to screen prominence with MGM during World War II; he often played the patriotic 'boy next door' and also appeared in a number of successful musicals with Esther Williams. Johnson's contract with the studio stretched over fifteen years and saw his roles develop from the affable 'everyman' to heavier character parts in films like 1954's *Brigadoon*.

12. Maurice Chevalier (1888–1972) was, to Hollywood audiences, the epitome of the suave and sophisticated French gentleman. Chevalier worked initially as an acrobat before finding work in early French cinema. He fought in World War I, but was captured and imprisoned, where he subsequently learned to speak English from his fellow prisoners of war. In 1928, he headed for Hollywood, where he made a series of successful features opposite Jeanette MacDonald. Resurrecting his American career after World War II, he made *Gigi* in 1958, which gave him his most recognizable signature song, 'Thank Heaven for Little Girls'. He was nominated for the Academy Award twice in 1930, for both *The Love Parade* and *The Big Pond*. In 1959, he was presented with an Honorary Academy Award.

13. Leslie Caron was born in Paris in 1931 and was already proving herself an accomplished dancer by the age of ten. She was seen dancing with the Ballets des Champs-Elysées by Gene Kelly, who was looking to cast his leading lady for *An American in Paris* (1951). Caron won the role and appeared in a succession of highly acclaimed films, including *Lili* (1953), which earned her a Best Actress Oscar nomination, *Daddy Long Legs* (1955) and *Gigi* (1958). In 1962, Caron proved that she was as much a straight actress as a fine dancer, when she starred in Brian Forbes's *The L-Shaped Room*—the role won Caron the BAFTA, a Golden Globe and an Academy Award nomination.

14. Joshua Logan (1908–88) began directing theatrical productions while still studying at Princeton—his graduation from which was delayed when he travelled to Russia to learn directly from the inventor of 'method acting', Konstantin Stanislavski. He balanced his Broadway career with his Hollywood career, often bringing to the big screen plays and musicals he had directed on stage. He was Oscar-nominated in 1956 for *Picnic*, in 1958 for *Sayonara*, and 1962 for *Fanny*.

15. French film director and playwright Marcel Pagnol (1895–1974) was the first filmmaker elected to the Académie Française. As a playwright, he is probably best known for his 'Marseille trilogy'—*Marius*, *Fanny* and *César*.

16. Directed in 1932 by Marc Allégret and starring Orane Demazis as Fanny, Raimu as César and Fernand Charpin as Panisse. An Italian version was released the following year, directed by Mario Almirante.

17. Charles Boyer (1897–1978) acted first on stage before making his screen debut in 1920 with *L'Homme du Large* and making his American debut in 1931 with *The Magnificent Lie*. He soon found himself promoted to lead roles and enjoyed equal success on both sides of the Atlantic. Determined to move beyond his matinée-idol status, Boyer took on increasingly heavy roles, even making a surprisingly sinister villain in George Cukor's 1944 melodrama *Gaslight*. He was nominated for an Academy Award on four occasions: *Conquest* in 1938, *Algiers* in 1939, *Gaslight* in 1945 and *Fanny* in 1962. In 1943, he was presented with an Honorary Academy Award for his part in the founding of the French Research Foundation.

18. In 1905, a group of young artists, Henri Matisse among them, exhibited in Paris; they became known as 'Les Fauves'—roughly translated as either 'Wild Beasts' or 'Savages'. Their style was marked by a disregard for the forms of nature and the use of vivid colour. Fauvism is recognized as having paved the way for both cubism and expressionism.

19. Lionel Jeffries was born in London in 1926. He was RADA-trained, and despite the fact that he is mostly remembered for his bumbling English eccentrics, his range was in fact far more diverse. His most prominent work included: Charles Crichton's *Law and Disorder* (1958), Ken Hughes's *Chitty Chitty Bang Bang* (1968) and Michael Winner's *A Chorus of Disapproval* (1988).

20. Among the film's many award nominations and wins were Academy Award nominations for Charles Boyer (Best Actor), William Reynolds (Best Film Editing), Morris Stoloff and Harry Sukman (Best Music for a Dramatic or Comedy Picture), Jack Cardiff (Best Cinematography, Colour), and Joshua Logan (Best Picture).

21. The system was originally named 'Scentovision', but Mike

Todd changed it to the somewhat less romantic 'Smell-O-Vision'. Commenting on the name change, Todd paraphrased Shakespeare by noting, '…you call a smell by any other name.'

22. The refurbished, 1100-seat Todd Cinestage Theater in Chicago was used as a test site for the system.

23. Hans Laube, a Swiss professor of 'osmics', who had previously worked as an advertising executive in Zurich. His 'Scentovision' system was an adaptation of an earlier invention for deodorizing the air in large auditoria, such as cinemas.

24. They were briefly married between February 1957 and Mike Todd's death in a plane crash in March 1958.

25. Peter Lorre (1904–64) made his screen debut in Fritz Lang's terrifying 1931 study of mob justice, *M*. He fled Germany in the 1930s and appeared in numerous British and American films, including two with Hitchcock: *The Man Who Knew Too Much* (1934) and *Secret Agent* (1936). His two most memorable roles were those opposite Humphrey Bogart: first as Joel Cairo in John Huston's *The Maltese Falcon* (1941) and then the following year in Michael Curtiz's *Casablanca*.

26. Initially the film was renamed and re-branded as *Holiday in Spain*. It first opened in May 1962 at the Boston Theater in Massachusetts.

27. The 'smelly' enjoyed a brief renaissance in 1981, when John Waters released his Baltimore-set schlock-fest *Polyester* in 'Odorama'. The film employed a card with numbered 'scratch-n-sniff' panels, which was handed out to audience members to scratch (and sniff) when the appropriate number was flashed on screen.

Chapter 7

1. D H Lawrence wrote his semi-autobiographical *Sons and Lovers* in 1913. His often-controversial treatment of sex is evident in *Sons and Lovers*, although it is less overt than in many of his other works (*Lady Chatterley's Lover*, for example, was banned during his lifetime.)

2. Jerome Irving Wald (1911–62) combined a highly successful 20-year producing career with a parallel writing career, penning such classics as *The Roaring Twenties* (1939) and *They Drive by Night* (1940), both directed by Raoul Walsh and starring Humphrey Bogart. He was Oscar-nominated for *Mildred Pierce* (1946), *Johnny Belinda* (1949), *Peyton Place* (1958), and *Sons and Lovers* (1961). In 1949, he was awarded the Irving G Thalberg Memorial Academy Award.

3. Harry Andrews (1911–89) appeared in almost 100 films between 1953 and 1986. In later life, he was also well known for his role as Tom Carrington in TV's *Dynasty*.

4. Buddy Adler (1909–60) was the recipient of the Irving G Thalberg Memorial Oscar in 1957 in addition to winning the 1954 Best Picture Oscar for *From Here to Eternity* (which is also the inscription on his tombstone). His other notable films include *Bus Stop* (1956), *South Pacific* (1958) and *The Inn of the Sixth Happiness* (1958).

5. Dean Stockwell, born in 1936, first made his name as a child actor, before revitalizing his career in his twenties and finally making something of a second comeback in later life as a solid character actor in films such as Wim Wenders's *Paris, Texas* (1984) and David Lynch's *Blue Velvet* (1986). He was Oscar-nominated (Best Supporting Actor) in 1989 for his role in Jonathan Demme's *Married to the Mob* and has twice won the Best actor award at the Cannes Film Festival; the first time in 1959 for *Compulsion* and the second in 1962 for *Long Day's Journey Into Night*.

6. Nottingham and the surrounding Midlands.

7. Freddie Francis, born in 1917, began working as a camera operator in the late 1940s before beginning his illustrious career as a cinematographer with *A Hill in* Korea (1956) and *Time Without Pity* (1957). His first Oscar win came in 1961 for Jack Cardiff's *Sons and Lovers* and his second, almost three decades later, in 1990 for Edward Zwick's American Civil War epic, *Glory*. He has worked with David Lynch on three occasions—*The Elephant Man* (1980), *Dune* (1984) and *The Straight Story* (1999)—in addition to shooting Martin Scorsese's *Cape Fear* in 1991. In a secondary career, Francis has also directed almost 30 films, predominantly in the horror genre; these include *The Evil of Frankenstein* (1964), *Dr Terror's House of Horrors* (1965) and *Dracula Has Risen from the Grave* (1968).

8. Italian composer Mario Nascimbene (1913–2002) enjoyed a career spanning almost half a century. He created memorable scores for films as diverse as Jack Clayton's *Room at the Top* (1959) and Don Chaffey's *One Million Years BC* (1966). In 1991, he was honoured with the prestigious David di Donatello Career award.

9. Thomas Clarke's (1907–89) most memorable work came during his contract period at Ealing, when he worked on the classics *Passport to Pimlico* (1949), *The Lavender Hill Mob* (1951) and *The Titfield Thunderbolt* (1953). Drawing on his own early career as a policeman he also wrote, *The Blue Lamp* in 1950, thus creating the British post-war television institution that was *Dixon of Dock Green*.

10. Famed British playwright John Osborne (1929–94), whose work included *Look Back in Anger* (1956) and *The Entertainer* (1957).

11. Mary Ure (1933–75) starred opposite Richard Burton and Claire Bloom in Tony Richardson's acclaimed screen

adaptation of John Osborne's *Look Back in Anger* (1958). She was nominated for the Best Supporting Actress Academy Award for her portrayal of Clara in Jack Cardiff's *Sons and Lovers* (1960) and was reunited with Richard Burton in 1968 for *Where Eagles Dare*, directed by Brian G Hutton. Ure was married to actor Robert Shaw from 1963 until her death from an accidental overdose.

12. Best Writing, Screenplay Based on Material from Another Medium (Thomas Clarke and Gavin Lambert), Best Picture (Jerry Wald), Best Director (Jack Cardiff), Best Supporting Actress (Mary Ure), Best Art Direction, Black and White (Lionel Couch and Thomas Morahan), Best Actor (Trevor Howard) and Best Cinematography, Black and White (Freddie Francis.) The latter, for Francis, won.

13. Steve Parker, to whom MacLaine was married between 1954 and 1982.

14. Italian-born actor and singer, Yves Montand (1921–91), was discovered by the legendary Edith Piaf, who cast him in her 1946 film, *Star Without Light* (directed by Marcel Blistène). But it was his role in Henri-Georges Clouzot's classic *The Wages of Fear* (1952) that brought him international fame. He was awarded the Best Actor BAFTA for his role in Claude Berri's *Jean de Florette* (1986).

15. Then as now, productions that seek cheaper countries in which to film are termed 'runaway films'. Foreign tax incentives, as well as cheaper crew and studio facilities, are the most common factors.

16. William Holden (1918–81) was signed to Paramount while studying chemistry at Pasadena Junior College. His first starring role was in Rouben Mamoulian's *Golden Boy* (1939), and after serving in World War II, he returned to Hollywood in the classic *Sunset Boulevard* (Billy Wilder, 1950), for which he was Oscar-nominated. Three years later, he won the Oscar for Best Actor, for *Stalag 17* (again directed by Billy Wilder) and was further nominated in 1977 for Sidney Lumet's *Network*; the latter role also earned him a BAFTA nomination.

17. Dale Carnegie's 1937, multi-million selling, people-skills book.

18. Lewis Milestone's 1962 adaptation starred Marlon Brando as Fletcher Christian and Trevor Howard as Captain Bligh.

19. French writer Joseph Kessel (1898–1979) had an illustrious career lasting almost 50 years. His novel *Belle de Jour* was adapted for the screen by director Luis Buñuel in 1967.

20. Richard Widmark, born in Minnesota 1914 and raised in Illinois, where he studied at Lake Forest College. It was

here that he began acting, returning after graduation to teach drama. He made his stage debut with *Kiss and Tell* in 1943 before making his unforgettable and uncompromising screen debut as the psychotic Tommy Udo in Henry Hathaway's *Kiss of Death* (1947), for which he was Oscar-nominated. The star turn led to a lucrative seven-year contract with 20th Century Fox, during which time he worked with Elia Kazan on the tense *Panic in the Streets* (1950) and Hathaway again on *Garden of Evil* (1954). His career continued unabated during the 1960s and 1970s, slowing only during the early 1980s.

21. Sidney Poitier, born 1927, made his first big impression on the screen in Joseph L Mankiewicz's *No Way Out* (1950), appearing opposite Richard Widmark (later his *Long Ships* co-star). His greatest successes were *Blackboard Jungle* (Richard Brooks, 1955), *The Defiant Ones* (Stanley Kramer, 1958, an Oscar nomination), *Lilies of the Field* (Ralph Nelson, 1963, an Oscar win), *To Sir with Love* (James Clavell, 1966), *Guess Who's Coming to Dinner* (Stanley Kramer, 1967) and *In the Heat of the Night* (Norman Jewison, 1967). The latter film's huge success resulted in two sequels: *They Call me MISTER Tibbs!* (Gordon Douglas, 1970) and *The Organization* (Don Medford, 1971). Despite still being a huge box office draw, Poitier all but gave up film acting, concentrating instead on directorial efforts such as *Stir Crazy* (1980). Poitier won a further, honorary, Academy Award in 2002 for his contribution to his craft.

22. Producer Irving Allen (1905–87) began his film career as an editor in 1929. During the 1940s, Allen directed a series of respectable adventure tales, including *Avalanche* (1946) and *16 Fathoms Deep* (1948). He won the 1948 Oscar for Best Short Film with *Climbing the Matterhorn* and was nominated two years later in the same category for *Chase of Death*. In the 1950s, he partnered Albert Broccoli to form Warwick Films.

23. Rod Taylor was born in Australia in 1930 and moved to Hollywood in the mid-1950s, where he played supporting roles for a number of years before starring in George Pal's 1960 film *The Time Machine*. He also took the lead opposite Tippi Hedren in Hitchcock's *The Birds* (1963).

24. *Battleship Potemkin*, Sergei Eisenstein's 1925 Russian classic, tells the story of the Kronstadt navy mutiny, an event that was a precursor of the Russian revolution of 1905. The film is considered a masterpiece of editing, and the central Odessa Steps massacre sequence has been much analyzed and repeatedly warmed over by subsequent filmmakers (for example, Brian De Palma for his 1987 film *The Untouchables*).

25. Born in 1925, Anne Coates first found film-related

employment (she had previously been a nurse) with Religious Films, where she worked restoring old prints. This led to work at Pinewood, where she worked, uncredited, on *The Red Shoes* before editing Noel Langley's *The Pickwick Papers* in 1952. She won her first Oscar in 1962 for her editing of David Lean's sweeping *Lawrence of Arabia*. She was later Oscar-nominated for *Becket* in 1965, *The Elephant Man* in 1980 (also BAFTA-nominated), *In the Line of Fire* in 1993 (again BAFTA-nominated) and for *Out of Sight* in 1998. In 1995, she was awarded the American Cinema Editors' Career Achievement Award.

26. David Lean's 1965 adaptation of the Boris Pasternak novel, which made a star of Julie Christie and a heartthrob of Omar Sharif.

27. Wilfred Hyde-White (1903–91) attended the Royal Academy of Dramatic Arts before making his stage debut in 1922. Although his film career stretched from 1934 (Herbert Smith's *Night Mail*) to 1983 (Gerry O'Hara's *Fanny Hill*), he will always be best remembered for his role as Colonel Pickering in 1964's *My Fair Lady*. Hyde-White constantly combined his film work with numerous television appearances, which ranged from *Peyton Place* to *Columbo* and *Battlestar Galactica*.

28. Daniel Mann's *Our Man Flint* (1966) and Gordon Douglas's sequel *In Like Flint* (1967) starred James Coburn as the tongue-in-cheek playboy spy, Derek Flint. The 'unofficial' entry in the Bond canon, *Casino Royale*, had also been released in 1967, featuring a multitude of 007s from Woody Allen to David Niven and Peter Sellers.

29. Born in 1946, Marianne Faithfull recorded her first song, 'As Tears Go By' (written by Mick Jagger and Keith Richards), in 1964. She later appeared in Kenneth Anger's seminal *Lucifer Rising* (1973) and Patrice Chéreau's equally controversial *Intimacy* (2000).

30. Alain Delon, born in 1935 in Sceaux, France, served with the French Marines in Indochina before making his film debut in 1957 with Yves Allégret's *Quand la Femmes s'en Mêle*. He came to international recognition with Luchino Visconti's *Rocco and his Brothers* in 1960, and later starred as the eponymous *Le Samouraï* directed by Jean-Pierre Melville in 1967. He has been nominated three times for the Best Actor César Award: 1977 for *Monsieur Klein*; in 1978 for *Mort d'un Pourri*; and winning in 1985 for *Notre Histoire*. In 1995, he was awarded the prestigious Honorary Golden Berlin Bear at the Berlin International Film Festival.

31. *Girl on a Motorcycle* was released on 21 June 1968 in France and 12 September 1968 in the UK.

Chapter 8

1. Born in London in 1944, Francesca Annis has enjoyed a remarkably varied career that has encompassed Shakespearean stage work, action-adventure films such as *Krull* (Peter Yates, 1983) and *Dune* (David Lynch, 1984), and television appearances on stock shows such as *The Saint* and *Magnum PI*. In the year before appearing in Jack Cardiff's *Penny Gold*, Annis had starred in Roman Polanski's bloody adaptation of *Macbeth*.

2. Written by Simon Beaufoy and directed by Peter Cattaneo, *The Full Monty* became one of the biggest hits of 1997 in both the UK and America. The film earned back its modest budget in its US opening weekend alone.

3. Donald Pleasance (1919–95) began his stage career in 1939, before World War II forced him into service in the RAF (he was shot down, captured and held as a prisoner of war). His first feature film appearance was in Muriel Box's *The Beachcomber* (1954) and Pleasance quickly found himself adding character weight to classic films as diverse as *Look Back in Anger* (Tony Richardson, 1958), *The Great Escape* (John Sturges, 1963), *Fantastic Voyage* (Richard Fleischer, 1966), *Cul-de-sac* (Roman Polanski, 1966) *You Only Live Twice* (Lewis Gilbert, 1967) and *THX 1138* (George Lucas, 1971). In the late 1960s and throughout the 1970s, his name became increasingly synonymous with the horror genre and perhaps one of his most memorable (if less challenging) characterizations was that of Dr Sam Loomis, who first appeared in John Carpenter's *Halloween* (1978).

4. Oliver Reed (1938–99) had already made several (largely uncredited) appearances in films during the latter half of the 1950s before making his first big impression in Terence Fisher's Hammer Horror movie, *Curse of the Werewolf*, in 1961. Managing, at least temporarily, to escape the clutches of the horror genre, Reed continued to make his mark on films such as *Oliver!* (Carol Reed, 1968), *Hannibal Brooks* (Michael Winner, 1969) and *Women in Love* (Ken Russell, 1969). He repeated his controversial teaming with Russell again in 1971 for the screen adaptation of *The Devils*. Throughout the 1970s, Reed became as famous as a drunk as he had ever been as an actor, and his roles and performances became increasingly mediocre. Ironically, what looked to be his comeback film, *Gladiator* (Ridley Scott, 2000), turned out to be his last, and much of his final performance was supplemented by computer-generated effects after his death on location.

5. Mark Lester was born in 1958 and made his first screen appearance at the age of six in Robert Dhéry's *Allez France* (1964), following it two years later with a small role in François Truffaut's cult-classic, *Fahrenheit 451*. Lester's

starring moment came when he was cast as the eponymous orphan in the all-singing, all-dancing *Oliver!* (Carol Reed, 1968).

6. Producer Ilya Salkind was born Ilya Juan Salkind Dominguez in Mexico City in 1947. He was the grandson of Michael Salkind, a pioneer of silent cinema and producer of Gina Lollobrigida's *Cervantes* (Vincent Sherman, 1966). Ilya Salkind inevitably entered the industry and by the mid-1970s, with the successful Richard Lester *Musketeer* films to his credit, he began developing the enormously lucrative *Superman* film franchise.

7. First published in 1882, *The Prince and the Pauper* was written by Twain as a respite during the writing of *The Adventures of Huckleberry Finn*.

8. Maurice Jarre, born in Lyon, France in 1924, is without doubt one of the world's greatest film composers. He has more than 150 films and nine Oscar nominations to his name; all three Academy Award wins— *Lawrence of Arabia* (in 1963), *Doctor Zhivago* (1966) and *A Passage to India* (1985)—were the result of collaboration with director David Lean.

9. *Death on the Nile*'s all-star cast included Peter Ustinov, Bette Davis, Mia Farrow, David Niven, Sam Wanamaker and Maggie Smith.

10. John Brabourne, who would later produce two further Agatha Christie adaptations, *The Mirror Crack'd* (1980) and *Evil Under the Sun* (1982), both for director Guy Hamilton.

11. Born in 1925, John Guillermin cut his directorial teeth during the 1950s on films such as *Miss Robin Hood* (1952) and *I Was Monty's Double* (1958), but is best known for his 1970s epics, which included *The Towering Inferno* (1974) and *King Kong* (1976).

12. Canadian director Mark Robson (1913–78) began his film career as a prop boy and then moved to editing, where among other things he helped the great Robert Wise to cut *Citizen Kane* (1941) and *The Magnificent Ambersons* (1942). By the mid-1940s, Robson was out of the cutting room and directing his own slate of low-budget horror films. His direction of the boxing film *Champion* in 1949 lifted him from the horror rut, and Robson went on to enjoy success with films such as *Peyton Place* (1957), *The Inn of the Sixth Happiness* (1958), *Von Ryan's Express* (1965) and *Earthquake* (1974). He was Oscar-nominated as Best Director for both *Peyton Place* and *The Inn of the Sixth Happiness*.

13. Robert Shaw (1927–78) was born in Lancashire and studied at the Royal Academy of Dramatic Art before making his stage debut in 1949. After fleeting appearances in *The Lavender Hill Mob* (Charles Crichton, 1951) and *Operation Secret* (Lewis Seiler, 1952), Shaw finally made his mark playing Flight Sergeant Pulford in Michael Anderson's *The Dam Busters* (1954). More than two decades of memorable character acting was to follow: *The Caretaker* (1963), *A Man for All Seasons* (1966)—for which Shaw was Academy Award nominated—*The Sting* (1973) and *Jaws* (1975) among them.

14. Ken Annakin was born in Beverley, East Yorkshire in 1914. He began his career working on documentaries, before graduating to feature films and finding his big break when Disney hired him to direct *The Story of Robin Hood and his Merrie Men* (1952). Other Disney live-action films followed, while his biggest post-Disney successes were, *Those Magnificent Men in Their Flying Machines* (1965), *Monte Carlo or Bust* (1969) and *Paper Tiger* (1975). He was co-nominated along with Jack Davies for an Academy Award in 1966 for the screenplay of *Those Magnificent Men*.

15. Sylvia Kristel was born in 1952 in Utrecht, The Netherlands. She came to international notoriety in 1974, when she starred in Just Jaeckin's glossy soft-porn 'classic', *Emmanuelle*. She followed the film with a succession of increasingly desperate (though undeniably lucrative) sequels: *Good-bye, Emmanuelle* (1977), *Emmanuelle 4* (1984), *Emmanuelle's Revenge* (1992), *Emmanuelle Forever* (1993) and others.

16. Based on the Frederick Forsyth novel and directed in 1980 by John Irvin, *The Dogs of War* starred Christopher Walken as a mercenary, Paul Shannon, leading an African revolt.

17. The tiny Central American country of Belize was a British colony that had fought for decades for its independence, a status that was finally achieved on 21 September 1981.

18. Born in 1926, producer-director Norman Jewison has been nominated for the Academy Award no fewer than seven times, the first for Best Picture for *The Russians Are Coming, the Russians Are Coming* in 1967. The following year he won the BAFTA UN (United Nations) Award for *In The Heat of the Night*. In 1999, he was awarded with the Irving G Thalberg Memorial Academy Award.

19. John Irvin was born in 1940 in Newcastle-upon-Tyne, England. As a director, he has successfully balanced film work such as *The Dogs of War* (1980), *Hamburger Hill* (1987) and *Shiner* (2000) with acclaimed television work, most notably *Tinker, Tailor, Soldier, Spy* (1980), which was based on the novel by John Le Carré and starred Alec Guinness as spy-master George Smiley.

20. Vincente Minnelli's 1953 scathing, cynical portrayal of the Hollywood machine remains one of the most poignant

depictions of filmmaking. Kirk Douglas stars as film director Jonathan Shields, who comments, 'Don't worry. Some of the best movies are made by people working together who hate each other's guts.' Ten years after the original film, Minnelli directed a semi-sequel companion piece, *Two Weeks in Another Town*.

21. Based on the Shirley Jackson gothic novel, Robert Wise's *The Haunting* (1963) is the epitome of understated terror. Conversely, Jan de Bont's risible 1999 remake was a blunt instrument, overly reliant on computer-generated effects.

22. Principal locations were Albany and Saratoga Springs (New York), and Woodstock (Vermont).

23. Cousins Yoram Globus and Menahem Golan have produced more than 150 films, dating back to the early 1960s. After working as a stage director in Israel, Menahem Golan moved to American to study under Roger Corman, later returning to Israel where he and his cousin built the foundations of the country's film industry. In 1979, the pair moved back to America and took control of the Cannon film group; releasing an often uneasy blend of respectable art-house films such as Cassavetes's *Love Streams* (1984) and Godard's *King Lear* (1987) mixed with schlock action films from Chuck Norris (*The Delta Force*) and Sylvester Stallone (*Over the Top*). Golan and Globus dissolved their partnership in 1989, the former leaving to head up 21st Century Film Corporation and the latter becoming CEO of Pathé International.

24. *The Last Days of Pompeii* was based on the novel by Edward George Bulwer-Lytton and directed by Peter R Hunt.

25. John Milius's 1982 sword, sandal and sorcery film is largely credited with making a star of Arnold Schwarzenegger, although he had previously made something of an impact in the 1977 bodybuilding documentary *Pumping Iron*.

26. David Lynch (born 1946) is America's foremost avant-garde director. His twisted, nightmarish visions of small-town America have been disturbing audiences since his breakthrough *Eraserhead* in 1977. He followed this with the Mel Brooks-produced *The Elephant Man* (1980) and his sprawling and almost incomprehensible adaptation of Frank Herbert's *Dune* (1984). He was Oscar-nominated in 1981 both as Best Director and for Best Writing for *The Elephant Man* (he was nominated in the same categories for the BAFTAs). In 1987 and 2002, he was again nominated as Best Director, first for *Blue Velvet* and then for *Mulholland Drive*.

27. Ultimately the cinematographer's job on *Blue Velvet* went to Frederick Elmes, who had worked on Lynch's *Eraserhead* and would later work on *Wild at Heart* (1990).

28. Based on the novel by David Morrell, Ted Kotcheff's powerful and often intelligent *First Blood* (1982) was less jingoistic and gung-ho than the Sylvester Stallone-penned sequels.

29. Australian actor Bryan Brown was born in 1947 in Sydney, New South Wales. Bruce Beresford's *Breaker Morant* (1980) gave Brown his first big break and he capitalized on it with appearances in two high-profile television mini-series, *A Town Like Alice* (1981) and *The Thorn Birds* (1983). His roles in crowd-pleasers like Robert Mandel's *F/X* (1986) and the Tom Cruise vehicle *Cocktail* (Roger Donaldson, 1988) have been balanced with more critically acclaimed work in films such as *Gorillas in the Mist* (Michael Apted, 1988).

30. *The Thorn Birds*, based on the novel by Colleen McCullough and starring Richard Chamberlain and Rachel Ward.

31. Raffaella De Laurentiis was born the daughter of producer Dino De Laurentiis and actress Silvana Mangano. As a producer, she has proved every bit her father's equal, and her largest-scale productions have included *Conan the Barbarian* (John Milius, 1982), *Conan the Destroyer* (Richard Fleischer, 1984) and *Dune* (David Lynch, 1984).

Chapter 9

1. Dar Robinson (1947–86) was considered by his peers to be the greatest stuntman in the industry. In 1973, he doubled for Steve McQueen in *Papillon*, making the spectacular 100-foot cliff-to-water jump. He provided the breathtaking stunts for *Rollerball* (Norman Jewison, 1975), *Turk 182!* (Bob Clark, 1985), *To Live and Die in LA* (William Friedkin, 1985) and *Lethal Weapon* (Richard Donner, 1987)—performing the 'suicide' jump-to-airbag stunt for the latter. A pioneer of stunt technology, Robinson developed the use of dragline cables which eliminated the use of airbags, a technique he put to brilliant use in the 1985 Burt Reynolds thriller *Stick* (Robinson also played the role of albino killer Moki in the film).

2. *Call from Space* and *The Magic Balloon* were produced and presented in a format called Showscan. The system employed an ultra-wide 70mm film stock and a shooting (and projection) rate of 60 frames per second—more than double the usual speed. The format was developed by special effects master Douglas Trumbull, who had created the groundbreaking optical effects for Stanley Kubrick's *2001: A Space Odyssey* (1968). Showscan was ultimately doomed as a mainstream presentation system because of the enormous cost of fitting and running custom cinemas; however, Trumbull's system lives on, in an adapted form,

in various theme-park rides across the world.

3. In 1973, Marlon Brando refused to accept his Oscar for Best Actor (in *The Godfather*), citing America's (specifically Hollywood's) treatment of Native Americans as his reason. He sent a woman called Sacheen Littlefeather to the awards on his behalf, although she was later revealed to be an actress by the name of Maria Cruz.

4. Christopher Coppola was born in 1962, the brother of Nicolas Cage and nephew of Francis Ford Coppola. In his teens, he worked with Carmine Coppola on the score of *Apocalypse Now* (1979) and later studied music at Redlands University, graduating in 1987. Among his subsequent feature films was *Deadfall* (1993) starring Nicolas Cage, James Coburn, Michael Biehn and Charlie Sheen.

Film Index

General Index